An Interpretation of American History

Samuel A. Johnson, Ph.D.

Former Professor of History and Government,
Harris Teachers College
Former Lecturer in History and Political Science,
Washington University
Former Lecturer in History and Government,
St. Louis University

Barron's Educational Series, Inc.

Woodbury, New York

CONTENTS

Contents

PREFACE

THIS IS *not* a textbook in American history. It does not narrate the history of our country in detail. Indeed, many relatively important events of our past are not even mentioned. Rather, this little book is intended to give meaning and added usefulness to any good textbook.

Reading or studying a well-written narrative history of our country can be interesting, and may have broad cultural value. However, it will not, of itself, apply the past to the present or make it a guide to the future. Mere knowledge of facts of the past is not enough to provide us with an understanding of the present, and to help us to cope more intelligently with problems we face at the ballot box and as participants in public opinion. To be meaningful, and to enable history really to function in our lives, the facts must be interpreted in their relation to each other, to what has gone before, and to what has come after. They must be put together to show the development of trends and patterns that still prevail, and often can be projected into the future.

This book undertakes to meet that need. Naturally, I have, in the main, followed my own interpretations, but these are not offered as final or authoritative. Rather, my purpose has been to illustrate the fact that interpretation of the past can make history more vital and meaningful for the present.

This book should prove valuable for use in connection with classroom courses in American history, either through collateral assignments by the instructor or through independent use by the student. It should also be useful (and, I hope, interesting) to non-academic readers who know the general story of our history.

I wish to express my gratitude to my wife, Winifred Feder Johnson, not only for general helpfulness and encouragement, but also for very specific and highly valuable assistance in proofreading, and in compiling bibliography and index.

SAMUEL A. JOHNSON

Peterborough, New Hampshire

1 | The Meaningfulness of History

HISTORY AND ITS VALUE

History as a Third Dimension. History is more than the traditional record of past events. It is all that is known of the human past. Just knowing about the past has cultural value and gives one emotional satisfaction. It also makes him a better conversationalist and a more interesting person to know. More specialized knowledge of an event or situation makes one something of an authority, able to clarify many misunderstandings. But probably the greatest value history can have for an individual is to give him a better comprehension of the present and its problems. To do this, though, history must be meaningful. A mere knowledge of names and dates is not enough. History must provide the third dimension—depth or perspective—in a study of any current problem.

What Gives It Meaning? How can history acquire this meaningfulness for an individual? First of all, he must approach history with an inquiring mind, always looking for meaning. He must see events, not as isolated happenings, but in their relation to each other, to what has gone before, and to what comes after. He must discern trends and behavior patterns. He must take account of psychological reactions and other influences. He must see historical developments in their broad sweep and their long-range implications, seeking to discover their relation to present situations. Although history never "repeats itself" exactly, the alert student will discern certain historical parallels, and will observe that similar situations will usually produce similar reactions and consequences.

The Need for Interpretation. In a word, to be meaningful, history must be interpreted. To some extent, each student must be his own interpreter, but he can be aided by the guidance of experienced historians. Such guidance can point out the fallacy of some misinterpretations, and the danger of reading meanings *into* history instead of out of it.

BASES OF INTERPRETATION

Preconceived Hypotheses. Most writers who have offered a systematic interpretation of history have begun with a hypothesis which they undertake to prove. They have come upon an element of truth, that a certain factor has had great influence in shaping the course of historical development. Then, ignoring other elements, they advance the doctrine that this factor has been the sole (or almost sole) determinant of the course of history, and set about to prove their doctrine from historical facts. Some of them have even distorted facts for this purpose. Short of that, they cite the facts which seem to support their thesis, and ignore those facts which point in another direction. As used by these people, the phase "history proves . . ." is utterly fallacious. Obviously, this is the wrong way to go about interpreting history.

Some Examples of Doctrinal Interpretation. Besides the numerous individuals who have written biased histories of some particular church, political party or movement, as well as untold biased biographers, there are several outstanding examples of this kind of interpretation of history.

Probably the best known was Karl Marx with his so-called economic interpretation of history. Marx was on solid ground in observing that economic conditions and economic pressures have been a major factor in shaping the course of history throughout all ages. His ignoring of other factors was bad enough, but when he distorted history to prove his theory of "economic determinism," the doctrine that economic forces make socialism the wave of the future and the culmination of all human development, he completely disqualified himself as a historian.

Late in the last century, U. S. Navy Captain (later Admiral) Alfred T. Mahan advanced his doctrine of sea power as an interpretation of history. He held that the country with the strongest navy has always been the dominant force in world affairs, and has sometimes been able to rule all of the then known world. Mahan's main concern was to use history to justify his belief in imperialism. He had much more influence on politicians than on historians, but for a time, some writers of history reflected his ideas somewhat.

A little later, Professor Frederick Jackson Turner announced his frontier hypothesis. By the frontier, he meant the ever advancing edge of settlement from East to West. According to Turner, just about everything distinctive in American history and American culture was a result of the influence of the frontier. For example, he attributed the high prevailing wage scale in America to the fact that migration to the frontier had drained off the labor supply. This is a part, but not all, of the true explanation. The germ of reality in Turner's theory was that the frontier undoubtedly had great influence in shaping the course of American history and the character of American institutions. Like other doctrinal interpreters, though, he overlooked or minimized other important factors. Turner's influence did bring about more stress on Western history and recognition of the real influence the West exerted. However, few present day historians accept his entire hypothesis.

Just before World War I, Sir Halford Mackinder, a British geographer, proposed a theory he called geopolitics. Not intended primarily as an interpretation of history, it nevertheless provided an interpretation of sorts. The heart of it was a doctrine of geographic determinism, comparable to Marx's economic determinism. Without going into Mackinder's elaborate notions about the "world island" and inner and outer crescents, we may note his idea that geographic conditions and geographic influences have been the overwhelming force in shaping the course of history and foreshadowing the future. A distortion of Mackinder's thesis by the German geographer, Karl Haushofer, tying it in with the German "master race" doctrine, had great influence on Hitler. Mackinder, and other writers who developed his thesis, rendered a real service in focusing attention on the already known fact that geographic considerations have played an important part in shaping the course of history, but like the other doctrinal interpreters, Mackinder went too far.

Rational Interpretation. Any sound interpretation of history must be rational in the sense that, instead of trying to prove a thesis, it reasons without bias (or with as little bias as is humanly possible) from known facts. In a given situation, it takes account of all the facts that are pertinent, though the judging of pertinence is, in itself, an act of interpretation. It then tries to determine, through careful analysis, the meaning of each fact and its bearing on the whole situation. Without looking for a direct "cause and effect" relationship between events, it recognizes that most things of importance are brought about by a combination of factors—economic, social, biological, psychological, ideological, and others—though, in a particular case, one or a few of these factors may exert greater influence than others. It will recognize, too, that different happenings, even though separated by considerable time or space, may be related to each other, and will seek to discover that relationship.

SOME PRINCIPLES OF HISTORY

The Importance of Principles. There are a few basic principles of history that must be taken into account in reaching a sound interpretation. These may not all apply equally in a given situation, but they should always be kept in mind when undertaking interpretation.

The Unity of History. One of these principles is the unity of history. All nations, races and areas are a part of what the late Wendell Willkie called "one world," and all interact upon each other. In the remote past, distinctive civilizations arose in different areas because there was little or no communication among them. Sooner or later, though, each civilization had its impact on the others. Even before the advent of modern times, Europe, through indirect contacts, acquired the art of printing, the formula for gunpowder, and the technique of paper making from far away China. Today, modern news media and electronic communications are tying the whole world together closely.

For several reasons, we split history longitudinally into national histories and histories of areas, institutions, ethnic groups and others. We also split it into aspects, such as political history, economic history, social history and numerous others, and we cut it up horizontally into periods such as ancient, medieval and modern, and shorter periods within each of these. There are adequate reasons for thus carving up history into segments, such as convenience in study and research, and the need to serve specialized interests, such as the interest of citizens in the history of their own country.

In thus segmenting history, however, we need to bear in mind that no segment is isolated. Each is related to and influenced by other segments. For example, in dealing with the history of the United States, we should never lose sight of the fact that, from the beginning to the immediate present, our history has been closely involved with the history of Europe and sometimes with that of other parts of the world. This segmentation does not invalidate the unity of history.

The Continuity of History. An equally vital principle is the continuity of history. From the earliest known beginnings of civilization right down to the present moment, history has flowed on in an unbroken stream. Conditions change, of course; indeed, changes in conditions come near to being the essence of history. These changes often provide the basis for division into time periods. One set of conditions dominates one period, while a different set prevails in the period that follows, and we designate the periods accordingly. The break between them, though, is never abrupt. For convenience in writing and study, we may arbitrarily pick a certain event as dividing periods, such as the discovery of America to mark the line between medieval and modern, or the inauguration of a President to divide periods in American history, but conditions are just the same after such an event as just before it. These landmarks do not really break the continuity of history.

The Selectivity of History. The historian must be selective, choosing as important enough to deserve his consideration only a comparatively few items out of the vast array of known events. Of those he decides to include, he evaluates some as being more important than others, and stresses them accordingly. This rating of importance depends, to a great extent, on the purpose the writer has in mind or the interest he intends to serve. Thus, in a history of sports, a baseball world series would probably loom large, but in a general history of the United States it would not be mentioned because it had little or no effect in shaping the nation's development. Similarly, the general writer will ignore as trivia items that may get major attention in news of the day, but are of only passing interest. To be meaningful, history must be selective.

The Relativity of History. Some facts in history have been established definitely and with finality, but for the most part, our knowledge of past events is relative. It represents only the weight of probability, and is always open to revision as new information comes to light. We seek to establish and clarify facts through research, using all the evidence available, but the job is never finished.

We can usually establish, beyond doubt, that the event occurred, but in many cases, we can not be sure just how and why it happened. Available evidence is of varying validity. Errors may have slipped into official records. Newspapers, either because of the editor's bias or through poor reporting, may give a distorted picture. Participants and contemporary witnesses may warp their accounts for personal reasons or, with completely honest intent, may be victims of faulty memory. Corroborating circumstantial evidence may be subject to different interpretations.

All of these factors must influence our interpretation of the meaning of the event and of its relation to other events. An interpretation that appears to be fully valid on the basis of knowledge available when it is made may become untenable in the light of later research. So, just as the "facts" of history are subject to revision, interpretations based on these facts are tentative and later may need to be revised. This is the meaning of the relativity of history.

WHY FOCUS ON AMERICAN HISTORY?

Various Reasons. In the light of some of these principles, a reader might ask, why focus on American history? Does it not do violence to the principle of unity? To some extent it does, so that we must always make a conscious effort to remember that American history does not exist in a vacuum, but is part of a greater whole. Despite this difficulty, there are several good reasons for dealing separately with the history of a single nation, in this case the United States.

Practicality. One very obvious reason is the matter of practicality. At the present time, it would be utterly impractical to undertake an interpretation, in any detail, of the whole broad scope of history. Such a general evaluation must be built step by step, first developing adequate understandings of various segments, and eventually synthesizing them into a general interpretation.

Serving a Particular Purpose. A more important reason is the serving of a particular purpose and specialized interests. We Americans are interested primarily in the history of our own country, and rightly so. We read, teach and study it more extensively than any other segment of history. Hence, there is a greater need for an interpretation of our own history than for that of any other area.

Convenience. Closely tied in with this is the reason of convenience. Material is more readily available for research than in any other segment, and usually there is no language problem. This means that an interpreter has more and better information available with which to work.

Moreover, although little has been written on interpretation as such, most writers of American history reveal distinctive ideas. Many of them, without quite saying that such-and-such means so-and-so, tell their story in a manner that leaves little doubt as to their evaluation. This is true particularly of biographers and writers on short time segments. The writer on interpretation has the convenience of comparing and evaluating these views of narrative writers.

Conclusion. For these reasons, then, and possibly for other reasons also, we focus our attention on American history. *Focus* seems to be a better word than *limit* or *restrict* because we shall not consider American history in isolation. As far as appears feasible, we shall observe the relationship of American developments to happenings and conditions elsewhere. In some cases, it will be necessary to stress developments outside America because of their impact on our own story. Indeed, we begin our account with happenings far removed in time and space from the continent of North America.

TOPICS AND QUESTIONS FOR DISCUSSION

Chapter 1

1. There are numerous definitions of history. Try to formulate a definition of your own which you consider adequate.
2. How can history be most useful to a person today?
3. To what extent can history provide a basis for forecasting the future?
4. Do you agree that history needs to be interpreted? If so, why?
5. What are some of the systematic interpretations of history that have been followed by certain writers? What, if anything, is wrong with each?

6. What constitutes a "rational" basis for interpreting history?
7. Examine the "principles of history" mentioned in this chapter. In what situations and to what extent is it practical to follow them in studying history?
8. In the light of these "principles," what is the justification, if any, for considering American history apart from world history?

2 | Genesis of the New World

A LONG PERIOD OF DEVELOPMENT

The Remote Background. Much in our American way of life traces back to the very early civilizations that developed between 4000 and 3000 B. C. in the valleys of the Nile and the Tigris-Euphrates. Much of it comes from the somewhat later civilizations of the Near East, especially those of the Hittites, the Hebrews and the Phoenicians. We owe a great deal, especially in the fields of letters, the arts and sports, to the classical Greeks, and many features of our political and legal institutions come from the Romans. We also derive a number of important features of our present-day scheme of things from medieval Western Europe. But all of this is the story of the development of Western civilization, of which we are a part. There is little or nothing in it which points specifically to the opening of the Western hemisphere and what is sometimes called the "expansion of Europe" into America.

The Crusades. The chain of developments that led to the opening of America began with the Crusades. These, as everyone knows, were a series of military expeditions of the knights of feudal Western Europe which aimed at conquering the Holy Land from the Moslem Saracens. Supposedly the motive was religious, to protect pilgrims. Actually, the hope of gaining new domains for the great feudal lords was an equally potent motivation. The first Crusade, which began in 1096, succeeded temporarily in conquering the whole eastern coast of the Mediterranean and set up four feudal states there. These, however, were lost in a few decades and left little permanent effect on the region.

At the time of the Crusades, most of Western Europe was a decentralized feudal society, living a self-sufficient hand-to-mouth existence. A few scholars, chiefly in the monasteries, kept alive some learning. In the city states of northern Italy, a surviving merchant class carried on limited commerce, chiefly with the Byzantine Empire, and so had some contact with the slightly higher Byzantine civilization. For the most part, though, the cultural achievements of the Greeks and Romans had been lost. All of the peasants and most of the nobles were entirely illiterate. At that same time, Moslems generally, and especially the Moors in Spain and the Saracens in the Near East, enjoyed a much higher culture. They lived better, had more commerce, and had kept alive the learning of the classical Greeks and of the Hellenistic age. They traded indirectly, through caravans to Persia, with India and China, and so had contact with those civilizations.

The real impact of the Crusades lay in bringing Western Europe into contact with this higher culture. North Italian merchants, sending out ships to carry supplies to the crusaders, imported as return cargo products of the Near East and even of the Far East. As feudalism broke down and Western Europe produced more wealth, the means were available for more and more people to buy these exotic products and to develop a taste for them. This was to have a direct bearing on the discovery of America. Even more important was the knowledge brought back by returning crusaders, pilgrims and merchants. Western Europe again became conscious of ancient Greek learning, philosophy and art. Soon contacts were made with Moslem Spain and European knowledge was enriched still further. Out of these developments came the Renaissance.

The Renaissance. The term *renaissance*, which literally means rebirth, was the name applied to the revival of learning and art which began in northern Italy in the thirteenth century. Gradually it spread northward, with the expansion of trade, to France, Germany and England. Not only did it produce great artists and writers, but it secularized philosophical thinking. It shifted the emphasis from a life after death to life here and now, a viewpoint called humanism. It raised questions about everything in the medieval pattern of life, including the Church. This, in turn, led to disturbances within the Church, beginning with the great "heresies," and culminating in the Protestant Revolt. These changes were not only a part of, but were also an important causal factor in the modernization of Western Europe.

The Modernization of Europe. The developments of the Renaissance were not the only factors in the modernization of Western Europe though, along with the expansion of trade, they contributed mightily toward bringing it about. Another factor, largely independent of Renaissance influence, was the decline and eventual collapse of feudalism with its accompanying manorial system of agriculture. The introduction of gunpower in the 1300's (probably indirectly from China through the Moors) dealt a death blow to feudal warfare by rendering the castles indefensible. The discovery that the cultivation of whole fields by individuals was more productive than the strip cultivation of the manor led to a gradual abandonment of the manorial system and enabled more and more peasants to rise out of the condition of serfdom into the status of independent farmers. This process was accelerated by the expanding money

economy which made it more profitable for the great land-
holders to rent their land to peasant farmers for cash, or even
to sell plots outright, than to receive the old peasant services
or payments in kind. As this change-over progressed, more
and more individuals, acquiring a little wealth and education,
were able to leave the ranks of the peasants and move into the
growing towns to become merchants or skilled craftsmen. The
growth of towns, in turn, created a new *bourgeoisie* or middle
class, whose members, living by industry and trade, were able
to acquire wealth, education and influence. Along with these,
as a by-product of the process, there developed a class of urban
workers, with varying degrees of skill and affluence, who
came to constitute a sizable urban population in most areas.
This process of modernization came about gradually over a
period of several centuries and proceeded at different rates in
different regions. In some places it was hardly complete before
the eighteenth century, but in most parts of Western Europe
it had gone far enough by about the year 1500 to say that the
modern pattern of life prevailed over the medieval.

Economic and Religious Factors in the Opening of America.
The wave of geographical exploration, that included the discovery of America, was prompted mainly by economic motives, though some of the men who took part in it were also
motivated by the religious goal of carrying the gospel to
heathen lands. Around 1400, the Ottoman Turks overran
Asia Minor and began pushing across into southeastern Europe.
In 1453, they captured Constantinople (present Istanbul) and
put an end to the tattered remains of the Byzantine Empire.
At about that time, the Portuguese began a series of explorations
aimed at finding an all-water route to the Far East. The old
theory was that the Turks had blocked the old overland trade
routes, making it necessary to find a new route to the Orient.

A research project of some years back demolished this

theory. Checking the prices of Oriental goods in Europe before and after 1453, this study found that these prices continued to drop after the fall of Constantinople, indicating that the old trade routes were still open. The Turks undoubtedly taxed the goods that passed through their domain, but increasing volume and the suppression of brigandage offset this addition to the cost.

The real explanation runs something like this. For a long time, Venice and Genoa had competed in the Oriental trade. In the middle 1400's, though, Venice, by methods which economists call "cutthroat competition," had squeezed Genoa out of the trade. Among other effects, this threw the Genoese mariners out of work and made them available for exploration service under European monarchs. Venice was prospering mightily, because the demand for Oriental goods, especially spices and silks, was increasing rapidly. Portugal was a poor country of mountains and seacoast. Her only exportable product was port wine, and her only market was England (which could not buy or drink enough port wine to make Portugal prosperous). The Portuguese, with a strong sense of nationalism, were worried about being able to preserve their independence in the process of unification of the Spanish Peninsula, which was then going on. They needed taxable wealth to support the armies necessary for defense. Someone hit upon the idea that, if they could find an all-water route to the Orient, they could import Far Eastern goods so much more cheaply than was possible by the land routes that they could capture the monopoly of this business from Venice and make Portugal wealthy and prosperous. In the middle 1400's, under the inspiration and guidance of Prince Henry (known as Henry the Navigator, though he probably was never out of sight of land) Portugal began sending expeditions, officered by Genoese mariners, down along the African coast in an effort to open up

the all-water route. Each expedition would push on a few
leagues beyond where the last one had turned back, when it,
in turn, would have to give up and turn about, either because
of weather or because of threats of mutiny by the illiterate and
superstitious crews. Before the Portuguese finally reached
India around Africa and across the Indian Ocean, Columbus
had made his famous voyage, and one Portuguese expedition,
carried off its course by adverse winds, had stumbled upon the
coast of Brazil. Before we turn to a discussion of how Columbus came into the picture, we shall glance briefly at some
other pre-Columbian explorations.

PRE-COLUMBIAN DISCOVERIES

Overland Journeys to the Far East. After the Crusades
had brought Western Europe into contact with the Near East,
and indirectly with the Far East, a sizable number of Europeans
made their way eastward to China, then ruled by the Mongols.
Most of them made the entire journey overland, though some
went partly by sea across the Indian Ocean. A large proportion
were merchants, seeking new trade relations, though some
were missionaries seeking to extend their religion. It is even
recorded that, around the year 1300, a young man from China
visited Paris on a diplomatic mission for the Mongol Emperor.
The tales brought back by these travelers whetted the interest
of Europeans in the Far East and stimulated a desire to increase
trade with the Orient.

The most famous of these travelers was Marco Polo, a
Venetian, who went out in the middle 1200's and spent twenty
years in China. After he got back to Europe in 1295, he wrote
a book giving an account of his travels and describing the
wealth and culture of China. His book had only limited in-

fluence until the introduction of printing a century and a half later, but, once in print, it was widely read and spurred new interest in geographical exploration to seek a new route to China. It is all but certain that Polo's overestimate of the distance from Western Europe to China, quite understandable in view of his devious route and slow transportation, had a direct influence on Columbus.

Unimportance of the Norse Discoveries. The Icelandic sagas tell how, in the late 900's, Eric the Red discovered and tried to settle Greenland and, about the year 1000, how his son, Leif Ericson, pushed beyond Greenland with a large fleet and found a land he called Vinland, undoubtedly North America. The sagas go on to tell how Leif founded a colony in Vinland. While these sagas are embroidered with a great deal of folklore, it is now well established that they are essentially true. Attempts to identify certain things as remains of Leif's settlement have not been successful, but he undoubtedly visited the coast of North America and may have launched a colony. If so, the colony had disappeared long before other Europeans arrived.

Some persons are inclined to argue that the credit for the discovery of America should go to Leif Ericson, rather than Columbus. The objection to this is that nothing permanent came of his discovery. In history, an event is important only if it has discoverable consequences or is a factor in shaping the course of developments that followed. By this test, the Norse discovery is unimportant. It did not lead to the opening of America to permanent European settlement. So far as we can tell, it had no influence on Columbus, since there is no indication that he had ever heard of Leif Ericson or Vinland. So we shall continue to begin American history proper (as distinct from its background), with the first voyage of Columbus.

THE DISCOVERY BY COLUMBUS

His Background and the Sources of His Idea. Christopher
Columbus (Italian *Columbo*) was born into a middle-class
family in Genoa. He received a good education, Renaissance
style, and became an omnivorous reader. For a time, he practiced his father's trade of a weaver, and then, like his oldest
brother, gave it up to become a mariner. As such, he sailed in
a number of expeditions in known waters around Europe. He
settled in Portugal and married a Portuguese woman whose
father later became governor of the Azores Islands.

We can not be sure just how or when he hit upon the idea
of reaching the Indies by sailing westward. There are a couple
of stories extant, the truth of which can not be verified, but
which, if true, would help to explain the matter. One is that,
on one of the Portuguese expeditions down the African coast,
he went along as a sort of apprentice mariner on a ship of
which his older brother was captain. Out of this experience,
he developed a desire to reach the Orient by a shorter and
simpler route than the one around Africa promised to be. The
other story is that, while he and his wife were living in the
Azores where his father-in-law was governor, a boat from a
wrecked ship, carrying the ship's log and a few survivors,
drifted ashore. The log, so the story goes, was turned over to
the governor and Columbus had a chance to examine it. It
showed that, in a longitude approximately that of part of the
east coast of North America, the ship had found land, but had
been wrecked on the return voyage. It would have been natural
to assume that this land was Asia, and that it was only about
three thousand miles west of Europe.

Errors That Influenced Him. It would be especially natural
to make this assumption in the light of two errors made by

others, which almost certainly influenced Columbus. He undoubtedly knew of these, not as errors, but (in his belief) as real facts. The classical Greeks, working without adequate instruments, had calculated the circumference of the earth at about one-seventh less than it actually is. This alone, had not the American continents intervened, would have shortened the sailing distance westward from Europe to Asia by several thousand miles. The other error was made by Marco Polo, who estimated the distance eastward from Western Europe to the east coast of Asia at about twice what it really is. If we combine these errors by measuring Polo's estimate on the smaller globe of the Greeks it brings the east coast of Asia about where the east coast of North America really lies. The accompanying chart will illustrate the point. If Columbus was fooled by these mistakes, as he very probably was, he would have figured that he could sail westward about the distance he did and reach the coast of Asia.

His Motives. The old legend that Columbus's prime concern was to prove that the earth is round is utter nonsense. In his day, all educated people believed that the earth is round. His motives were much more personal and self-centered. He was a very ambitious, not to say avaricious man. He wanted to break into the nobility, he sought wealth, and he coveted power. An examination of the contract he was able to get with Queen Isabella shows this clearly. He was to be given the rank of a noble, was to be made an admiral, and was to be viceroy of all non-Christian lands he should discover and acquire for Spain, and this viceroyalty was to be hereditary in his family. He was to receive a large share in all profits of trade with lands he might discover and a larger share in all loot he might seize on behalf of the Spanish Crown. Along with seeking these material rewards, he hoped to achieve fame and glory.

A secondary, but real, motive was religion. He was always conscious that his baptismal name, Christopher, means "Christ bearer," and he had a real enthusiasm for carrying Christ to the heathen. This enthusiasm undoubtedly helped to sustain him in several crises of the first voyage when the superstitious crews of his ships threatened mutiny.

Significance of Spanish Sponsorship.   In the late 15th century, there was little chance that anyone but a monarch could be induced to finance such an expedition as Columbus en-

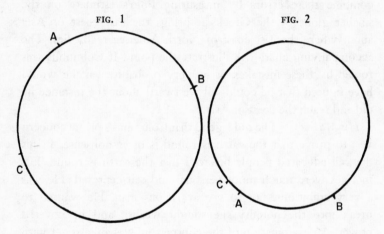

FIGURE 1 represents the real circumstance of the earth and the real distance from the westernmost point of Europe to the easternmost point of Asia.

FIGURE 2 represents the circumference as underestimated by the Greeks and the distance across Eurasia as overestimated by Marco Polo. In both figures, A represents the westernmost point of Europe; B represents the easternmost point of Asia; C represents the longitude of the Bahama Islands and central Cuba. Measurements are not mathematically accurate, but are approximate enough to illustrate the point.

visaged. None of the few private capitalists who could have raised the required funds could be expected to risk so much on such an uncertain venture. Consequently, Columbus made the rounds of the monarchs of Western Europe. He first tried King John of Portugal who was definitely interested in an all-water route to the Orient. To John, however, the project appeared too visionary, and he preferred to keep all of his eggs in the one basket of seeking a route around Africa. The King of France saw no point to it all and refused even to give Columbus an audience. Henry VII of England, who had just become king as the final outcome of the Wars of the Roses, was not only tight-fisted, but had his hands full putting England's internal house in order. The Spanish monarchs, Ferdinand and Isabella, were just completing the unification of Spain, and were engaged in a war to capture Granada, the last Moorish foothold in the Spanish Peninsula. Through influential ecclesiastical mediaries, Columbus got the ear of Queen Isabella. She could give him only vague encouragement so long as the war continued, but immediately following the fall of Granada in January, 1492, she persuaded her husband, King Ferdinand, to agree to back the project on Columbus's own terms. Thus, it was not mere coincidence that the fall of Granada and Columbus's great voyage of discovery occurred in the same year.

We can not, of course, know all the considerations that were taken into account by the Spanish monarchs in reaching this decision. Zeal to carry their religious faith to remote areas may have played a part. It is certain, though, that, as a newly united country with few natural resources and almost no foreign trade, Spain stood to profit enormously by opening a new route to the Orient. If, in the process, new lands could be annexed to provide new revenues, that would be all the better. Whatever the reasons, though, the results are obvious. Spain

had a full century head start over other countries in colonizing and exploiting the new world. She gained control of what
was then the most important part of it. Better (or so it seemed)
than a new trade route to the Far East, Spain had the opportunity to plunder the gold of Mexico and Peru, which brought
in great wealth and made Spain, for a century, the most powerful country in Europe. It is unlikely that, in the 16th century,
any other country in Europe could have made the headway
that Spain did in developing the parts of America that lie between the tropics.

Success in Failure.   In terms of what he was trying to do,
Columbus's work was a failure. He never knew that he had
discovered America. He believed that he had reached the true
Indies, and so called the natives Indians. But the wealth of
China and India still lay beyond, and all of his attempts to
pierce the barrier failed. He also failed as an administrator
when he tried to govern the first Spanish colony. At one time,
he was sent back to Spain in chains. Though restored briefly
to royal favor, he was later deprived of all of his offices and
emoluments and died in obscurity and relative poverty.

In terms of history, though, his work was a huge success. He
opened up the Western Hemisphere to development by Europeans, and a part of this development has been the building of
the United States.

MOTIVES AND MEANING OF THE
FOLLOW-UP EXPLORATIONS

Staking National Claims.   The voyages of Columbus, followed by other explorers, established Spain's prior claim to the
parts of the Western Hemisphere south of present Georgia,
with the exception of Brazil. The Papal Line of Demarcation
of 1493 awarded the tip of Brazil to Portugal and in 1500

Cabral sailed along part of the coast and claimed the region for Portugal. In 1494, without much knowledge of the real geography, Spain and Portugal made a treaty drawing a north-south line through the mouth of the Amazon confirming the area east of this line to Brazil. Columbus's brother had been trying to interest Henry VII of England in Columbus's venture, and apparently succeeded a bit too late. However, when Columbus returned from the first voyage, bringing some gold trinkets and a few kidnapped natives, Henry decided that he would try to grab some of this land to the west. Accordingly he sent out two successive expeditions under John Cabot, in 1496 and 1497. Cabot sailed along the coast of present New Brunswick and New England, and possibly as far south as the Carolinas, called the whole coast the New Found Land (a name, combined into one word, which is now restricted to the large island off Nova Scotia), and claimed it all for England. In 1524, the French king sent out Verrazano to search for a route to China. He sailed along the coast from Newfoundland south to present New York Harbor and claimed the region for France. Ten years later, the then French king sent out Cartier to seek a waterway to China. He sailed up the St. Lawrence River for some distance and claimed all land drained by that river for France. The Dutch, who did not gain their independence until after the Armada battle of 1588, began, in the early 1600's, to claim and settle land along the Hudson River. Little was done to occupy these national claims until after the Armada battle, but in the 1600's they all became important.

Spanish Explorations.   There is an old saying that the motives of Spanish explorers were "Gospel, glory and gold," but the order should be reversed. All of them, except the missionaries, were concerned mainly with acquiring wealth. A few were merchants who hoped to open up valuable trade, but most of them were Spanish knights and soldiers who, deprived of their military occupation in Spain after the fall of Granada, sought wealth, adventure and glory in the new lands. The missionaries, members of religious orders of the time, had as their prime concern the conversion of the Indians to their faith, but they were often content with very superficial conversion and did not hesitate to use the forced labor of their converts to build up wealthy monasteries and mission stations. Cortez and the Pizarro brothers struck it rich by conquering the wealthy native realms of Mexico and Peru, opening the vast gold supplies of these areas to plunder by Spain for more than a century. Whatever their motives, though, they did open up and bring under effective Spanish control all of the Americas between the tropics.

One Spanish exploration that was of particular importance was the voyage of Magellan around South America and across the Pacific to the true Indies. This forced Europe to make a distinction between the East Indies and the West Indies, terms still in use. Magellan was killed in the Philippines, which he discovered and named for Philip II of Spain, in 1521, but a part of his expedition made its way across the Indian Ocean and around Africa back to Europe, thus completing the first circumnavigation of the globe. The great importance of the voyage was that it showed that America was not a part of Asia, but was a separate land mass farther from Asia than it was from Europe.

French Explorations. As already noted, the earliest French explorers, sent out by the king, were seeking a waterway to China. It was not long, though, until they discovered the possibilities of the fur trade and most of the later French explorers were seeking new sources of furs. After France and England began fighting over North American territory in the 1700's, some French explorers were sent out by their government to push French holdings into the Ohio Valley and down the Mississippi.

English Explorations.   After Cabot, most English exploration during the 1500's was done by the buccaneers. These buccaneers, who operated during the reign of Queen Elizabeth I, were a queer combination of patriot, pirate and religious zealot. As pirates, they plundered the Spanish treasure ships, mainly for their own enrichment. But as staunch English patriots, they shared their loot with the Queen, who bestowed knighthood on most of them, providing her with the means to build the English navy which triumphed over the Armada. At the same time, they were such zealous Protestants that they felt that they were serving the Lord by massacring Catholic Spaniards. Their exploration was incidental to their other activities. When they sought out new areas or tried to plant settlements, they were either fleeing from Spanish warships or trying to set up secure bases for their operations. They included such persons as Sir Walter Raleigh, Sir John Hawkins, and Sir Francis Drake. They penetrated several then unknown water areas around North America and occupied, at least temporarily, several islands of the West Indies. They helped to prepare the way for English colonization.

TOPICS AND QUESTIONS FOR DISCUSSION

Chapter 2

1. Can you see any justification for beginning the consideration of American history with the Crusades, and tracing developments down through the Renaissance and the modernization of Europe?

2. How did various kinds of motives (economic, religious, pa-

triotic, love of adventure, and quest for "glory") inter-
mingle to produce the geographic explorations of the 1400's
and 1500's?

3. It is fairly well established that the Norsemen reached North
America about the year 1000. Why, then, should not they,
rather than Columbus, be given credit for the discovery of
America?

4. How was Columbus qualified by his background and early
life to undertake the voyage of discovery?

5. What errors (made by others, but accepted as true by
Columbus) led him to believe that he could reach the "Indies" by sailing westward about the distance he did?

6. Why was sponsorship by some important government necessary for the undertaking?

7. Considering the contract Columbus made with Queen Isabella, what would you say were his predominant motives?

8. What was the impact on the later history of the Western
Hemisphere of the fact that Columbus was sponsored by the
government of Spain?

NOTE: Since this chapter was written, a scholar has announced the "discovery" that the Phoenicians reached Central
America about 500 B. C. and established trading posts which
lasted long enough to give the natives a basis for the culture
which flowered into the civilizations that the Spanish found in
Yucatan, Mexico and Peru. His evidence appears very tenuous.
Even if his thesis is correct, the fact remains that the Phoenicians did not open the Western Hemisphere to development
by Europe, so it is unimportant as background of the history
of the United States.

3 | The Significance of Colonization

NON-ENGLISH COLONIES

Why Non-English Colonies Are Included. In attempting an interpretation of the history of the United States, it is obvious that consideration must be given to the English (later British) colonies, but one may well ask, why include any discussion of the non-English colonies? There would appear to be at least two good reasons. One is that the contrast between conditions in the English colonies and those in colonies of other European countries goes far to explain why the colonists in English America were able to develop as they did and to prepare themselves for successful independent nationhood. Another reason is that an adequate understanding of the relations between English America and other parts of the hemisphere requires some knowledge of the other areas.

Brevity of Treatment. This does not mean that we need to examine these other colonies as fully as we do the English. It will suffice to point out in rather general terms those conditions of their settlement and those features of their social, economic, and political structure which made them different from English America.

SPANISH AND PORTUGUESE

Basis of Settlement. Settlement in the Spanish and Portuguese colonies was government directed but privately promoted. Royal officials in Madrid or Lisbon decided where a settlement should be made and then granted land to a promoter with authority to impress into service the natives on the land. The Crown retained full authority to govern the colony through royal officials. The promoter financed the venture privately. He rarely went to the colony himself, but recruited settlers with promises of land and sent them out under a trusted lieutenant. Where gold or silver were to be found, the ownership of the mines was reserved to the king. He granted a patent to someone to work the mines, with impressed native labor, and received a fifth of all the precious metal extracted.

What Rulers and Promoters Sought. Rulers and promoters alike had financial gain as their prime objective. The king and his top administrators were also, no doubt, thinking in terms of bringing prosperity and power to the kingdom at home. This was especially true of Spain. The kings of Portugal continued to look to the Far East to attain these objectives, and paid scant attention to the colony of Brazil. Everyone involved expressed a concern for the Christianizing of the natives. The condition was always imposed in grants to the *encomenderos* (colonizers who received land grants) that they should see that their Indian wards were taught Christianity. All too often, though, in practice they met this condition only to the extent of maintaining a priest in the native village, who persuaded the natives to attend mass, without understanding much of what it was all about.

Effect of Conditions in Areas Colonized. In the first two centuries of their colonial era (the 1500's and 1600's), the

Spanish (and, for the most part, the Portuguese also) established agricultural settlements, based on plantation agriculture with servile labor. Not until the south temperate zone was settled in the 1700's did individual small farms appear, and that was only because that region was not suitable for plantations. The planters grew general food crops for use in the colonies, but, since nothing could be exported to Spain or Portugal which could be produced in those countries, they concentrated, where climate and soil permitted, on exportable commodities, chiefly sugar and tobacco. The planters were not affected much by the mines, where these existed, because mining was the monopoly of a few licensees. A few towns grew up, inhabited chiefly by merchants and their employees, though the planters sometimes maintained town houses.

In the Caribbean islands, where the Indian population was sparse and the Indian cultural development very low, the Spaniards attempted to enslave the Indians, but the net result was to exterminate the natives. In the early 1500's, the Dominican Friar Las Casas launched an appeal, supported by many other ecclesiastics, to protect the Indian. These reformers were able, in 1542, to achieve the issuance of the "New Laws of the Indies," which required the Christianization and protection of the Indian, and forbade his enslavement. About the only improvement, though, was that, on the mainland, instead of being made a slave (chattel property which could be bought and sold), the Indian was reduced to something like serfdom. There was, however, another factor which had more to do with determining the Indian's condition than did the New Laws.

In Mexico and Peru, and to a less degree in the area in between, the Indian population was relatively dense, and the natives had achieved a degree of civilization comparable to that of Egypt in the Pyramid age. The Mayas of Yucatan even had a system of hieroglyphic writing. Into such an area, it was probably inevitable that the Spanish should come as conquerers, rather than as colonists, just as the French and British later went into India. There was already a feudal type of society, so the Spaniards simply displaced the native aristocrats as lords of the land and rationalized the servile condition of the peasants into their system of *encomiendas*.

Why Negro Slavery Was Introduced. Anywhere and everywhere, plantation agriculture requires servile labor. In the Caribbean islands and along the north coast of South America, the Indians were never satisfactory workers on the plantations, and their numbers rapidly diminished to the vanishing point. Consequently, very early, the Spanish and Portuguese planters began importing Negro slaves from Africa to replace the natives. Some of these Negroes had been kidnapped by slave traders, but many of them were war captives, bartered from victorious tribal chiefs. After Negro slavery had become well established in the Caribbean, a few slaves were introduced into Mexico and Peru, mainly as household servants, but they never became a signficant element in the population there.

Mercantilism and Absolutism Applied to Colonies.   In the 16th, 17th, and 18th centuries, all the governments of Western Europe accepted the doctrine of mercantilism. Without going into the faulty economics on which it was based, it will suffice to say that the doctrine of mercantilism held that a government should regulate all foreign trade very strictly to bring more wealth and prosperity to the home kingdom. Governments differed greatly, though, in the application of mercantilism to their colonies. The Spanish and Portuguese treated their colonies as external dependencies to be exploited for the benefit of the homeland. Portuguese regulations were neither as strict nor as well enforced as the Spanish, mainly because Portuguese interests were chiefly in the Far East and there were no gold mines in early Brazil, but they were of the same general character. Spain regulated the economic life of the colonies very rigidly and to the detriment of the colonies. Colonists were forbidden to produce any commodity which could be produced in Spain or could be supplied from Spain. At one time, they were even forbidden to grow grapes, except for table use, in order to force them to buy Spanish wine. Only licensed merchants could engage in trade. When the buccaneers became active, as a protection against their depredations, Spain adopted the fleet system. Trade between the colonies and Spain could be carried only in annual convoyed fleets, which touched at only four colonial ports. Gold, of course, had a priority on cargo space, and other commodities had to make do with whatever space was left.

Since Spain and Portugal were both absolute monarchies at the time, it was natural that they should extend absolutism to their colonies. This the Portuguese did in a haphazard manner, so that Brazilians were a somewhat disorderly society. Spanish absolutism was systematic and as thorough as the venality of most of the lower officials would permit it to be. Spanish rule in the colonies has been characterized as despotism tempered by corruption. The planter or other well-to-do colonist, if he found regulations oppressive, could usually secure relief by well placed bribes. We need not go into the structure of colonial government. It was all organized from the top down, heading up in a royal Council of the Indies in Spain, through appointive officials, mostly sent over from Spain. The Church was largely under the control of the Spanish monarch, who used it as an instrument to maintain absolutism. It did, however, provide schools of various grades for the sons of upper class families, and even operated several colonial universities of a medieval type. Writers and artists were encouraged so long as their writings and artistic creations were in line with the royal scheme of things. Most of the printing had to be done in Spain, where it was subject to rigid censorship, since there were very few printing presses in the colonies and these printed almost nothing but legal and ecclesiastical documents.

Consequences for Later History. As a result of these arrangements, the Spanish (and to a lesser extent the Portuguese) colonists were deprived of economic freedom and an opportunity for economic development. They did not even have the concept of self-government and their cultural development was circumscribed by a tradition of rigid conformity. This meant that, when they acquired independence in the early 1800's, they had no preparation or developed capacity to operate as independent countries, and so fell under military dictatorships. The old habit of corruption carried over under independence, and so made the situation worse. They had no established trade relations, very little capital, and almost no economic know-how. Most of their land was held in huge estates, many of them owned by the Church, and agriculture was extremely backward. Their lower classes, in a class-stratified society, were illiterate and many were still living in a condition approaching serfdom. It was almost a century before any of them could achieve even a modicum of political or economic stability. Many of them have not done so yet.

The bearing this has on United States history lies, first, in the contrast with the English colonies; second, in conditioning the relations of the United States with Latin America from the time of our independence down to the present.

FRENCH

Nature and Location of French Colonies. At first, the French established agricultural colonies along the St. Lawrence River, in present New Brunswick and Nova Scotia and, later, in some of the West Indies islands. The locations were selected because they were accessible and, for a time, no other country was in a position to challenge French claims. Except in the West Indies, where sugar plantations became the pattern, French colonial agriculture was never very successful. At best, they produced only enough food to feed the colony, and often not even that. The pattern was manorial. A tract of land sufficient for a manor was granted to a manorial lord called a *seigneur*, who expected to settle peasants in a manorial village, parcel out land to them in medieval type strips, and live by their labor. The peasants were legally free (not serfs), but this meant little. Most of them were illiterate and had to depend on the village priest to write and read their letters, and to arrange whatever limited social activity they had. In many cases, the *seigneurs* were unable to recruit enough peasants to put their manors into operation, and so turned to fur trading, exploring, military life, or some other activity. Many became licensed fur traders; others, called *coureurs du bois* or forest rovers, were clandestine fur traders. Living among the Indians and often marrying Indian women, they traded their furs at the licensed trading posts under the pretense that they were Indians themselves.

The only thing that made the French colonies valuable economically was the fur trade. It was carried on by licensed traders who could export their furs to France only through a government monopoly. Partly for this reason, the French were on cordial terms with all of the Indians except the Iroquois, who were allied with the English. The Indians were necessary to successful fur trade. Other factors were that the Indian tribes were useful as allies in the wars against the English, and that missionaries had converted most of them to Catholic Christianity. Still another factor was that the Indians were too few and too wild to be impressed into agricultural labor. Theoretically, government was from the top down, but it was less effective than in the Spanish colonies because authority was divided among too many officials, and there was no effective machinery for enforcing orders from Paris.

Retarding Factors. There were several factors which retarded the development and expansion of the French colonies in North America. One of the most important was sparsity of population. Except for fur traders, there was no economic inducement for settlement in Canada. Agriculture, as practiced by the French at that time, was not profitable and there were no 'opportunities for business. The peasants hand made practically everything they used or wore, so they provided no market for merchants. Nor, until 1685 when Louis XIV abolished toleration for the Huguenots by revoking the Edict of Nantes, was there any internal pressure in France, as there was in England, for emigration. Had the Huguenots who fled France been permitted to settle in the French colonies, their skill and industry (most of them were either skilled craftsmen or successful business men) might have given Canada a real boost toward economic development, though for this to happen the law would have had to be changed to permit them to engage in foreign trade. As it was, they went mainly to England and the English colonies, where they contributed greatly to economic progress. The population of Canada grew very slowly. At the beginning of the 1700's the French were able to settle lower Louisiana, where the attractions were greater than in Canada. Later in that same century, though, when the French government, in rivalry with the British, undertook to occupy the Ohio valley, only enough settlers were available to launch about a dozen tiny settlements around fortified trading posts.

Another retarding factor was the bungling French absolutism. In theory, the absolute power of the French monarch extended to the colonies. In practice, the king's ministers in Paris took little interest in the colonies and permitted royal power to be dissipated by divided authority. The effect was inefficient government in the colonies, and this hampered their development and expansion. A third factor was French mercantilism.

French Mercantilism as Applied to Colonies. In general, French mercantilism was directed toward increasing products for export, but the colonies were too poor to buy many French exports. Like the Spanish and Portuguese, the French regarded their colonies as dependencies to be exploited for the benefit of the mother country. However, aside from the fur trade which was placed in the hands of a government monopoly, there was nothing to exploit. Mercantilist laws restricted (almost to the point of prohibiting) free enterprise in the colonies, and outside trade, except with France, was prohibited. The effect was to hamper the development of the colonies with no corresponding benefit to France.

Beginnings of Colonial Imperialism. With only brief intervals, from 1689 to 1763 France was at war with England (Britain after 1703) in what are known in American history as the intercolonial wars. The wars were fought in America, in India, and in Europe. The European phases grew out of old world power rivalries, but in the last two, France and England were fighting primarily over colonial competition and joined forces with countries that were fighting each other in Europe. Indeed, the fourth war, called the French and Indian in the British colonies, began in America two years before it opened in Europe. This "Second Hundred Years War," as the series of wars is sometimes called, was the real beginning of colonial imperialism in America (though it was already going on in the Far East). Colonial imperialism means the deliberate effort of a country, usually in competition with other countries, to acquire colonies and dependencies for the benefit of the home country. Each imperialist country was usually concerned with tipping the balance of power in its own favor, but the compelling motivation was commercial advantage. The final outcome of this eighteenth-century struggle, the elimination of French rule in North America and in India, had a profound effect in helping to cause, and in shaping the course of, the American Revolution.

ENGLISH

English Background as Contrasted with Others. The contrasts between English colonization and that of other countries goes far to explain the success of British America, both as colonies and later as an independent nation. First off, the English national background was entirely different. Since Anglo-Saxon times, the English had been evolving institutions and attitudes that fitted them well to succeed as colonizers. Around the year 1600, France and Spain were both absolute monarchies with many aspects of feudalism surviving in their social structure. Their foreign trade was very limited. Their commercial classes were small, and soon to be depleted even further by the expulsion of the Moriscos (Moors converted to Christianity) in Spain (the Jews had already been expelled) and the suppression of the Huguenots in France. In neither country was there a tradition of personal liberty or of free enterprise.

In contrast, England had developed the system of common law which guaranteed every person legal protection. It had an elected Parliament which shared power with the monarch and was often able to dominate him through its control of taxation. It had strong traditions of personal liberty and free enterprise. It had a wealthy and powerful merchant class which engaged in extensive foreign trade, and well developed handicraft industries which produced surpluses for export. There was an internal incentive to emigration in the fact that an early inclosure movement had crowded thousands of small farmers off their land and there was not enough work available in the towns to absorb them. This provided a ready source from which colonial promoters could recruit settlers, and many displaced farmers found the means to migrate to the colonies by binding themselves as indentured servants.

The Spanish Armada in American History. Although the defeat of the Spanish Armada in 1588 occurred in the English Channel three thousand miles from American shores, it was a decisive event in American history. We have already noted how the depredations of the buccaneers, in preparation for the Armada battle, cut down Spain's supply of gold from her colonies and forced her adoption of the restrictive fleet system which hampered all colonial commerce. The actual defeat of the Armada broke the sea power of Spain and made the English navy mistress of the Atlantic. As long as Spain controlled the seas, she could and did prevent other countries from colonizing the Western Hemisphere. With Spanish power broken, the English, French, and Dutch soon began further exploration and actual colonization.

Two by-products of the defeat of the Armada also deserve mention. As an indirect result, the Dutch, within a few years, won Spanish recognition of their independence. This enabled them, almost immediately, to become rivals of the English in international commerce and in the settlement of territory within the area of the later United States. Furthermore, the thwarting of the schemes of Philip II for the conquest of England insured the survival of that country as an independent Protestant nation and this affected the whole course of colonization.

Colonization by Free Enterprise. English colonization (except for the belated settlement of Georgia) was all by free enterprise. The promoter of a colonizing project would obtain a charter from the Crown granting him a tract of land with authority to plant and govern a colony. This promoter might be an individual, such as George Calvert and William Penn, or a corporation such as the Virginia Company and the Massachusetts Bay Company. In the cases of Maryland and the Carolinas, the King took the initiative in making grants to favorites, but left it to the proprietors to plant and develop the colonies through their own resources. In several cases, settlers from older colonies migrated into a new area and launched a self-governing colony of their own. With the single exception of Vermont, however, these were shortly either brought within the scope of an existing charter or obtained charters for themselves.

Economic, Political, and Religious Motives. Again with the exception of Georgia, where the original purpose was altruistic, all promoters of colonization projects were motivated largely, and some of them entirely, by the hope of financial gain. John Winthrop, in the launching of Massachusetts, hoped to improve his financial condition, but he also wanted to get away from a political situation in England which was obnoxious to him, and he had an ambition for personal power. The Quaker William Penn, along with hoping to make money out of his colony, had an altruistic desire to provide a refuge for religious groups who were suffering from what they considered persecution in Europe. In almost every case, the actual settlers were likewise motivated by a hope of bettering their economic condition, though some of them also wanted to get away from political and religious situations in their homeland which they disliked. The "Pilgrims" who settled Plymouth, along with a hope of economic betterment, had a patriotic desire to remain English; they were being assimilated into the Dutch population of the Netherlands to which they had fled from England several years before. Moreover, they wanted a community of their own, tailored to their religious and political ideas. In a word, while the economic motive was always present, political and religious considerations also helped to motivate the colonization of English America.

Distinctive Character of English Mercantilism. A vital factor in making the English colonies different from those of other countries was the distinctive character of English mercantilism. Like everyone else in the colonial era, the English accepted the doctrine of mercantilism. Unlike the other countries, though, instead of regarding their colonies as dependencies to be exploited, they considered the colonies a part of the English economic community. With a few exceptions, English mercantilist legislation protected the trade and enterprise of the colonies along with that of the English homeland. This may not have been due entirely either to altruism or pure reason, or a combination of the two. From the beginning, the great value of the colonies to England lay in profitable trade. Not only did the colonies supply many things that England needed, but prosperous colonies provided a big market for English manufactured goods. So long as this trade was thriving, to the great benefit of the mother country, it was only good sense not to hamper it with petty restrictions.

Under pressure from certain lobbyists who feared colonial competition, Parliament did enact a few restrictive laws, such as the one that forbade the shipping of beaver hats from the colonies to England, but these either had no real application or were never enforced. The much discussed Navigation Act, aimed at barring the Dutch from English colonial trade, was a great boon to the colonial merchants and ship owners who were regarded as English, and so gained protection against

Dutch competition. An Enumerated Articles Act forbade certain colonial products, items badly needed in England, being exported to any foreign country. This worked no hardship on the colonists, however, because England was their natural market for these items. The later Staple Act, passed as the result of lobbying by English merchants, required the colonists to buy all goods of certain types imported into the colonies only in England. With the connivance of the home government, this law was universally ignored, and it was this fact which, technically, made smugglers of most colonial merchants. In the early 1700's, the first prime minister, Sir Robert Walpole, secured the enactment of the famous Molasses Act, which required colonial merchants to buy all the molasses for their very lucrative rum, molasses, and slave trade in the British West Indies. Walpole was willing to put this law onto the books to appease the West Indian planters, but he had no intention of enforcing it. Enforcement would not only have antagonized the colonial merchants, but would have shattered the trade which provided most of the money with which the colonists paid for imports from Britain. Thus English (later British) mercantilism brought great benefit to the colonies and, until the quarrel with the mother country began in 1763, did them no harm.

Effects of American Environment. Naturally, the colonists were influenced by the environment in which they lived. In New England where, in most areas, the land was hilly and heavily forested and the soil was rocky, many colonists turned to other occupations to supplement the meager earnings of agriculture. For several reasons, including terrain, the urban background of so many of the settlers, and the influence of Calvinism, most of the colonists lived in villages and governed themselves democratically through town meetings. The harsh environment combined with Calvinism to produce a spirit of rugged individualism. New Englanders believed in education, mainly to enable every person to read his Bible, so free public schools were open to almost every child. Private secondary schools were open to those who could afford them, and there were two full blown colleges, Harvard and Yale, to which Dartmouth was added near the end of the colonial period.

In the Middle Colonies, climate and soil were better suited to general agriculture. These came to be known as the "bread colonies," and produced a surplus of cereals to help feed other sections and for export. The population was heterogeneous in national origin and in religion so, of necessity, the people developed a spirit of tolerance. Because of the availability of materials, and skills introduced by some of the early settlers, the Middle Colonies become centers of handicraft industry.

South of Pennsylvania, a broad coastal plain extended southward to the limits of English colonization. Here the mild climate and the rich alluvial soil along the many rivers combined to foster a plantation type agriculture with tobacco, for which there was a growing market in England, as its staple crop. The planters needed servile labor. Land was too accessible and too easily obtained to hold free labor on the plantations at wages the planter could afford to pay. At first the planters depended on white indentured servants, who proved unsatisfactory in many ways, but gradually they changed over to Negro slaves. This situation led to a semi-feudal, class-stratified society. Small farmers in the South far outnumbered the plantation owners, but the planters formed an aristocracy which copied the ways of the old aristocracy of England, and dominated politics, the Church, and life in general.

The Germ of North-South Sectionalism. These colonial differences contained the germ of that North-South sectionalism which culminated in the Civil War. This sectionalism did not become acute in colonial times, but after independence each section developed in its own direction and sectional interests became more and more antagonistic. This, in turn, produced sectional loyalties which almost amounted to two discordant nations living under a single government which each sought to control.

TOPICS AND QUESTIONS FOR DISCUSSION

Chapter 3

1. What were the motives of the Spanish explorers and conquerors? To what extent, if at all did commercial motives enter in?
2. To what extent were the characteristics today of the area between Texas and Argentina predetermined by: the nature of Spanish and Portuguese settlements; the early policies of the Spanish and Portuguese governments; climatic conditions?
3. Why was Negro slavery introduced?
4. What characteristics of French colonization retarded the successful development of French colonies?
5. In what ways were the English better qualified than other nationalities to develop strong colonies based on the principles of a free society?
6. In what ways was the defeat of the Spanish Armada in the English Channel in 1588 important in shaping the course of American history?
7. Compare the influence of each of these factors in shaping the character of the English colonies: historical developments in England during the 1600's; environmental factors in America; the policies of the English government.
8. In what ways did the germ of later North-South sectionalism appear in the early English colonies?

4 The Old Colonial System and Its Meaning for Later America

TRANSPLANTED INSTITUTIONS

In General. It must be obvious even to the most casual observer that many of our American institutions had their roots in England. It should help our understanding of American history to see how, and with what modifications, some of these institutions were transplanted. It was very natural that colonial settlers should try to reproduce in their new homeland, as nearly as they could, the institutions to which they were accustomed before they migrated. Neither is it surprising that officials in London should use what power or influence they had to see that colonial institutions conformed to those of England.

Governmental and Legal. Different colonies went through different stages, but by the early 1700's each had a colonial legislature which was considered a modified replica of Parliament. Each had a representative lower house, elected by the voters, and corresponding to the House of Commons. In most of them, a colonial Council, which also served as executive council to the governor and the supreme court of the colony, acted as upper house of the legislature. The hereditary feature of the House of Lords was never introduced into America, but functionally the Council corresponded to that body. Each colony had a charter, granted by the Crown, which made it a "body corporate and politic," and gave it extensive rights of self-government. The legislature could enact laws within the scope of this charter. Each colony had a governor who corresponded to (and in eight of the thirteen, represented) the King. In these eight crown colonies, the governor was appointed by the Crown, which meant in practice by the Lords of Trade or Department of Commerce. In the three proprietary colonies, he was appointed by and represented the proprietor. At first in four, eventually only two corporate colonies, he was elected by the legislature. Thus, the government of the colony as a whole was a modified facsimile of the government of England. The cabinet system (with the ministers responsible to Parliament and required to resign when out-voted in the House of Commons) was never introduced into the colonies because, by the time it developed in Britain, colonial institutions had already crystallized into a permanent pattern.

Local administration in England was through counties and boroughs. The county, which administered rural areas, was mainly an administrative unity, with only a modicum of self-government surviving. Most towns, however, were chartered as boroughs, with almost complete self-government in local matters. The county was introduced into every colony. In the plantation South it differed from its English counterpart only in having more elective officials. It was the only unit of local administration since, until near the end of the colonial period, the South had no towns larger than villages. In New England, though, the settlers developed the town (or township) as the unit of local self-government, and the counties had only limited administrative functions. The middle colonies developed a mixture of the two systems, with the township more important in New York, and the county in Pennsylvania. The

New England town was the English borough, adapted to local conditions.

By the time the earliest colonies were being settled, the common law had crystallized into permanent form in England, and a system of courts had been developed to administer and enforce it. The common law was transplanted totally to every colony, and each had a system of courts modeled on the courts of England. The common law guaranteed and enforced the basic civil liberties, including trial by jury and freedom of speech.

Economic. Seventeenth century England had what was essentially a free enterprise economy, and this too was transplanted to the colonies. There was some government regulation, particularly of foreign trade, in line with the doctrine of mercantilism. For the most part, though, this regulation benefited English merchants by shutting out foreign competition. In general, a man was free to amass capital in any legal way, to invest it in any enterprise of his own choosing, and to run his business with a minimum of government interference. In sharp contrast with the colonies of other countries, this same situation prevailed in the English colonies.

Social. England in the seventeenth and eighteenth centuries had distinct social classes and was very class conscious. Even so, the lines were less rigidly drawn than in most countries of the time, and it was easier to pass from one class to another. This class structure was brought to the colonies by the settlers, but what happened to it on this side of the ocean varied with the region. In the plantation South, it took firm hold. In New England and the middle colonies, hereditary class tended to give way rapidly to an aristocracy of wealth. In New England, along with the deference paid to the wealthy, a superior status was generally accorded to "old families"—descendants of the earliest settlers.

Religious. When the colonies were being settled, just about everyone in England believed in a state church, though different factions wrangled bitterly over what that state church should be. The early Stuart kings insisted it should be high church Anglican. Puritans differed among themselves. The low church element would be content with reforms within the Anglican Church, leaving the episcopal system intact. During the period of the English Revolution, the Presbyterian Puritans set about to make the Church of England Presbyterian, and failed only because of a *coup d'état* by Cromwell. Even the so-called Separatists (they called themselves Independents and are best described as Congregationalists) wanted the state to support the church, but to leave each congregation free to decide its own beliefs and form of worship.

Naturally, then, most of the colonies began with a state church: Anglican in the South; Congregationalist in New England. Neither had much tolerance for dissenters. Lord Baltimore decreed tolerance between Catholics and Protestants in Maryland from the beginning, but this was less a matter of principle than for a practical reason. Baltimore was Catholic and most of the gentry who settled in Maryland and became the planter class were Catholics, but English Catholics generally were not looking for a place of refuge (they were favored by the Stuart kings) and few would migrate. If Baltimore's colony were to succeed, then, it must attract Protestant settlers, so they were promised toleration. Half a century later, William Penn insisted on toleration in Pennsylvania, partly as a Quaker principle, but also to attract all kinds of settlers. It may be noted, too, that both Baltimore and Penn were adherents of religions that were unpopular in England, so it stood them in hand to be tolerant of other faiths than their own.

The first actual separation of church and state occurred in Rhode Island in the 1630's under the influence of Roger

Williams. This is interesting as a "first," but the American tradition of religious liberty does not really stem from Rhode Island. Rather, it developed in the late 1600's and early 1700's in the middle colonies as a very practical adaptation to a situation. In these colonies, there were so many diverse religious groups that no one was strong enough to impose restraints on the others, so religious freedom came to be taken for granted.

DEGREE OF COLONIAL FREEDOM

In General. Not only were the people of the English colonies freer than people in the colonies of any other country; they were also freer than the people of most of the countries of Europe at the time. In general, this flowed from the traditions and attitudes of the people of England, along with English government policy, though local environment had some influence.

Political. There was complete political freedom in the colonies for all who could qualify as voters. Even those who could not vote often could make their influence felt through the force of public opinion. The right to vote was restricted in all the colonies, very drastically in some of them, but the restrictions were imposed by laws of the colony, not by laws of England. The voters elected representatives in their legislatures and numerous town and/or county officials. In doing this, there was complete freedom of campaigning and of discussion, and the elections, conducted by local officials, were usually fair and honest. When political parties appeared in England during the Restoration Period, party politics did not spread to the colonies. Almost all of the colonists, except the few royal officials, considered themselves Whigs, but with no opposition party, they preferred to carry on their politics, as they were accustomed to doing, on a personal rather than a partisan basis. A group of leading men of a community would get together in a "caucus" and propose a slate of candidates. Another group would propose a rival slate, and the voters then chose between the two slates. If there was any trace of a consistent difference between the rival groupings, it was between conservatives and radicals, but neither grouping had a party organization. The real point is that the London government never interfered.

Economic. As already noted, the English colonies operated under a free enterprise economy with very little interference from London. Of the three mercantilist laws, discussed previously, one benefited the colonial merchants, one made no difference, and the third was ignored. The few restrictive laws passed by Parliament at the behest of lobbyists either had no real application or were not enforced. The sea ports of the northern colonies developed a class of wealthy merchants with trade all over the world, though their heaviest trade was with Britain. The colonies had what economists call a "colonial economy." This means that they devoted themselves to producing and exporting agricultural products and raw materials, and importing most of their manufactured goods. Other than fishing, shipbuilding, forest products, mining and smelting, and distilling, the colonies had no industries of significant size. Local craftsmen produced goods of many kinds for a local market, but never enough to supply the demand. Although the industrial revolution had brought factories and machinery to England by the mid-1700's, these were not introduced into the colonies. On the other hand, the colonists wanted more manufactured goods from Britain than their normal exports would pay for, so the balance of trade ran strongly in favor of England and against the colonies. This called for the shipment of gold or silver to Britain, but where was this money to come from?

This gap was bridged by the rum, molasses, and slave trade, carried on mainly by Boston merchants, but also engaged in by merchants of other seaport towns. The pump was primed by shipping molasses casks (cooperage was an important part of New England's forest products industry) to the West Indies, especially the Spanish islands, and exchanging them for molasses. The molasses was brought back to New England and distilled into rum. Some of the rum was consumed locally, by sailors for the most part, but most of it was shipped to the west coast of central Africa where it was exchanged to war chiefs for their captives. When one African tribe was defeated by another, the entire defeated tribe, if not massacred, was taken captive to be sold into slavery. The unfortunate victims of this barter, those who survived the notorious "middle passage," were carried to the West Indies where they were traded, partly for more molasses and partly for Spanish silver money. The process was then repeated interminably. Any slaves not sold in the Indies, where demand did not always equal supply, were sold along the coast of the English plantation colonies, where demand usually exceeded the supply.

One may wonder that the Puritan conscience would tolerate such business, but it did. There was nothing in Calvinism to condemn either slavery or the liquor trade. At first, the trade was illegal under Spanish law (a matter of small importance to the Yankees), but in 1713, as one penalty of defeat in the War of the Spanish Succession (Queen Anne's War in the colonies), Spain gave England a monopoly of the slave trade with her colonies.

This trade created a highly favorable trade balance between the English colonies and the Spanish Indies, which brought great quantities of Spanish silver money into English (or British) America. This provided the means to pay the unfavorable trade balance with Britain. It also had another interesting effect. The colonists carried on much more of their business with Spanish dollars than with English pounds and shillings. The Spanish dollar was divided into eighths, the Spanish name of which was too much for the English-speaking colonists who called them bits; hence our expressions "two bits," "four bits" and "six bits." When, during the Revolutionary period, the Americans adopted their own currency system, the dollar became the unit of value.

Personal. The colonists enjoyed all the personal freedom of the England of their day. The completeness of freedom of speech and the press (especially after 1688) is indicated by the fact that when, during the time when the revolution was brewing, neither the newspapers nor the spellbinding orators like James Otis and Patrick Henry who thundered denunciations of the British government and even the King, were even threatened with prosecution. The colonists objected to the presence of British troops, whom the British government considered necessary for the defense of the colonies, but the absence of any real military oppression is shown by the fact that, at the time of the so-called Boston Massacre, the commander of the troops involved permitted his soldiers to be arrested by the town authorities of Boston and placed on trial before a jury of Bostonians. Another freedom regarded as important in colonial times was the right to organize and maintain militia units. Since these were not equipped by the colonial governments except in time of war, the individual militiaman regarded "the right to keep and bear arms" as essential. It was largely the enjoyment of these personal freedoms that made the Revolution possible, and perhaps inevitable.

EFFECTS OF EVENTS IN EUROPE

The Puritan Revolution. Inevitably the colonies were affected by events that transpired in Europe, especially in England. The first of these that had major repercussions on this side of the Atlantic was the so-called Puritan Revolution. In this upheaval, supporters of Parliament, the traditional constitution, and the established civil liberties, a grouping which coincided fairly well with the adherents of some variety of Puritanism, revolted against the King and his royal usurpations and his effort to impose high church Anglicanism on the kingdom. The royal dictatorship, which Charles I maintained from 1629 to 1639, was the chief spur to the founding of Massachusetts and the "great Puritan migration" to New England. During this period, too, settlers in Connecticut, New Haven, and Rhode Island, unwilling to apply to the dictatorial King for a charter, organized their own colonial governments. During the next two decades, the period of Puritan ascendancy in England, migration to New England slowed down, but the colonies there had time to get their local institutions into good working order without royal interference. During that period, too, thousands of Anglican gentry fled to Virginia, thus strengthening both Anglicanism and the plantation system in that colony. In 1649 the last Maryland legislature in which Anglicans and Catholics together held control passed the Maryland Toleration Act in the hope of protecting these two faiths when the Puritans should gain control. However, it came nearer to being the end of toleration in Maryland than the beginning. The next year, the Puritans did gain control of the legislature and subjected both Anglicans and Catholics to political disabilities from which the Catholics did not escape until the American Revolution.

The Restoration.   The restoration of the monarchy in 1660, followed by the "Restoration Period" which lasted until 1688, brought a number of repercussions in the colonies. To Virginia, which had been the most loyal to the Stuarts of any of the colonies, Charles II sent the tyrannical Governor Berkeley, who provoked Bacon's Rebellion. Massachusetts was penalized for harboring "regicides," persons who had taken part in condemning Charles I to death, by being deprived of her liberal corporate charter and being given a much less liberal one as a crown colony. This charter granted equal status in the colony to Anglicans and annexed the Plymouth colony to Massachusetts. Connecticut, to which New Haven was annexed, and Rhode Island received charters making them self-governing corporate colonies. In 1664, Charles II granted the land occupied by the Dutch to his brother James, Duke of York, later James II, who in turn granted part of it, now named New Jersey, to two favorites, Lord John Berkeley and Sir George Carteret. New Netherland was seized from the Dutch and renamed New York. James extended the common law with the basic civil rights to his colony, but refused to grant any self-government. Charles also granted the Carolina region (already named for his father, Charles I) to a group of eight favorites. In 1681, Charles granted the region he named Pennsylvania to William Penn, including what became Delaware. Thus were born the "restoration colonies."

The "Glorious" Revolution.   The Revolution of 1688 (the English call it the "Glorious Revolution"), which deposed James II and brought William and Mary to the English throne, affected the colonies and the later United States in several ways. First, it set a pattern of government which lasted less than half a century in England, but which took firm root in the colonies and was later embodied in the governments of the states and the federal union. It did not quite go the length of separation of powers, as we understand that term, because it implied the power of Parliament to depose and elect kings. It did, however, provide a basis for separation of powers. The King was the single supreme executive, with all other executive officers subordinate to him. He could recommend legislation and veto Acts of Parliament, but Parliament held the real legislative and financial power.

The revolution settlement included a Toleration Act for Protestant dissenters and a Bill of Rights. The Toleration Act had little influence in the colonies, which were working out religious toleration in their own ways, but the Bill of Rights took a firm hold in America. When the colonies became states, they included it, with modifications, in their state constitutions, and later the same idea was applied in the first nine amendments to the Constitution of the United States.

A third effect of the revolution was to restore self-government to the New England colonies and to give it to New York. This aspect went far to shape the character, in America, for the first two of the Intercolonial Wars.

The Intercolonial Wars. The balance of power wars, which went on intermittently from 1689 to 1763, were fought in America as well as in Europe, and were known here as the Intercolonial Wars. A bit of background is needed to explain colonial participation in the first of these, 1679–1697, called in America King William's War. James II not only violated the traditional English constitution to favor his Catholic co-religionists, but sought to introduce absolutism into the northern colonies. He annulled the charters of all the New England colonies and combined them with his proprietary colony of New York as the Dominion of New England. He then sent over Sir Edmund Andros as viceroy of the Dominion, with instructions to rule it arbitrarily.

When James was deposed, the New England colonists seized

Andros and bundled him off to England, and resumed self-government under their old charters. The new King, William, at once granted a liberal charter to New York. James fled to France where Louis XIV, about to start an aggressive war on his own, promised to restore James to his throne. The New York and New England colonists figured that if France were victorious and James restored to the English throne, he would reestablish absolutism in their colonies. To help prevent this, they were willing to carry on war against the French in Canada. They were fighting for their own liberty.

A continuation of this same fear impelled them to take part in the second war, 1701–1713, called in Europe the War of the Spanish Succession and in America, Queen Anne's War. The South Carolinians also took part in this war because the Spanish, who were allied with the French, had been raiding their territory from Florida. In both of these wars, the colonists who took part considered that they were fighting in their own defense, not merely taking up a quarrel of the mother country.

The third war, 1744–1748, grew out of the aggression of Frederick II of Prussia against Austria and was called in Europe the War of the Austrian Succession. France got into it to influence the balance of power in Europe, but the British were interested mainly in expanding their colonial holdings. Incidentally, we should say Britain and British, rather than England and English, after 1703 when the separate kingdoms of England and Scotland merged to form the United Kingdom of Great Britain. In America, where the struggle was called King George's War, the colonies which had western land claims under their charters, claims that were challenged by the French and Spanish, took part in the war to defend their western claims.

The fourth war of the series, called the French and Indian War in America and the Seven Years War in Europe, began in America and India two years before it opened in Europe. In India, Britain and France were fighting to control that subcontinent with its great commercial value. In America, the colonists themselves began the conflict in an effort to gain control of the area west of the Appalachian Mountains. When war started in Europe, with France, Spain, and Austria on one side and Prussia on the other, the British aligned themselves with Prussia in the belief that the destruction of the power of France in Europe would cripple that country's ability to hold its colonial possessions. The outcome of this war in 1763, the end of French rule in North America and India, was a major factor (in several ways, to be discussed in the next chapter) in precipitating the American Revolution.

Dutch Colonization. The Dutch colonization of the Hudson Valley, already touched upon, had considerable influence in shaping the course of development in English colonies. New Netherland, as the Dutch colony was called, was the property of a private corporation, the Dutch West India Company. This company refused to extend to the settlers in the colony the personal liberty and self-government which the Dutch people enjoyed at home. Like the French government in Canada, it maintained a monopoly of the fur trade through licensed traders, and thus deprived the agricultural settlers of the means, always open to them in the English colonies, of supplementing their earnings from farming in undeveloped frontier areas. The company also sought to set up a semi-feudal agricultural society through its *patroon* system. This was never very successful, but it did create discontent among the settlers. So dissatisfied were the colonists with Dutch rule that when the English fleet appeared before New Amsterdam in 1664, they defied the call of the governor to resist and welcomed the English.

While New Netherland existed, it drove a wedge between New England and the Southern English colonies, and so prevented the development of a feeling of colonial unity. Dutch ships and merchants of New Amsterdam (later New York City) made great inroads into the trade between the two sections of the English colonies and between the colonies in England. It was against this trade that the English Navigation Act was directed. When the English took over the Dutch colony, all this was changed. Rather than being a barrier, New York became a bridge between the sections of English colonies. It opened up an important new area for settlement and development by English colonists and provided a passageway to Canada which figured militarily in the Intercolonial Wars and later in the War for Independence.

During the Thirty Years War in Europe, the Swedes planted settlements on both sides of the Delaware River at about the point where it begins to broaden out into Delaware Bay, and called the place New Sweden. Since the Dutch were allied with the Swedes in the war in Europe, they did not molest New Sweden until the war was over. Then, however, they seized it by military force, claiming that it trespassed on Dutch territory, and incorporated it into New Netherland. It passed into English possession along with the rest of the Dutch colony. Aside from a slight infiltration of Swedish blood in the area, the chief contribution of the Swedes was the introduction of the log cabin into America.

BACKGROUND OF THE
AMERICAN CONSTITUTIONAL SYSTEM

In Relation with England (Great Britain After 1703). We have already noted that the beginnings of many of our constitutional institutions were transplanted from England. Several important features of our constitutional system, though, grew out of the relationship that existed between the colonies and the mother country during the later part of the colonial period.

"Imperial" and "Colonial" Powers. The basis of our federal scheme of government lay in the distinction between "imperial" and "colonial" powers. The colonists called the London government, in its relation to the colonies, the "imperial" government because it functioned for the whole British Empire. By tacit consent, never formally provided for, certain powers of government were conceded to be "imperial," or to belong to the "imperial" government, while others were regarded as "colonial," or belonging to the government of the individual colony. In general, the "imperial" powers were those later given to the federal government under the Constitution of the United States. They included the conduct of foreign relations, making war and peace, the regulation of commerce, and the postal service. "Colonial" powers, with which the British government rarely interfered, included control of suffrage, laws on education, laws on religion, the legalizing of slavery and, in general, laws governing the internal affairs of the colony,—the powers "reserved to the states" under our federal system.

The taxing power was never clarified, and finally became the chief issue in the revolutionary quarrel. Certainly the individual colony had taxing power, granted in its charter, but the British government never conceded that it did not have power to tax the colonies. It always levied regulatory duties, in its function of regulating commerce, but these were not expected to produce more revenue than enough to pay for their administration. Prior to the famous Stamp Act, however, Parliament never levied a tax for revenue on the colonies, and the colonists denied that it had the power to do so.

The important aspect of the matter is that the colonists were accustomed to living under two levels of government, each with its own sphere of powers. All that was necessary to turn this into true federalism was to provide that each level of government should hold its powers in full sovereignty.

The Royal Disallowance. All of the colonial charters, along with granting some specific powers to the colonial government, had a provision that the colonial legislature could pass laws "not in conflict with the laws of England." To determine questions of conflict, either with the charter or with the "laws of England" (a term interpreted to mean basic constitutional laws only), an "imperial" court developed, miscalled, from its historic origin, the Judicial Committee of the Privy Council. Anyone in Britain or the colony involved who wished to challenge a colonial statute, could bring a case before the Judicial Committee. If this body found the statute to be in conflict with either the charter or British constitutional law, it would recommend to the King that the law be disallowed and, since the King always acted on the advice of his ministers, the disallowance followed as a matter of course.

Stripped of technicalities, what this amounted to was that a high court declared a colonial law unconstitutional, and therefore void. The colonists became accustomed to this concept and, under independence, carried it over as judicial review of legislation.

The Royal Veto. The charters of the seven crown colonies reserved to the Crown the right to veto colonial legislation. In the three proprietary colonies, the proprietor had the same right. This veto was exercised by the governor of the colony in the name of the King or the proprietor, but the colonists regarded it as the executive veto of the governor. The veto disappeared in Great Britain with the coming of cabinet government, but it took firm hold in America and was carried over into the state and federal constitutions.

Developments in America. There were also some developments in America in colonial times that helped to shape our constitutional institutions. These had to do mainly with our republican form of government.

The Mayflower Compact and "Plantation Covenants." The Mayflower "Pilgrims" had no charter and they settled in an area where they had not been authorized to locate. They therefore felt it necessary to create some legitimate basis for their community. The men of the group met in the cabin of the Mayflower and signed the famous Mayflower Compact. By this document, they associated themselves together in a "civil body politic" and agreed to obey the laws. They had never heard of the social contract theory (Hume and Locke had not yet formulated it), but their act was the first instance in recorded history of a political community being formed by the explicit agreement of its members. The Mayflower Compact was not a constitution, since it did not provide a framework of government, but it might well have served as the preamble to one. What it did do was to set up the principle of government by the consent of the governed, a principle which, by the time of the Revolution, had been accepted in all the colonies and became a major factor in all American constitutions.

The example of the "Pilgrims" was followed many times in the settlement of New England. Whenever a group of settlers would locate outside the charter boundaries of a colony, they would draw up a document similar to the Mayflower Compact. These were so numerous that they acquired a general name: plantation covenants. Later in Connecticut and Rhode Island, and still later in Vermont, the idea was expanded into drawing up constitutions of self-governing colonies. This set the pattern for the drafting of state constitutions.

Charters as Constitutions. The concept of a written constitution was an outgrowth of the colonial charters. The idea of granting charters to colonial proprietors, and later to colonies themselves, was a carry-over from the chartering of trading corporations, begun by Queen Elizabeth I, and these corporation charters were, in turn, an outgrowth of the charters of English boroughs.

The colonial charter served as the constitution of the colony, and was so regarded by the colonists. It outlined the framework of government and granted or restricted the powers of that government. Hence, the colonists became accustomed to living under a written constitution and to regard that as the normal state of affairs.

The Fundamental Orders of Connecticut. Until the time of the Revolution, the grant of a charter by the English Crown was considered the proper basis for colonial government. However, there were three instances in which (because of the royal dictatorship in England in the cases of Connecticut and Rhode Island, and the fact that the American Revolution was going on, in the case of Vermont) settlers in a new area could not obtain a charter. In this situation the settlers drew up a provisional constitution of their own to serve until a charter could be obtained or, in the case of Vermont, until the region could be admitted as a state. The first of these was the Fundamental Orders of Connecticut in 1638. Two years later, two of the Rhode Island towns united and adopted a similar provisional constitution and in 1644 Roger Williams obtained a charter from Parliament uniting all four towns. In both colonies, the government set up was modeled closely on that of Massachusetts. In the early years of the Restoration, both Connecticut and Rhode Island received regular royal charters as corporate colonies. Although these provisional constitutions were regarded only as makeshift substitutes for charters, they set precedents for the adoption of constitutions by the states during the Revolution.

Corporate Colonies. A corporate colony was itself a corporation, with autonomous corporate status and rights of self-government conferred by its charter. It is not to be confused with a proprietary colony whose proprietor was a corporation, such as Virginia under the London Company. The corporate colony developed in Massachusetts. About a year before Charles I abolished Parliament and set up his royal dictatorship, a group of London merchants, headed by John Winthrop, obtained a charter for the Massachusetts Bay Company, which authorized the Company to settle and govern a colony on Massachusetts Bay. Winthrop was "Governor" (President) of the Company and was to manage its affairs with the help of a "Council of Assistants" (Board of Directors). A periodic "General Court" (stockholders' meeting) was to elect the officers, levy assessments on stockholders (referred to as "freemen"), and have the final word on questions of policy. The intention was to govern the colony by remote control from England. A group of settlers was sent out under John Endicott who founded Salem in 1629.

When Charles announced his royal dictatorship, Winthrop with many of his associates decided to migrate to the colony, take the charter with them, and govern the settlement on the ground. In 1630, Winthrop with about a thousand settlers arrived in Massachusetts and founded Boston. As the colony grew and prospered, funds were needed to meet the expense of governing it, so the General Court levied a tax on the settlers. Several well-to-do colonists, who were not "freemen" of the Company, refused to pay the tax until they were permitted to see the charter to determine whether or not the tax was authorized. When they found that it was not, they demanded that they be admitted as "freemen," and this was done. Other groups then made the same demand and very soon, the General Court voted that all adult male colonists, who were members in good standing of the Congregationalist Church, should be considered "freemen." Thus the term freeman changed its meaning from stockholder to citizen. As more towns were started, it became impractical for all the freemen to go to Boston for the General Court, so town meetings began electing proxies to represent them. This was too complicated, so a systematic scheme of representation was soon adopted.

By thus making practically all the colonists voting members of the Company, colony and Company became identical. What had been the charter of a private corporation became the charter of a self-governing colony. The Assistants, along with serving as a governor's council and a court of law, became the upper house of the legislature, and representatives of the towns were the House of Representatives. Massachusetts still calls her legislature the General Court. During the Restoration Period, Massachusetts lost her privileged position as a corporate colony but, in the meantime, corporate charters had been granted to Connecticut and Rhode Island, and they remained corporate colonies until they became states. Indeed, both of them used their colonial charters as state constitutions for a long time after independence, changing only the preamble. Thus, it is obvious that the corporate colony became the model for the later states.

TOPICS AND QUESTIONS FOR DISCUSSION

Chapter 4

1. What institutions that we regard as typically American were transplanted almost unchanged from England by the early colonists? What historical principle does this illustrate?
2. How much personal, political and economic freedom did the

English colonists have? What bearing did this have on the later history of the United States?

3. What effects did the Puritan revolution and the "Glorious Revolution" in England have on developments in America?
4. How were the colonies affected by the "balance of power" wars in Europe?
5. Compare English (later British) mercantilism with that of other countries as applied to colonies of the respective countries.
6. What feature of the old colonial system laid the foundation for later American federalism?
7. What was the colonial background of the distinctly American institution of judicial review of legislation?
8. Trace the origin and development of American-type written constitutions.

5 | Realities of the American Revolution

REVOLUTION IN GENERAL

Meanings of the Term. The word *revolution* is used with several different meanings. Literally, of course, it means turning around, and it always implies turning around in one sense or another. Sometimes it is used to mean merely an extensive change, as in the term *Industrial Revolution.* This was a change, over a period of time, from handicraft production to mechanized production. As a technical term in political science, it means any change in the structure or personnel of a government by illegal or unconstitutional means. The word is often used in the press to mean a change in the headship of a government by acts or threats of violence. In history, though, the term revolution is usually restricted to those great upheavals that have brought about major changes in the life or government of a country, or sometimes in both. In this sense, the revolutions of history have not been numerous. No country has ever had more than one, and many countries have had none at all.

Where Most Apt to Occur. Contrary to a common notion, revolutions are most apt to occur, not among the most oppressed people, but among the least oppressed. The first in modern history was the so-called Puritan Revolution in England, where the people were a century ahead of most other countries in liberty and prosperity. Next was the American Revolution where the people were well off indeed. Then came the French Revolution. Certainly the Old Regime left much to be desired, but the French people generally were much better off than the people of any other country in continental Europe except the Dutch. A revolution is apt to occur when rights or privileges long established are curtailed or threatened. Normally, the people rise up to preserve existing liberties, not to gain new ones.

A Discernible Pattern. No two of the great revolutions of history have been exactly alike, but there is a discernible pattern that runs through them all, except a few that developed out of some external situation, such as defeat in a foreign war. The revolution normally starts with protests of moderate groups against the curtailment or threatened curtailment of their liberties. A radical group then appears that demands very extreme changes and usually resorts to mob violence. Moderates and radicals manage to work together, but rarely without friction, until some untoward event precipitates armed conflict—either civil war or war with outside countries. This brings a period when the radicals hold sway and resort to some measure of terror to compel support. They may decree drastic changes in government or social structure. Up to a point, they are able to carry the moderate leaders along. Then a reaction sets in that brings the moderates back into the dominant role and there is a distinct swing back toward conservatism. At some point, the "strong man" appears, and what happens next depends largely on his character. He may be a benevolent dictator like Cromwell. He may, like Washington, refuse to be a dictator and use his influence to guide his country back to stability. He may, like Napoleon, seek personal aggrandizement and try to become a world conquerer. Sooner or later, in any case, the country settles down to a state of affairs that is quite different from that which prevailed before the revolution, but falls far short of the extreme desires of the radicals.

AN OVERVIEW OF THE AMERICAN REVOLUTION

How Long It Lasted. In the broadest sense, the Revolution lasted from the beginning of the quarrel in 1763 to stabilization under the Constitution in 1789. In the usual sense, it ended with the attainment of independence, *de facto* (practically) in 1781, *de jure* (legally) in 1783. The period of the quarrel, down to the "Boston Tea Party" in December of 1773, may be considered the incipient stage. During this decade, few if any of the colonial leaders intended to go beyond protests and economic pressure to secure changes in British policy. The strategy worked twice in securing the repeal, first of the Stamp Act, and later of all but one of the Townshend taxes. With the "Tea Party," attitudes on both sides of the Atlantic stiffened. Parliament passed the Coercive Acts, and the colonial leadership determined, at least in Massachusetts, to resort to rebellion to force the British government to change its policies. The decision to strike for independence came as an afterthought more than a year after open rebellion had begun. Popular usage identifies the Revolution with the War for Independence. The war was a phase of the Revolution, but is not identical with it. It is permissible to call the armed conflict the Revolutionary war, but hardly to call the war itself the Revolution.

The Pattern It Followed. With some variations, the American Revolution followed the typical pattern. It began with protests by moderate elements against changes in British policy toward the colonies following the Peace of Paris in 1763, because these changes appeared to them to curtail their liberties. They wanted to make it clear to the British government that they objected to these policies and would resort to economic pressure in the form of boycotts to get them changed, but they were unwilling to resort to illegal or violent methods. Soon a radical element appeared, led by such men as Samuel Adams, John Hancock, and Patrick Henry, who were willing to back up the protests by mob violence. As usually happens, it was this radical group which first formed a revolutionary organization in the form of "committees of correspondence." When, following the repeal of the Stamp Act and again following the repeal of the Townshend taxes, the excitement tended to die down and the moderates were inclined to let well enough alone, the radicals used various propaganda devices to keep antagonism alive, hoping to push the British government into an even further retreat.

When the North Tea Act of 1773 precipitated a crisis, the radicals gained the upper hand. It was a group of them that executed the "Boston Tea Party" and, when the Coercive Acts were passed, led Massachusetts and then all the colonies into open rebellion. They were usually able to dominate the Continental Congress. However, the moderates were able to hold the strategic spots, in the army with Washington and in diplomacy with Benjamin Franklin and John Adams.

With the attainment of independence, the moderates, or conservatives as they were usually called, gradually regained the ascendancy. It was they who brought about the adoption of the Constitution and so stabilized the post-revolutionary situation. The epilogue to the Revolution, corresponding to the "Glorious Revolution" in England and the Revolution of 1830 in France, came with the advent of Jacksonian democracy in 1828.

Major Factors Involved.   As already noted, prior to 1763 the colonists enjoyed a very large measure of economic, political, and personal liberty. Most of them were well contented with their relationship with Great Britain, and practically all of them were loyal to the King and to the British connection. However, at the conclusion of the French and Indian War, the British government began to adopt policies which seemed to threaten or even impair the traditional liberties of the colonists. Several points of conflict developed, but in the early stages of the quarrel, the most irritating was the assertion by Britain of the right to tax the colonies. To the colonist, taxation was a colonial, not an imperial power. If they should concede the right of Parliament to tax even a few luxuries, this could be an opening wedge to lead to really oppressive taxation. It was to safeguard what they considered their legal rights, that they first protested and then rebelled. Another factor was that, with their prosperity and their military experience in the war against France, they felt strong enough to defy London. Just before the outbreak of violence, another grievance was added which aroused those colonies which had western land claims and enraged those individual colonists who wanted to migrate to lands west of the mountains. As early as 1763, a royal proclamation restricted fur trade and land purchases west of the mountains, and the Quebec Act of 1773 annexed the whole region west of the mountains and north of the Ohio River to the Province of Quebec, which was under what the English colonists considered arbitrary rule. This was a major factor in arousing the Virginia planters against Britain. These planters had another grievance in that the price of tobacco had dropped, because of overproduction, until their tobacco crop would no longer pay for the goods they wished to buy in Britain. This was a particularly strong element in persuading the planters, in 1776, to get behind the movement for independence. Independence would permit their own legislature to cancel debts owed to British commission merchants. What all of these things add up to is to explode the old "worm turned" doctrine that the colonists suffered ever increasing oppression until they could not stand it any longer, and rebelled.

DEVELOPMENTS 1763 TO 1775

Effects of the Peace Treaty of 1763. The Peace of Paris, which ended the war known in Europe as the Seven Years War and in America as the French and Indian War, was embodied in several treaties, not just one, but we need not concern ourselves with this detail. French rule and influence were eliminated in North America and in India. France ceded the territory west of the Mississippi, including New Orleans, to her ally Spain to keep it from falling to the British, with a secret understanding that it should later be restored to France. The important thing, for our present purpose, is that this settlement changed the relationship between the continental colonies and Great Britain, and set in motion the chain of developments that produced the American Revolution.

Change in British Policy. Except for a few minor spots like Gibraltar and Malta, the British Empire, prior to 1763, had consisted of the continental colonies in North America, the sugar islands in the West Indies, and only a tenuous foothold in India. Except for India, where the military ruled the British holdings, an ultraliberal colonial policy served well for this homogeneous empire. With the Paris peace settlement, though, British authorities felt, in line with the mercantilist thinking of the time, that the now polyglot empire should be welded together into an economic unity. India and Canada were not ready for self-government and British style personal liberty, and it appeared necessary to impose new restrictions on the American continental colonies.

Misguided British Legislation.   In a misguided attempt to do this, Britain enacted several items of legislation which aroused the ire of the colonists. The British ministry decided that a standing army should be maintained in the colonies as a precaution against Indian uprisings in the West or a possible revolt of the French Canadians. A Quartering Act provided that, if the colonial governments should fail to provide quarters for the soldiers, any troop commander could commandeer outbuildings and unoccupied buildings as quarters, but radical propaganda made it appear that the troops were actually being billeted in the homes of colonists. Moreover, the British government took the position that, since the troops were for the protection of the colonies, the colonists should help pay the cost of maintaining them. When the colonial legislatures refused to provide the money, the famous Stamp Act was passed to raise it. To prevent the Western Indians from being aroused by an influx of settlers, the proclamation line severely restricted migrating to or trading in the Western territory. Besides arousing would-be settlers and some colonial governments, this was a blow to influential groups of speculators who had hoped to make big money by speculating in Western lands. As still another blow, Britain decided to crack down on the almost universal practice of smuggling in the colonies in violation of the Staple Act. To this end, "Writs of Assistance" (general search warrants) were authorized. A "writ of assistance" permitted a revenue officer to enter any premises during daylight hours to search for smuggled goods. To the colonists, this seemed to violate the common law principle that "a man's house is his castle," and it was against these writs that James Otis thundered so violently.

Change in Prevailing Attitude in the Colonies. Largely because of these changes in British policy, but also because their
participation in the war had given the colonists a feeling of
strength and self-sufficiency, the prevailing attitude among
articulate colonists now underwent a change. There was still
no thought of complete independence, but most people in positions of leadership were ready to protest with sufficient vigor
to secure a hearing in London. There were, of course, some
"loyalists," though not as many as later when independence
became the issue, whose loyalty to the King and the British
authority outweighed their feeling of grievance, but these were
not the people who made themselves heard.

Division Into Conservatives and Radicals. It was probably
inevitable that a division should appear among the protesting
colonists into moderates, usually called conservatives, who
insisted that all protest activities be kept within the bounds of
strict legality, and radicals, who were willing to use more
drastic methods, even (on occasion) mob violence. Rather than
being divided by a sharp line, the two groups shaded out one
into the other. Even so, a clear distinction is evident in the
leadership of the two wings.

Committees of Correspondence. It was the radical group
which formed a revolutionary organization of sorts in the
committees of correspondence. Samuel Adams organized the
first committee in Boston at the time of the Townshend Acts,
and the example was copied throughout the colonies. Eventually, there was a local committee in each important community, and a central committee in each colony. Ostensibly,
the purpose was for each committee to keep in touch with
others by correspondence, so that they could coordinate their
activities. In addition, though, the committees served as planning groups for revolutionary activities and a channel for dis-
seminating revolutionary propaganda. Incidentally, it was these

committees of correspondence that provided the model for political party organization under the later federal government.

Chain Reaction of Developments. We need not follow in detail developments down to 1773, but a few observations are in order. The first British move that produced a general reaction in the colonies was the Stamp Act of 1765. This act required all newspapers and legal documents to be printed on stamped paper, the sale of which would provide revenue for the Crown. The radicals were vehement. Patrick Henry denounced the act in the Virginia legislature and Samuel Adams organized the Sons of Liberty and formed his "trained mob" which broke into the house of the Lieutenant Governor and destroyed the stamped paper. The conservatives called the Stamp Act Congress, in which nine colonies participated, to register a formal protest. The thing that turned the trick, though, was a general boycott of imports from Britain, to which both radicals and conservatives subscribed. The Stamp Act would have been resisted anyway, as an attempt of Parliament to tax the colonies, but it was a political blunder in that it made involuntary tax collectors of the newspaper men and lawyers, two of the three groups (the third was the clergy) who were in a position to arouse public opinion.

The Stamp Act was repealed before it actually went into effect, but soon thereafter, in 1767, Parliament passed the Townshend Acts. There were three of them. One reorganized the revenue service in the colonies, and provided that colonists be replaced with men from Britain as customs agents. The second set up admiralty courts, which did not use juries, for the trial of smuggling cases. The reason is obvious enough: colonial juries would not convict on smuggling charges, whatever the evidence. To the colonists, though, it was an infringement of their common law right of trial by jury. The third Townshend Act laid duties on paint, glass, paper, and tea imported from

Britain. In opposing the Stamp Act, the colonists had argued that Parliament could not impose an *internal* tax in the colonies. In all of their earlier experience, *external* taxes, which they conceded that Parliament could levy, had been strictly regulatory in character. But the Townshend Tax Act levied external taxes for revenue. Again there was an outburst of protest. The committees of correspondence were formed and an even tighter boycott of imports from Britain was organized than the one against the Stamp Act. Partly because British merchants protested the loss of trade, but also because of political changes in Britain, Parliament, in 1770, repealed all of the Townshend taxes except the one on tea, and calm returned to the colonies. The colonists smuggled in Dutch tea rather than pay the Townshend tax, but all other boycotts were dropped and trade returned to normal. The radicals tried to keep the agitation alive, playing up distorted versions of such incidents as the street brawl which they called the "Boston massacre," but it took the North Tea Act of 1773 to produce another general outburst in the colonies.

The East India Company, which had enjoyed a monopoly of the importation of tea into the colonies until the Townshend Act boycott, was threatened with bankruptcy and blamed its troubles on the loss of the American tea trade. Most important Britishers, from the King down and including most members of Parliament, were stockholders and would suffer financial losses if the Company should fail. To cope with this situation, the North Tea Act was devised to force the East India Company tea onto the colonial market. The tax arrangements were so modified that this tea could be sold to colonial consumers at a considerably lower price than the smuggled Dutch tea. To by-pass the boycotting colonial merchants, the tea was to be shipped to special agents of the Company in America, who would distribute it to peddlers and other retailers.

Down to this time, the colonial merchants, with a few rare exceptions like John Hancock, had been aligned with the conservatives. Now, however, they were fully aroused and supported drastic actions by the radicals to prevent the landing of the tea. If these merchants could be by-passed in the sale of tea, they might also be by-passed in the sale of other goods they imported from Britain, and their business would be ruined. Different things happened in various ports. In some, the colonial governor was persuaded to deny landing permits for the tea. In Charleston, South Carolina, the tea was landed, but was seized by the radicals and later sold to help defray the expenses of the colony in the Revolution. The most spectacular and violent action, though, was the "Boston Tea Party." This produced a violent reaction in Britain and Parliament passed the Coercive Acts, also called the Retaliatory Acts and referred to in America as the Intolerable Acts. The Boston Port Bill closed the port of Boston to commercial shipping until the tea should be paid for. The Massachusetts Government Act annulled the colony's charter and provided for military rule. The Transportation Act provided that British officials in Massachusetts, accused of crimes, could have their cases transferred to Britain for trial, since they would not be able to have a fair trial in the colony. Radical propaganda represented this as authorizing the sending of colonists to Britain for trial. The Quartering Act repeated the provisions of the similar act of 1763, and again propaganda misrepresented it as authorizing the billeting of troops in the homes of the people. Another act, passed about the same time, was not intended to have any connection with these four, but was regarded in the colonies as a fifth intolerable act. This was the Quebec Act, which annexed the territory between the Ohio River and the Great Lakes to the Province of Quebec, and reorganized the government of that province in a manner pleasing to the French Canadians, but regarded by the British colonists as denying the basic civil liberties. These acts touched off open rebellion in Massachusetts and led to the calling of the First Continental Congress.

Degree of British Tolerance to 1774. Until after the Boston Tea Party, British authorities were extremely tolerant of colonial protests and even acts of violence. None of the spellbinding orators or newspaper editors was ever prosecuted for his denunciations of Parliament or even of the King. Except for denying jury trial in smuggling cases, no civil liberty was infringed. After the so-called Boston Massacre, not only did the military commander permit his soldiers who had been involved to be arrested by town authorities and placed on trial before a Boston jury, but the troops were removed from the town to an old fort on an island in the harbor, and they were not returned until the passage of the Coercive Acts. Clearly, while the British authorities bungled, they had no real intention of oppressing the colonists. As for the slogan, "taxation without representation is tyranny," it did not mean what it seemed to say. The colonists did not want representation in Parliament; this was offered them off the record. What they were arguing was that they could be taxed only by their own legislatures: that taxation was strictly a "colonial" power; not a concurrent "colonial" and "imperial" power.

THE OUTBREAK OF VIOLENCE

Tradition of "Loyal Rebellion." Throughout English history, there had occurred, from time to time, rebellions with limited objectives which professed their loyalty to the King. Their formula was that they were appealing from the King, ill advised, to the King better advised. They were not considered treasonous and their participants were rarely punished. Thus there had developed the tradition of "loyal rebellion." The American revolt began against this background and, for the first year, had no other object than to force changes of policy on the British ministry.

The Revolt in Massachusetts. When General Thomas Gage, military governor under the Massachusetts Government Act, dissolved the colonial legislature in accordance with that act of Parliament, the members, instead of dispersing to their homes, reassembled outside Boston, declared themselves the "Provincial Congress of Massachusetts," and proceeded to prepare for armed rebellion by accumulating war supplies and enlisting a new militia called the "minute men." As other royal governors dissolved their legislatures, on one ground or another, these followed the example of Massachusetts. Indeed, it was the Virginia legislature, meeting in defiance of the governor, that issued the call for the First Continental Congress. This gathering, with delegates from all of the colonies but Georgia, met in Philadelphia in September of 1774. It adopted resolutions affirming loyalty to the King, but defying the Coercive Acts, summarizing grievances, calling for a complete boycott of British goods, and calling a Second Continental Congress to meet the following May unless grievances should be redressed in the meantime.

In Massachusetts, General Gage, after delaying until the middle of April (possibly on orders from London), decided to send a military expedition to seize supplies accumulated at Concord and to try to arrest Samuel Adams and John Hancock, ring leaders of the revolt. The result was the Battle of Lexington and Concord, "the shot heard round the world." There is reason to believe that Adams and Hancock stage-managed the resistance to force the British to fire the first shot so that they could appeal to their fellow colonists to defend their homes and firesides.

"De Facto Coup d'État" by the Continental Congress. When the Second Continental Congress met, the Battle of Lexington and Concord had occurred, so armed rebellion was a reality in Massachusetts. So the Congress, under influence of the radicals, carried out what amounted to a *coup d'état* by adopting the revolt as "continental" and assuming its direction. The militia clustered around Boston, mainly from Massachusetts but with contingents from other New England colonies, was adopted as a "continental army," and the Congress selected its commander. John Hancock wanted the job, but there were several reasons for passing him by. Probably the best reason was Hancock himself. He was far too impetuous and lacked military experience. Moreover, Hancock was from Massachusetts. If a New Englander, especially a Massachusetts man, were selected as commander-in-chief, the whole affair might look to colonists in other areas like a localized revolt in which they need not take part. Preferably, a Southern planter should be chosen to win over the many planters who were still wavering. George Washington fitted the requirements perfectly. He was a Virginia planter—one of the few solvent ones—and his choice would assure the active participation of Virginia. He had commanded large forces in the French and Indian War and had demonstrated great military capacity. Moreover, he had a character and personality that would hold the loyalty of his troops and enable him to get along with civilian authorities. So Washington was chosen. Hancock was "appeased" by electing him President of the Congress, which was the reason he signed first on the Declaration of Independence. From this point until the adoption of the Confederation in 1781, the Continental Congress served as the *de facto* government.

SIGNIFICANCE OF THE
DECLARATION OF INDEPENDENCE

Circumstances That Led to It. As already noted, independence was an afterthought. By the late spring of 1776, the outlook for the success of the revolt seemed very promising. The British army had evacuated Boston, and this was interpreted to mean that they were giving up the struggle. Actually, they had only been withdrawn to Nova Scotia for regrouping and reinforcement, to prepare for a major drive later in the summer. A pamphlet, *Common Sense*, by Thomas Paine (a congenital revolutionary recently arrived from England, who later took part in the French Revolution) helped to arouse sentiment for independence. Southern planters were ready to rally to the idea as a means of repudiating their debts to British merchants. Virginia had already declared for it, and it was the Virginia delegation that introduced the independence resolution into the Continental Congress. The Congress set up a committee of five to prepare a formal declaration, but it was Thomas Jefferson (a Virginian) who drafted the document with some help and advice from Benjamin Franklin.

The Document. After the preamble, which says in effect that the purpose is to inform world public opinion, the document falls into three parts. The first part is a concise statement of John Locke's version of the social contract doctrine, including the right of revolution. This was intended to give "natural law" legality to the assertion of independence. The second part is a long, detailed statement of grievances, and the third is the declaration proper, asserting that "these united colonies are and of right ought to be free and independent states." It may be noted that it was now necessary to place all blame on the King in order to justify repudiation of his sovereignty. In the early stages of the quarrel, the blame had been placed on Parliament for enacting unjust laws. During the period of "loyal rebellion," the ministry was blamed as befitted tradition.

In Effect, a Political Party Platform. In effect, the Declaration was a political party platform, and it served as a pattern for many later party platforms in the United States. It set forth the aim of the independence party, which now called itself "patriot." It not only sought to justify the aims of this party to world public opinion, but it was intended to win adherents at home. As such, it was, of necessity, a propaganda document. It exaggerated, and in some cases distorted, grievances. Actions were blamed on the King which were entirely beyond his control, such as "conspiring with others," which meant only that the ministers had acted in his name, and "giving his assent to Laws," a mere formality since the monarch had lost the power of veto. The Declaration is an important historic document, in the proper frame of reference, but is not to be taken literally.

Effects of the Declaration. The principal effect of the Declaration was to make independence the issue of the war. It did not, in itself, create any more independence than already existed on a *de facto* basis. This independence could become *de jure* or legally established only when the war should be won and independence recognized by Great Britain. It made success of the revolt more imperative, since war against the King would be treason. There was much truth in the statement attributed to Franklin that "now we must hang together or be hanged separately." A side effect was to draw a sharper line between Patriots and Loyalists (or Tories as the Patriots called them). Many of the common people still remained relatively apathetic, appearing to favor whichever army was in their vicinity or was paying for supplies with good money, but it became difficult for important people to avoid taking a stand. Many Loyalists were subjected to varying degrees of terrorism and, after the war, many of them left the United States to go to Britain or migrate to Canada.

HOW THE AMERICANS WERE ABLE TO WIN THE WAR FOR INDEPENDENCE

The Military Task. It sometimes seems amazing that Washington could lose so many battles and still win the war. This followed from the nature of the military tasks involved. To win, the British had to conquer the rebellious colonies. The Americans, on the other hand, had only to keep the rebellion alive. So long as they could keep an army in the field and keep the state governments functioning, they were not losing, and they could "play for the breaks" to give them an opportunity to achieve final success. Partly because of successful diplomacy, and partly because of British bungling, they had this opportunity at Yorktown.

Obstructive Factors. Washington and his generals faced many obstructive factors which hampered their activity and delayed final success. Several of these deserve our consideration.

Lack of Coercive Power. The most serious of these was the lack of coercive power. The Continental Congress, as the instrument of a *de facto* confederation, directed the war and undertook to provide the necessary men and supplies, but it had to depend on the governments of the separate states for everything. It could appeal for enlistments, but it could not draft soldiers. It could raise money to pay the army and buy supplies and equipment only by requisitions on the states, and the states never contributed all they were asked for. Washington, as military commander, punished deserters when he could catch them, but there was no overall civilian government with power to apprehend and punish them, and the state governments were reluctant to do so. British commanders in the field could buy supplies from the farmers for hard money, but Washington could pay only with paper of doubtful value. The states had coercive power, but could rarely be depended upon to use it in the common cause.

Degree of Apathy and Selfishness. For the most part, the farmers, who made up the great majority of the population, were apathetic except when some special interest was threatened. They might enlist in the continental army in a spurt of enthusiasm, but enlistments were for a few months only, reenlistments were rare, and desertions were all too frequent. Militia units would turn out and fight valiantly when their area or its interests were threatened, but after the battle they returned to their farms. As a case in point, the farmers along the Mohawk turned out to resist Burgoyne's invasion because British control of the area would imperil their land titles, but after Saratoga they all went home.

Among business men, profiteering was rampant. The suffering of the army at Valley Forge was due, not to deliberate neglect by the Continental Congress, but to profiteers withholding supplies to extort higher prices. We should like to think of the Revolution as characterized by self-sacrificing patriotism on the part of all Americans, but unfortunately such was not the case.

Degree of Loyalism. Still another obstructive factor was the degree of loyalism. Over the whole period of the war, almost as many colonials enlisted in the royal army as in the continental forces. When Benedict Arnold changed sides, he was given command of a whole division of Loyalists. In the Southern hinterland especially, the small farmers tended to be Loyalists because they were jealous of the tidewater planters.

The struggle was really more of a civil war than we are apt to think.

British Military Bungling. An important factor in enabling the Americans to succeed was British military bungling. This was probably due in part to the ineptitude of some of the British commanders, but there was also a political explanation. Authorities in London wanted to end the revolt with a minimum outlay of men and money, and on a basis that would encourage a restoration of the valuable colonial trade. We can not document some of the orders from London, but there is every reason to believe that they were issued.

At any time during Washington's retreat across New Jersey in the fall of 1776, vigorous action by Howe's forces could have destroyed Washington's ever shrinking army, and probably have ended the revolt then and there. The Continental Congress was discouraged and would probably have decided to bargain for the best terms it could get. Instead of taking vigorous action, Howe held his army in comfortable winter quarters in New York and merely sent out two regiments of Hessian mercenaries to Trenton and Princeton as a formal occupation of the territory. Washington was able to save the situation by his surprise capture of these Hessians. Howe's inaction may have been due, in part, to his ineptitude, but it was almost certainly based on the belief in London that the revolt was collapsing, as it showed every sign of doing, and that it would be better for a restoration of trade to let it collapse, so the colonists would feel that it was their own failure, than to crush it by a military blow and give the Americans the feeling that they were being held in unwilling subjection.

In 1777, the obvious strategy for the British was to drive south from Canada along Lake Champlain, and north from New York along the Hudson, and so seal off New England, the hotbed of discontent. It was so planned in London, and Burgoyne's expedition moved south according to plan. Howe, however, moved his army by sea and occupied Philadelphia. We have only hearsay evidence that the dispatch from London, ordering him to move north, was delayed and did not reach New York until after he had gone, but this is highly plausible. Howe's decision to seize Philadelphia was probably not, as often supposed, just the old European tactic of winning a war by capturing the enemy's capital. Philadelphia was the capital of Pennsylvania, but was not a national capital such as London or Paris. It was only the meeting place of the Continental Congress, not a government in any real sense, which could and did move elsewhere when the city was threatened. The decision was almost surely based on the belief that, despite the activities of such patriots as Franklin and Robert Morris, Pennsylvania was overwhelmingly Loyalist and would rally around a British army in its capital. When the mistake became obvious, Howe was replaced with General Clinton who, the next summer, moved the British army back to New York. Burgoyne's failure at Saratoga was due in part to his incapacity, but it is doubtful if the most capable general, without Howe's support, could have won the campaign.

The sending of the Cornwallis expedition into the South in 1778 was likewise based on the belief that the section was overwhelmingly Loyalist and only needed the presence of a British army as a rallying point. There was enough loyalism to hamper the Americans, but not enough to hand the area over to British control. This situation assured Cornwallis's failure to achieve his purpose, but not the disaster that befell him at Yorktown. We shall touch on the reasons for that presently.

Diplomatic Achievement. While the Americans were barely holding their own militarily, they were achieving great success diplomatically. As early as the spring of 1777, Franklin had been able to persuade the French foreign minister, Vergennes, that the American war offered France an opportunity to redress the balance of power and possibly to regain some lost territory. Only after the American victory at Saratoga, however, was Vergennes able to persuade the King and the other ministers to recognize American independence and enter into a treaty of alliance. Vergennes was already sending supplies to the American army secretly, through a dummy corporation, but after the treaty France made loans to the Continental Congress and sent supplies openly. A French army under General Rochambeau was sent to America, but saw no action until the Yorktown campaign. With great difficulty, Vergennes drew France's ally Spain into the conflict, and the Spanish fleet was put under French command.

By the spring of 1781, Cornwallis had given up hope of regaining control of the South. He withdrew his army into the York Peninsula where a British fleet was to take his troops on board and transport them to New York to join forces with Clinton. It was now that Washington's generalship and the French alliance paid off. A combined French and Spanish fleet under Admiral De Grasse intercepted the British flotilla that was to rescue Cornwallis's army, and left him stranded at Yorktown. Washington, skillfully avoiding a confrontation with Clinton, moved his own army and the French army to the York Peninsula, gathered in all Southern contingents, and laid siege to Yorktown. After a futile effort to fight his way out of the trap, Cornwallis surrendered.

Colonial Rebellion Turned Into "World War." At a superficial glance, there would appear to be no compelling reason why the surrender at Yorktown should have ended the war and assured American independence. There were several reasons why it worked out that way. One reason was British politics. Lord North, the Tory Prime Minister who had precipitated the conflict by his tea act of 1773 and had headed the administration ever since, felt that he had failed and insisted on resigning. This brought a Whig ministry into power. The Whigs were somewhat divided among themselves. One faction, led by Charles James Fox, had opposed the war all along and had done what they could to hamper it. Even the Whig elements that were less extreme than Fox had supported the war only half-heartedly and had favored conciliation at every turn. Moreover, the Whigs represented the merchant class (the Tories spoke for the country gentry) and the merchants were anxious to have the war ended to restore their trade with America. All of this meant that the new ministry was willing to talk peace.

However, there was another very weighty factor that influenced both Lord North and the Whigs. This was the fact that the American rebellion had been expanded, largely due to the success of American diplomacy, into what, for that day, was a world war. Britain was at war with France and Spain, and was losing valuable holdings in the Mediterranean and the West Indies to Spain. The Netherlands had entered the war against Britain independently to protect Dutch commerce. Several other countries, headed by Russia, had formed a "league of armed neutrality," with the implied threat that they would enter the war unless British privateers should stop molesting their merchant ships. Even the Irish contributed their bit by revolting to gain more freedom from British control.

In the face of such a coalition, continuation of the war seemed hopeless. On the other hand, if Britain could make peace with her former colonies on a basis that would win them away from French influence, she stood not only to regain their trade, but to render the power relationship in Europe less unfavorable. So peace negotiations began and American independence was assured.

TOPICS AND QUESTIONS FOR DISCUSSION

Chapter 5

1. Why are revolutions more apt to occur among the least oppressed people?
2. In what ways and to what extent did the American Revolution follow a "discernible pattern" that runs through other major revolutions?
3. Instead of listing "causes," trace the chain of developments that led to the American Revolution.
4. For what reasons, both theoretical and practical, was the Declaration of Independence written and adopted?
5. Analyze the Declaration of Independence in the light of the circumstances of the time. What effects did it have?
6. What obstructive factors hampered the conduct of the War for Independence?
7. How was it possible for Washington to lose most of his battles and still win the war?
8. Analyze the role of diplomacy in determining the outcome of the War for Independence.

6 | The Aftermath of Revolution

HOW THE AMERICANS WON THE PEACE

Really Part of the Revolution. In the proper sense of the term, the developments discussed in this chapter were a later phase of the Revolution, rather than its aftermath. Certainly, the negotiation of the peace treaty, which made the already *de facto* independence *de jure* also, was a part of the revolution. Even so, as a matter of convenience, we are following common practice and treating the Revolution proper as ending with the establishment of the Confederation and the end of hostilities in 1781, and the developments of the next eight years as the follow-up.

The Problems. When Vergennes summoned delegations from Great Britain, Spain, and the United States (the Confederation) to Paris to negotiate peace, it was a foregone conclusion that American independence would be recognized. There were questions, though, as to what territory the United States should include. The Americans were asking for Canada, but had little chance of getting it. They did not have military possession, the French Canadians preferred British rule to American, the Loyalists had begun the settlement of Ontario, and Britain would not relinquish Canada unless forced to do

87

so. Moreover, France and Spain looked with disfavor on giving Canada to the United States lest it make the new country *too* independent in power relations. Spain not only demanded the return of the Floridas, which she had ceded to Britain in 1763, but claimed all territory west of the Appalachians and south of the Ohio River, an area claimed by the southern states. In working out these problems, the power situation was a major factor.

The Power Situation. For the moment, the balance of power was tipped heavily against Great Britain, but the British hoped to retrieve the situation somewhat in the peace settlement. The United States would not, of course, be a major power for a long time to come, but its strategic location in America and its potential strength made it worth cultivating by both sides in the European power conflict. France, on the basis of the wartime alliance and American gratitude for French help, hoped to hold the new country in its own power orbit. This would weaken materially the power position of Great Britain. If, on the other hand, Britain could, in the peace settlement, win the good will of her former colonists and hold the new country in her own power orbit, this would go at least part way in restoring the power relationship of 1763. It would also be to the advantage of Britain to hold Spanish gains in America to a minimum. For these reasons, as well as because of economic considerations, it behooved the British to be generous to the Americans in peace negotiations.

British Economic Concern. It will be recalled that the principal value of the colonies to Britain had been their trade. There were, naturally, British who, as a matter of national pride, were reluctant to see the Union Jack give way to the Stars and Stripes across the Atlantic, and who would have liked to be as tough as they could on the Americans. To the hard-headed business men, though, national pride should be subordinated to profits, and it was these business men who largely controlled British government policy. If the good will of the Americans could be won by liberal peace terms, so that they would resume their pre-Revolutionary trading habits, this might go far toward nullifying the economic effects of the Revolution.

British Political Situation. A less important, but hardly negligible factor in American success at Paris was the British political situation. Politics in Britain was in a state of confusion. The makeshift Whig ministry, headed first by Rockingham and later by Shelburne, which took over when North refused to go on, was badly divided within its own ranks, and its Parliamentary support was tenuous. Its leaders were politicians of mediocre ability. Because of this situation in the Cabinet, the British delegation at Paris was made up of men of little diplomatic ability who worked at cross purposes. In contrast, the American delegation, Franklin, John Jay, and John Adams, showed remarkable genius at negotiation.

The Negotiations. Only a few observations are in order about the actual negotiations. At the urging of Jay, the American delegation persuaded the British delegation to negotiate with them separately, rather than in conference of the four countries. The treaty of alliance with France bound the Americans not to make a separate peace. Technically they did not do so, since the final treaty was not signed until France and Britain and Spain and Britain were also ready to sign treaties, but actually the terms of the "preliminary agreement," worked out by the Americans and British without consulting the French, were embodied almost exactly in the final treaty. Vergennes protested feebly, but there is reason to believe that he was not displeased at the separate negotiations because it got him out of the difficulty of trying to mediate the conflicting claims of his two allies.

The treaty not only recognized the independence of the United States, but granted the new country all land westward to the Mississippi between the Great Lakes and the Florida border. It developed later that there were a great many ambiguities in the drawing of the boundary, but, except in the case of the Florida boundary, where the British were trying to favor the Americans at the expense of the Spanish, all of these arose from an inadequate knowledge of the geography involved rather than from design. The Americans were to retain the right to fish in Newfoundland waters, though disputes arose later as to just what this involved. Two clauses were included to save face for the British: no "legal impediment" was to be imposed against the collection of debts owed by Americans to British merchants, and Congress was to recommend to the states that they stop discriminating against Loyalists. Neither of these was ever effective. Most authorities agree that the terms were much more favorable to the United States than the military situation in America justified.

THE "CRITICAL PERIOD," 1781–1789

What Was Critical About the "Critical Period"? The historian John Fiske named the eight years from 1781 to 1789 the Critical Period, and critical it was in several ways. Independence was a fact and the states, after much haggling, had accepted the Confederation, but much was wrong. The Radicals wanted to push on to a social revolution, against the staunch hostility of the Conservatives. Most of the small farmers were deeply in debt and were looking for an easy way out. The merchants were having a difficult time getting their business back onto a paying basis. They found themselves barred from the lucrative trade with the British West Indies, and Britain was imposing trade regulations that favored British merchants to the detriment of Americans. The states were jealous of each other and would not cooperate, even to the extent of levying common tariffs which would have put pressure on the British to ease their restrictions on American trade. The money situation was chaotic. Hard money was scarce, and both the Continental currency and the paper money issues of the separate states had depreciated almost to worthlessness. All of these things added up to the question, could the Americans make a success of independence?

Aims and Activities of the Radicals. Not only were the radicals demanding more democratic suffrage (it was relatively democratic only in Rhode Island), but they wanted cancellation of the debts of small farmers. Since these debts were owed mainly to merchants of the towns in the North and to planters in the South, cancellation would have been disastrous to the already hard pressed merchants and planters. The actions of the Radicals in Rhode Island and Massachusetts were a major factor in frightening the Conservatives into launching a movement for a central government with real power.

The "Know Ye" Episode. In Rhode Island every landowner could vote, and this enabled the debtor farmers to control the legislature. First an act was passed making the "lawful money of the State of Rhode Island" legal tender (at face value) in payment of all debts. This was followed by an act which stated that, if a debtor offered to pay his creditor in this money and the offer were refused, he could post a notice declaring this fact and his debt would be cancelled. Since this notice began with the words, "Know ye," the act was nicknamed the "Know Ye Law." Lawyers for the creditor merchants reasoned that, if Rhode Island were still a colony, the Judicial Committee would disallow this law as contrary to the charter. Now that Rhode Island was a sovereign state, they argued, the courts of the state held all the powers ever

exercised by British courts. Accordingly, they brought suit
in the state supreme court and the Know Ye Law was declared
unconstitutional. This, incidentally, was the first instance of
judicial review of legislation by an American court.

The Shays Rebellion. In Massachusetts, few of the debtor
farmers owned enough property to qualify as voters, so they
could not elect a majority of the legislature. Finding a leader
in Daniel Shays, they took up arms in open rebellion to try to
seize control of the state government. The Shays rebels were
defeated in a pitched battle by loyal militia, but it was a close
call. The situation did not get out of hand in other states, but
the discontent and grumbling were present everywhere, and
the creditor classes lived in fear of overt acts.

Inadequacy of the Confederation. It was once a common
practice to compile lists of the defects of the Articles of Confederation. The only thing wrong with the Articles was that
they provided for a confederation: an association of sovereign
states. The Congress of the Confederation, made up of delegations sent by the state legislatures and bound by the instructions of the legislatures, was, like the General Assembly of the
United Nations today, a diplomatic body, not a government
body. Except in procedural matters and one other matter to be
discussed a little later, the Congress could take binding action
only by unanimous agreement of the states. Its only source
of revenue was requisitions on the states (this in the very nature of a confederation), and states never contributed as much
as they were asked for. The Congress never had enough
money available to meet the expenses of the Confederation,
much less to pay anything of the Revolutionary War debts.
It could not even pay the soldiers discharged from the Continental army. An attempt to amend the Articles to permit
Congress to levy a small import duty was vetoed by Rhode
Island. Just because it was a confederation, not a government,

the Confederation was incapable of coping with the problems of the time.

Economic Pressures.   Along with other factors, there were strong economic pressures to create a general government with actual power. Some of these have already been hinted at. The merchants felt that, if the United States could levy tariff duties and perhaps make other trade regulations, pressure could be put on Britain to give us more favorable trading terms. Britain was refusing to make a commercial treaty with us, giving as an excuse the failure of the states to live up to the promises in the peace treaty regarding debts and the Loyalists. This proved, British officials argued, that if they should make a commercial treaty, they would bind themselves to concessions, but that reciprocal promises by the United States could not be enforced on the separate states. Hence, the American merchants felt the need for a government that could not only *make* treaties, but would have power to enforce them. The Southern planters also felt the need for means to put pressure on Britain to reopen their former unrestricted market for their tobacco. Other needs that were recognized by most thinking people were for a uniform sound currency and for some authority to regulate interstate commerce, so that the jealousy of the states would not hamper the economic development of the country.

A Conservative Reaction.   The movement for a federal union was a conservative reaction against the confusion that prevailed under the Confederation. As such, it was typical of the later phases of revolutions. The conservative elements in the population, drawn mainly from the better educated people of the upper social and economic levels, felt that it was inexcusable to try to go on without a general government that could cope with the existing problems. They had a background for federalism in their colonial experience. In a sense, they felt the need of a substitute for the old imperial government of colonial days. The main difference would be that this new government would be truly federal in that it would be based on the sovereignty of the people, and its powers, as well as those retained by the states, would be fully sovereign powers. Since these people controlled the legislatures of most of the states, it was possible for them to set in motion the calling of a convention of the states, ostensibly to propose amendments to the Articles of Confederation, but actually to draft a federal constitution.

THE CONSTITUTION

Nature and Composition of the Constitutional Convention. The convention that met in Philadelphia in the summer of 1787 was a convention of states. Each state legislature was to send a delegation of any size it chose, and each state was to have one vote. Most of the delegates were men of good education and high standing in their respective states. Such outstanding leaders as Washington and Franklin were among them. Most of them were conservative in their leanings, but they differed greatly in their ideas. All of them belonged to the propertied classes. One of the Radical leaders, Patrick Henry, was named a delegate, but refused to serve. Samuel Adams and John Hancock were not named to the Massachusetts delegation. Rhode Island would have no part, partly because of pique over the "Know Ye" affair, and its legislature did not name a delegation. New York presented a particular problem. George Clinton, who was both Governor and political boss of the state, was opposed to a central government lest it diminish his power and prestige. Only the skillful parliamentary maneuvering of Alexander Hamilton was able to wangle through the Clinton-dominated legislature a resolution to send a delegation of three. As author of the resolution, Hamilton was named to the delegation, but the other two were Clinton men who attended only the opening sessions of the Convention in the hope of disrupting it. Thus Hamilton was the only delegate from New York, and he was not able to be present much of the time. He did, however, play an important role in shaping the Constitution. Of the sixty-three delegates designated, fifty-five attended more or less regularly. Thirty-nine signed the completed document.

Problems of Drafting. We need not follow in great detail the problems with which the Convention coped in drafting the Constitution. Much preliminary work had been done by the Virginia and Pennsylvania delegations before the Convention opened. At the opening session, it was agreed, wisely as it turned out, to hold only closed-door meetings and to pledge the delegates to secrecy. We might never have known what went on in the Convention (the official journal tells almost nothing) but for the publication of James Madison's notes after his death. Older textbooks spoke of the three great compromises of the Constitution. In a way, the whole document was a bundle of compromises. There was one, however, that was so basic that it may well be called *the* great compromise. The delegates were in agreement that the old Articles should be abandoned and a new document written. They were in agreement, too, that the new regime should have sovereign powers to cope with existing problems. But here agreement ended. One group, made up of small state delegations, proposed, in effect, to continue the structure of the Confederation. The one-house Congress would consist of state delegations, with each state having one vote, following the doctrine of the sovereign equality of states. This Congress would elect an executive committee. The delegates from the large states wanted a federal republic based on popular sovereignty.

Under the Virginia Plan, representatives in the lower house of a bicameral Congress would be apportioned among the states according to population, and would be elected by the voters in each state. This house would select an upper house, and the two jointly would choose a single executive. Under the great compromise, these viewpoints were reconciled. The lower house of Congress would represent the voters, as in the Virginia Plan, but the Senate would represent the states. Not only would each state have the same number of Senators (two), but the Senators would be chosen by the state legislatures. Down almost to Civil War times, Senators were considered to be bound to vote in Congress according to instructions from their state legislatures.

Rather than picking out the three compromises to be considered greatest, it is more to the point to note the three types of compromises. The substantive compromises, of which there were several, compromised the substance of the disagreement, as in the great compromise. Compromises by ambiguity consisted of using ambiguous phrases, such as "necessary and proper." Most interesting are compromises by omission. In a few instances, when agreement could not be reached on a point, the delegates simply left it out, leaving later developments to fill the gap. A good example was the failure to say whether or not the courts should have the power of judicial review of legislation. Those who favored judicial review regarded the power as existing by implication; those who opposed it, held that if the power were not granted, it would not exist.

How Adoption Was Achieved. The adoption of the Constitution was, by political science standards, a revolutionary process. The Articles of Confederation, which could be amended or supplanted only by unanimous consent of the states, were ignored. A pretense of unanimity was preserved by persuading at least one delegate from each of the twelve states represented to sign the document. The Convention set up its own procedure of ratification. Instead of asking the legislatures to ratify, each state legislature was to call a state convention to pass on ratification. This was good politics, since it enabled the legislators to shift responsibility. The Constitution could be put into effect, among the states ratifying, when it had been ratified by any nine states. This arrangement also enabled the voters to express themselves by voting for delegates who favored or who opposed.

People who concerned themselves with the matter, divided into two groups: those who favored ratification called themselves Federalists, and dubbed their opponents Anti-Federalists. These are not to be regarded as our first political parties; neither had a permanent or countrywide organization. It is especially a mistake to identify the later Jeffersonian Republicans with the Anti-Federalists, as is sometimes done. In the ratifying conventions, a third grouping appeared, whose members may be called conditional Federalists. They favored ratification only if certain additions were assured. A series of essays were written and published by Hamilton and Madison (one by Jay) urging ratification. These essays presented strong, logical arguments, and they have become a classic under the name *The Federalist Papers*, but it is doubtful if they had much influence in securing ratification.

All of the state legislatures except that of Rhode Island called state conventions and, in several of the twelve, much the same thing happened. The conditional Federalists voted for ratification upon receiving pledges from the unconditional Federalists to work for desired amendments. Each convention then adopted a set of resolutions setting forth the amendments desired. In North Carolina, the conditional Federalists were not satisfied with promises. In that state, the convention adopted resolutions setting forth desired amendments, and then, without voting on ratification, recessed until such time as appropriate amendments should be submitted.

Within a few months, nine states had ratified, but two of the big three, New York and Virginia, had not acted, and it would have been futile to try to launch the new federal union without them. In New York it took more skillful maneuvering by Alexander Hamilton to obtain ratification. In Virginia, the Anti-Federalists, led by such Radicals as Patrick Henry and George Mason, put up such a fight that the end was very much in doubt. Finally the prestige of such men as Washington, Madison, and John Marshall prevailed. By the late summer of 1780, all of the states but North Carolina and Rhode Island had ratified and the Congress of the Confederation, accepting the *fait accompli*, began taking steps to set the new government in motion. North Carolina fell into line as soon as amendments were submitted, but Rhode Island held out until the spring of 1790. Even then, it required a statement by the new Congress that, unless Rhode Island should ratify within a specified length of time, that state should be considered a foreign country.

In retrospect, it is clear that, much as we should like to believe that the Constitution represented the will of an overwhelming majority of the people, it was actually the work of a determined minority, made up of highly influential men, who used every device they could think of to get it written and adopted. As such, it marked the completion of the Revolution.

The First Ten Amendments. It has been said, very aptly, that the first ten amendments should not be thought of as amendments in the ordinary sense, but as contemporary addenda. They were actually a condition of ratification. One of the first acts of the new Congress was to submit amendments in line with the pre-ratification agreements. The various state conventions had drawn up 124 proposals, but these contained much overlaping and duplication. The House of Representatives boiled down the contents of most of them into seventeen proposed amendments. The Senate cut the number down to twelve (and the House concurred) by eliminating items which the Senators regarded as trivial, or which had been asked for by only one or two states. Of the twelve submitted, the necessary number of states promptly ratified ten.

We usually refer to these ten amendments as the Bill of Rights. Actually, only the first nine deal with civil rights. The tenth makes explicit what was already implicit in the Constitution, the basis for apportioning powers between the federal government and the states. A complete federal bill of rights would also contain several rights protected in the original document of the Constitution, such as restrictions on prosecution for treason. Whatever we call them, though, the first ten amendments completed the process of constitution making.

TOPICS AND QUESTIONS FOR DISCUSSION

Chapter 6

1. In view of all the circumstances, how were the Americans able to get such favorable peace terms at the close of the War for Independence?
2. What was critical about the "Critical Period"? How did the future of the country depend on finding solutions of the problems of the time?
3. In what ways were the Articles of Confederation inadequate? What was the basic defect?

4. What effect did such "radical" movements as the "Know Ye" affair and the Shays Rebellion have in spurring the demand for a strong central government?

5. In what sense was the movement for a federal union a conservative reaction? How did it fit the "discernible pattern" of revolution?

6. What do you think of Beard's "economic interpretation" of the making of the Constitution?

7. In what sense was the adoption of the Constitution a revolutionary process?

8. Why are the first ten amendments regarded by many scholars as "contemporary addenda," rather than true amendments?

7 Launching the Federal Union

PROBLEMS OF SETTING
THE GOVERNMENT IN MOTION

Filling Gaps in the Constitution. The Constitution had left two major gaps in the structure of government to be filled by Congress. One of these was in the judiciary. It provided only that there should be one Supreme Court and such inferior courts as Congress might establish. Presumably, Congress could also determine the size and structure of the Supreme Court. Probably some of the delegates in the Constitutional Convention favored this provision as providing elasticity to meet changing needs, but there is some reason to believe (though Madison's notes are not clear about this) that it was a compromise of sorts. There seems to have been a question whether the federal government should have its own separate system of courts or should (as is done in some federal unions) leave the handling of federal cases to the courts of the states, up to the final appeal. The effect of the provision was to leave the answer to Congress. Congress decided on a separate system. It established a Supreme Court of five members, a chief justice and four associate justices, and two levels of courts of a lower grade. With some modifications, including the en-

largement of the Supreme Court, the arrangement continues
to the present day.

The other gap was in the structure of administration. The
Constitution alludes to "executive departments" and "heads
of departments," without making specific provision for them.
This obviously was to be left to Congress. The first Congress
created three departments, State, Treasury and War, with a
fourth officer of what today we should call cabinet rank, the
Attorney General. Congress also created civil service offices of
various grades and gave the appointment of such officers to
the President without requiring consent of the Senate.

Washington's Administration.   It was taken for granted in
the Constitutional Convention that Washington would be the
first President, and someone remarked that the office was
tailored to fit the man. The Constitution gives the President
all executive power. It stipulates certain things that he shall
do or may do, but he is not limited to these things. Clearly,
the attitude Washington should take toward the office and the
precedents he should set would go far toward shaping the
character of the presidency.

Washington conceived of his position as much like that of
the English King in the time of William III. He laid great
stress on the dignity of the office as personifying the sovereignty of the country. He was the effective head of government. He might seek the advice of department heads or other
persons, but he reserved all final decisions to himself. To head
the top departments of State and Treasury, he selected two
political giants, Thomas Jefferson and Alexander Hamilton.
He consulted them on all major problems, sometimes together
but more often separately. He usually supported Jefferson in
foreign relations, and Hamilton on domestic matters. The
term cabinet (borrowed from the British) was sometimes used
in Washington's day to designate the four ranking executive

officers, but the cabinet as an advisory council to the President did not come into being until Jefferson's administration. The concept of the presidency has changed through succeeding generations, but much of the pattern that Washington set has remained permanent.

Financial Problems. One of the first and most urgent needs of the new government was to create financial stability, such as the Confederation had never had. That there must be taxes was obvious, but there were questions as to what kinds of taxes should be levied and what uses, if any, other than raising revenue, should be made of them. As soon as the executive branch was organized, Congress asked Alexander Hamilton, as Secretary of the Treasury, to report to it an analysis of the problems with recommendations as to solutions. Hamilton issued three reports in succession, each of which stirred up controversy and helped to draw the lines of the first political parties.

Beginning of the Tariff Issue. Hamilton's first report was on tariff. He urged that tariff duties be used not only to raise revenue, but to regulate commerce, and he wanted the rates made high enough to encourage the development of American industry. This was the viewpoint of protective tariff. There was, as yet, no American industry to protect, but Hamilton believed it would grow up behind a wall of high import duties. This position was challenged by representatives from the plantation section, who found a Congressional leader in James Madison. Madison argued for a level of rates not high enough to discourage imports, but calculated to produce the most revenue. This was the idea of tariff for revenue only. When, after long debate, Congress enacted a tariff law, it was said that Hamilton got the preamble and Madison got the bill. The preamble stated, as one of the purposes of the act, the encouragement of industry, but the rates were those advocated by Madison. Thus the issue was raised. For the next century and a quarter, tariff—high *versus* low—was a major issue in American politics.

The Excise and Its Side Effects.   In his second report, Hamilton proposed excise taxes on a number of items produced in America, including all kinds of liquor. Despite the efforts of Congressmen representing the Western farmers to provide for some exemptions, the measure passed Congress almost exactly as Hamilton had proposed it. The excise is a sound form of taxation, and we have used it ever since. However, this first excise produced some significant side effects.

The natural way for the pioneer farmers of western Pennsylvania and the Kentucky region to market their grain was to float it down the Ohio and Mississippi Rivers to New Orleans. This was blocked by Spanish possession of the lower reaches of the Mississippi. The Kentucky farmers could get their grain to the Atlantic seaboard, partly by water and partly by primitive roads, but there were no roads across the mountains in Pennsylvania—only narrow trails. The farmers of the Pittsburgh area devised a scheme. They distilled their grain into whiskey. A train of pack mules, each with two casks of whiskey slung across his back, could be led over the mountain trails to eastern Pennsylvania where the whiskey was sold for enough cash to meet the farmers' needs. The excise tax would take all the profit out of this trade. Consequently the farmers took up arms in what was called the "whiskey rebellion."

Hamilton wanted to send an armed force to suppress the rebels, but Washington insisted that he wait. The farmers had a real grievance, and Washington undertook to remove it through negotiations with Spain. After a few months, we obtained the Pinckney Treaty with Spain opening the Mississippi, giving us the right of deposit at New Orleans, and accepting our claim as to the Florida boundary. Our minister,

Thomas Pinckney, was able to get this treaty largely by misleading Spanish officials about the contents of the commercial treaty that John Jay had just negotiated with Britain. With the rivers open, the whiskey rebellion lost momentum, but the farmers still refused to pay the excise. At that point, Washington directed Hamilton to send a militia force into the area to uphold federal authority, but insisted that the force be large enough to overawe the farmers without firing a shot. It worked.

The Public Debt. Hamilton's third report stirred up the most controversy of all. It dealt with the Revolutionary War debts, in two parts: the "national" debt and the state debts. The Constitution provided that the debt of the Confederation should be an obligation of the federal government. Hamilton demanded that all of the bonds be redeemed or "refunded" (replaced with new federal bonds) at face value, as a means of establishing the "national" credit. In Congress, Madison conceded that the "foreign debt," bonds held abroad, should be paid at face value to uphold the country's credit, but he argued that the "domestic" debt, bonds held by Americans, should be redeemed only at their depreciated market value. Practically all of these bonds, he insisted, were in the hands of speculators who had bought them at a fraction of their face value. The people who had advanced the money during the war had already taken a huge loss, and to pay the bonds in full now would only enrich speculators. On this point, the Hamilton forces carried the day.

Hamilton also urged that the federal government assume the war debts of the separate states, arguing that these debts had been incurred in a common cause. Madison objected to assumption on the ground that it would benefit only some of the states, and would benefit them unequally. Several of the states had either paid a part of their debts or, like his own

Virginia, had arranged to pay them in full. While this question was being debated in Congress, Jefferson, who had been American minister to France under the Confederation, returned to take up his duties as Secretary of State, and Hamilton persuaded him to make a deal. Another question pending at the moment was the location of the federal capital. The Northern states wanted it located on the Delaware River near Philadelphia; the Southern states wanted it on the Potomac. Hamilton agreed to support the Potomac location, and Jefferson promised to urge his friends in Congress to drop their opposition to assumption of state debts. So assumption carried, and the District of Columbia was located on the Potomac.

Centralism versus *"States' Rights."* Out of these differences on financial policy, along with differences on other questions, there arose an issue which was very much in evidence in various guises right down through the Civil War, and even has its reverberations today. That was the issue of centralism *versus* states' rights. Hamilton and his supporters wanted to make the federal government overwhelmingly strong and to hold the powers of the states to a minimum. Jefferson and Madison, with their following, wanted to make the federal government strong enough to succeed, but to preserve as much as possible of the sovereignty of the states. This difference can be explained in part, but only in part, by the fact that Hamilton spoke for the commercial interests, and potential industrial interests, of the North, while the Jeffersonians were the voice of agriculture, primarily the Southern planters. State pride, especially in rural areas, was a strong factor, of course, but beyond this, farmers and planters felt that their interests could best be protected by strong state governments.

During the first decade of the federal government, the issue took the form of loose construction *versus* strict construction of the Constitution. Centralists interpreted the grants of power in the Constitution very broadly to permit the centralizing actions they wanted to take. Opponents of centralization took refuge in a narrow interpretation of these grants of power to deny the constitutionality of centralist proposals. It has been true ever since that opponents of a pending measure have often challenged its constitutionality, interpreting the provision of the Constitution that applied narrowly to uphold their position. Not since the 1790's, though, has this issue consistently followed political party lines. Needless to say, as time has gone on the Constitution has been interpreted ever more broadly, and we have had more and more federal centralization.

Emergence of Political Parties. It was probably inevitable that the differences we have been discussing should crystallize into political parties. Washington, thinking in terms of the British parties of his day, opposed the whole idea of political parties. In his "farewell address," refusing to run for a third term, he warned against the "spirit of faction," meaning the division into parties. There is every reason to believe that his real reason for refusing to try for a third term was the fact that he would have had to run as a party candidate, rather than any scruples about more than two terms for a President. If space permitted, much circumstantial evidence could be cited to show that, until the parties jelled, Washington had every expectation of continuing in the presidency indefinitely.

The Hamilton party seized npon the name *Federalist* to hint to voters that it was the only party that really upheld the Constitution. Jefferson called his party Republican, thus hinting that the Federalists were monarchists at heart. Jefferson's opponents dubbed his party "democratic" as a term of opprobrium; the terrorists of the French Revolution had called themselves "democrats." It is a mistake to refer to Jefferson's party as Democratic-Republican, as is sometimes done; *Demo-*

cratic Republican did not appear as a party name until 1828. It is an even greater mistake to confuse the Jeffersonian Republicans with the Anti-Federalists; all of their leaders had been staunch Federalists on the issue of adopting the Constitution.

Like the English parties a little over a century earlier, both parties began as "parliamentary" parties. Each consisted of a group of members of a legislative body, Congress or a state legislature, who organized as a "caucus," elected a party floor leader, and appealed to voters to support them in elections. Until the election of 1824, it was the Congressional caucus of each party that nominated the candidates for President and Vice President. The Federalists never got beyond this stage of development. By the election of 1800, though, the Republicans, following the pattern of the Revolutionary committees of correspondence, had organized in each state, in which they had much support, as a pyramid of committees. For nominating candidates for local offices, including members of the legislature, the pre-Revolutionary local leaders' caucus turned into a party caucus; candidates for state offices were nominated by a legislative caucus.

THE WESTWARD MOVEMENT
AND INDIAN RESISTANCE

Migration Beyond the Mountains. Settlement in the areas that were to become Kentucky and Tennessee began just as events were moving rapidly toward open rebellion in Massachusetts. Indeed, Lexington, Kentucky, was named for the battle of Lexington. Since these areas were still parts of Virginia and North Carolina respectively, these states had full authority to convey land to settlers and to set up local governments. Some of the settlers made an abortive attempt to set up an independent "State of Franklin," but the scheme soon collapsed.

North of the Ohio River, migration proceeded more slowly. It was hampered by British regulations (until these collapsed in the Revolution), by hostility of the Indians, and by the lack of adequate communication lines across the mountains. During the Confederation period, though, the settlement of what is now Ohio proceeded rapidly. Settlers, as individuals and in small groups, swarmed in and established "squatters'" claims by building a cabin and getting an acre of land under cultivation. Two large land grants, one to General Symmes and one to the Ohio Land Company, were made by Congress, and Virginia war veterans poured into the Virginia Military Reserve between the Scioto and Little Miami rivers. All of this called for governmental action to provide for disposition of land and to organize local administration.

The Northwest Ordinances. The area bounded by the Ohio River, the Mississippi, the Great Lakes, and the still undetermined western boundary of Pennsylvania, was the one place where the Congress of the Confederation could act as a sovereign government. As a condition of getting the Articles of Confederation ratified, all the states with western land claims had agreed to cede their western lands, with the exception of the Kentucky area and an area along the southern shore of Lake Erie reserved by Connecticut, to the United States. The Southern states delayed until after the federal union was set up, but the states with claims northwest of the Ohio River ceded immediately. Virginia reserved the land title, but not the sovereignty, in the Virginia Military Reserve. This land was the property of the Confederation, so Congress could legislate for it with full authority. In 1784, Jefferson drafted an all inclusive ordinance dividing the territory into ten future states and covering all matters of land and government. Congress, however, decided to enact a land ordinance first and leave government problems for later consideration.

The Ordinance of 1785. This first ordinance covered several aspects of land matters. It provided for the rectilinear system of land survey, later extended to almost all of the United States west of the Appalachians. The scheme gets its name from the fact that tracts of land are bounded by straight lines. It divides land into mile-square "sections" and six-mile-square "townships." Townships are numbered north and south from a base line, and ranges (lines of townships running north and south) are numbered east and west from a principal meridian. The ordinance provided for surveying the western boundary of Pennsylvania (that state had agreed to a straight line boundary), which should serve as the first principal meridian, and the southern boundary of the Connecticut Reserve, which should be the base line. West and south of these lines, seven ranges were to be surveyed. Within the seven ranges a settler could buy one section at auction at a minimum price of one dollar per acre. This was the beginning of a public land policy which was liberalized in successive steps until it culminated in the Homestead Law of Civil War times. It was also the Ordinance of 1785 (rather than that of 1787, which merely declared that education should be encouraged) which foreshadowed federal aid to education. It set aside one section in each township as school land. This land could be sold by local school authorities and the proceeds used to build a school house.

The Ordinance of 1787. The better known Ordinance of 1787 organized the area as the Northwest Territory and provided for its government. In general, it followed the pattern of the old colonial system, substituting the word territory for colony because that term had become repugnant. Until the territory should have six thousand white male residents, it was to be governed by officials appointed by Congress (by the President, when the ordinance was reenacted by the first Congress under the Constitution). After that, the voters were to elect the lower house of a territorial legislature and an upper house or territorial council would be appointed by Congress (later by the President). The governor, other territorial officials and judges of the territorial courts would be appointed by Congress (later by the President). The great difference from the old colonial system was that, when the territory should have sixty thousand inhabitants, it could be admitted by Congress as a state on full equality with the existing states. Eventually, the ordinance provided, not less than three nor more than five states should be formed out of the Northwest Territory.

Another difference from the old colonial pattern was that, unlike the colonial charters, the ordinance contained a bill of rights for the territory, modeled on those in the state constitutions, and prohibited slavery in the territory. As the country expanded, this territorial pattern was extended across the continent and to Alaska and Hawaii. In the later territories, the voters were permitted to elect the upper house of the territorial legislature also.

The Indians.   The Indians of the area resisted the encroachment of white settlers. Repudiating all earlier treaties, they made repeated attacks on frontier settlements. Several military expeditions were sent against them during the Confederation period, but these either failed in their purpose or met with disaster. Not until 1795, when they had been badly defeated by "Mad Anthony" Wayne in the Battle of Fallen Timbers, did the Indians agree to the Treaty of Greenville by which they gave up all of what is now the southern half of Ohio. These events set the pattern of a United States Indian policy, not unlike that of the British, which was followed for about a century. Under this policy, the Indian tribes were treated as semi-independent nations to be dealt with through war and treaties. The federal government undertook to acquire Indian land for settlement through treaties, often imposed by military force, and forbade individuals to acquire land from the Indians directly. The federal government also assumed the responsibility for protecting the frontier against Indian attack.

UNAVOIDABLE INVOLVEMENT
IN POWER POLITICS

Situation in Europe: The French Revolution. The situation in Europe in the early years of the federal republic made it impossible for the United States to avoid involvement in the power politics of the day. On the whole, Washington's administration was able to turn this to American advantage. The French Revolution, which had been brewing for several years, got under way just as Washington was beginning his presidency. Within two years, the French revolutionaries were at war with Austria and Prussia, and a year later with Britain also. One of Washington's first major problems in foreign relations was the question of recognizing diplomatically the revolutionary government of France. In advising the President to extend such recognition, Jefferson, as Secretary of State, laid down the rule that the United States should recognize any government that is in actual control of a country, provided only that such a government meets its international obligations.

Involvement with France and Britain. Our treaty of alliance with France, coupled with our recognition of the French Republic, soon produced complications. Washington believed that the alliance treaty was still valid, but would apply only if France were attacked. He therefore issued a formal proclamation of neutrality, the first ever issued by a chief of state. Soon thereafter, the French revolutionary government sent over, as minister to the United States, "Citizen" Edmund Charles Genêt. Without bothering to present his credentials, Genêt, assuming that the treaty of alliance automatically made the United States an ally of France in the European war, began commissioning American ships as privateers to prey on British commerce, and recruiting an American force to invade Florida. After much bickering, Jefferson requested the French government to recall Genêt, which it did readily enough since his party, the Girondins, had lost power to the more radical Jacobins. Fearing the guillotine if he should return to France, Genêt asked for and received political asylum. The episode set a precedent for demanding that diplomats accredited to the United States conform strictly to their diplomatic obligations.

American shipping took full advantage of our position as a neutral to carry on trade with the belligerents, and this was to the advantage of France whose ships were subject to seizure by the British. The British regarded most of the goods carried to France in American ships as contraband of war. Claiming a "right of search" under international law, British naval vessels stopped American ships on the high seas and seized the "contraband" cargo. They also began the practice of "impressment": taking off American ships sailors who were British subjects and who were alleged to be deserters from the Royal Navy. These activities infuriated Americans and, coupled with British distrust of American intentions because of the alliance treaty with France, threatened to bring on war between the two countries. To avert this danger, Washington persuaded John Jay to resign his position as Chief Justice and go to London to try to negotiate a treaty. In the retrospect of history, Jay's treaty of 1794 brought great benefit to the United States. War was averted, Britain gave up the forts she held in the Northwest Territory, British restrictions on American trade were removed (except in the British West Indies), and other issues were compromised. Also, as previously noted, by letting Spanish officials believe that the Jay treaty meant that we would support Britain in a war against Spain unless Spain should make major concessions, the Jay treaty enabled us to get the Pinckney treaty with Spain a few months later. At the moment, Jay's treaty was extremely unpopular in the United States because Britain did not give up the right of search and impressment and because trade with the British West Indies remained so restricted. It was only with great difficulty that the Senate was persuaded to ratify it and, in doing so, we struck out as insulting the provision for very limited trade with the West Indies.

Beginnings of a Foreign Policy. In coping with these problems, we were making the beginnings of a more or less permanent foreign policy. We could not practice isolation. We would play whatever role in world affairs circumstances seemed to require. We would try to maintain friendly relations with all countries, relying on diplomacy to achieve our aims, but we would threaten or even use force if our national interests were transgressed. We would not interfere in the internal affairs of other countries, nor would we tolerate foreign interference in our internal affairs. This pattern changed somewhat as time went on, but this was the point of departure.

DEVELOPMENTS TO 1828

A Period of Adjustment. The thirty-two years between the presidencies of Washington and Jackson were a period of adjustment. The federal union was reaching maturity of a sort, and the stage was being set for the developments of the next half century. We can not trace the events of this period in detail, but a few items deserve brief comment.

The "X. Y. Z. Affair." At the urging of Jefferson, Washington sent James Monroe as minister to France, just as the Directory was taking over from the revolutionary Convention, with instructions to seek compensation for damage done to American shipping during the height of the French Revolution. Monroe performed his mission badly. Expecting Jefferson to be elected President in 1796, he endeared himself to the Directors by telling them to hold off until after the election when all friction between the United States and France would disappear. Washington learned of this about the time that Adams was winning the election. Without waiting to turn over the presidency, he recalled Monroe and sent Charles C. Pinckney, a Federalist, to replace him. The Directors refused to receive Pinckney and ordered him out of the country. This produced a war fever among some of the Federalists. In the hope of averting war, President Adams sent two special commissioners to join Pinckney in another try. The Directors did not receive the commissioners officially, but three agents of the Directors met with them unofficially and made the famous demand for bribes as a condition of restoring diplomatic relations. In reporting the matter to Congress, President Adams, for reasons known only to himself (probably just a whim), deleted the names of the three French agents and substituted the letters X, Y and Z. This gave the name "X. Y. Z. Affair" to the whole episode.

There was now no restraining the war faction. They pushed through Congress legislation to create a Department of the Navy, to speed the building of naval vessels, to recruit an army, and another packet of laws which we shall discuss presently. The President was able to dissuade Congress from an actual declaration of war, but for two years, American naval vessels and privateers attacked French shipping. Late in 1798, Napoleon was preparing for his *coup d'état,* and had infiltrated the Directory. Since it would serve his purpose to quiet the American war threat, he had the Directors send word through the Netherlands that an American minister would be received with all due respect. In negotiations which followed, France agreed to the termination of the treaty of alliance. Thus the X. Y. Z. Affair not only freed us from this embarrassing commitment but, even more importantly, it served notice to the world that the United States could not be browbeaten and must be treated with the respect due to a strong, independent country. Moreover, it dealt a blow to the Federalists from which they never recovered, though the actual death of the party came only with the War of 1812.

The Alien and Sedition Laws. The packet of legislation that did the most to damage the Federalist Party was the group called the alien and sedition laws. There were three of these. The Alien Act authorized the President to deport undesirable aliens; the Sedition Act imposed penalties for publishing criticism of the President or Congress; a Naturalization Act extended to twenty-one years the time a foreigner must live in the country before he could be naturalized. Ostensibly intended to guard the security of the country, the way these laws were applied indicated strongly that they were politically motivated, with the intent of undermining the Republicans. The Republicans struck back with the Virginia and Kentucky Resolutions, written by Jefferson and Madison respectively, in which the legislatures of these states (which could not be prosecuted under the Sedition Law) denounced the acts as unconstitutional. The net effect, along with a general reaction against the Federalists for pushing the country to the brink of war, was to drive hundreds of thousands of voters from support of the Federalists over to support of the Republicans. This was a major factor in bringing about Jefferson's election to the presidency in 1800.

Jefferson and Marshall. One of the last acts of John Adams as President was to appoint John Marshall Chief Justice of the Supreme Court, a position he held until his death during the administration of Andrew Jackson. Marshall remained the embodiment of Federalism long after the party was dead. Jefferson and Marshall were bitter antagonists in shaping the institutions of the United States. This antagonism was exemplified in the trial of Aaron Burr for treason. Burr, Vice President during Jefferson's first term, was a dubious character, never trusted by Jefferson, who engaged in intrigue with Federalist extremists in New York and New England and who, in the summer of 1804, killed Alexander Hamilton in a duel. After that, he went west and concocted some sort of conspiracy, the real goal of which is still unknown (because Burr told conflicting stories to different people), but which apparently aimed at setting up an independent state with Burr as ruler, either in the new Louisiana Purchase or in Spanish Mexico. Burr was arrested and charged with treason. Jefferson was anxious to have him convicted. In those days, Supreme Court Justices spent part of their time presiding over circuit courts, and Marshall's circuit (which included Virginia) was the one in which Burr was brought to trial. Marshall, as presiding judge, so interpreted the Constitution and the evidence as to make Burr's conviction impossible. Marshall's interpretations may have been good law, but it is a safe bet that he also had the political motivation of wanting to embarrass Jefferson.

While Jefferson and his immediate successors were trying to shape the meaning of the Constitution to conform to Jeffersonian doctrine, Marshall was handing down Supreme Court decisions that imposed Federalist interpretations. Out of this conflict, or more accurately, out of the interplay of these conflicting efforts, there developed what is often called our "unwritten constitution." This is a cluster of traditions, based on precedents, and interpretations, that determine how the federal government shall operate in practice.

Effects of the Napoleonic Wars. The Napoleonic Wars, which followed the Wars of the French Revolution and lasted until the downfall of Napoleon, affected the United States in several ways. It was Napoleon's decision to resume war against Britain that led him to sell Louisiana (which he had just pressured Spain into ceding back to France). During the wars, both Britain and France molested our shipping and violated what we regarded as our neutral rights. The British did us the more damage because of their control of the sea. They not only seized cargoes of "contraband," but impressed sailors from American ships; several clashes occurred between British and American naval vessels. Jefferson, at first, tried to bring both belligerents to terms by withholding all American goods. It was probably the failure of his embargo that caused him to decide against trying for a third term as President. During Madison's first term, things went from bad to worse until we finally declared war on Britain—the War of 1812.

In the long run, the most important effect of the Napoleonic Wars on the United States followed from the reduction of our trade with Britain to a mere trickle. Down to this time, we had continued a "colonial" economy, shipping foodstuffs and raw materials to Britain in exchange for manufactured goods, for the simple reason that it was more profitable than creating our own industries. With the high cost of labor in America, due at least in part to the drain of westward migration, American factories could not have produced goods cheaply enough to compete with imports from Britain. War activities cut down the supply of these goods to such an extent that prices skyrocketed. So high were prices that old established New England merchants could afford to lose one ship in three, and still make a profit. For this reason, they opposed the War of 1812 and, while it was going on, supported a movement for the secession of New England. However, younger men, who normally would have invested their capital in ships and merchandise, not only considered the risk too great, but saw an opportunity to earn large profits in manufacturing. So factories, especially textile mills, began to spring up throughout the Northeast. Thus the Napoleonic Wars brought about the beginning of American industrialization.

The War of 1812. The War of 1812 has been called a needless war, and it really was, though it did have some significant consequences. Had the Atlantic cable existed in 1812, it probably would not have occurred because the British revoked their orders in council to which we objected a week before Congress declared war. To some extent, we were maneuvered into the war situation by the duplicity of Napoleon, reinforced (until it was too late) by the hesitancy of the British, but the decisive factor was the clamor of the "war hawks." These were younger politicians from the West, who wanted war as an excuse to conquer Canada, though they failed miserably in the attempt when war gave them the chance. They pressured Madison into agreeing to a declaration of war by threatening to defeat him for a second term.

Old time textbooks presented the War of 1812 as a great American victory—our "second war for independence." Actually, it was nothing of the sort. For two years, the Canadians, with little more than moral support from Britain, fought the war to a draw along their frontier. In 1814, when Napoleon was presumably eliminated after the Battle of Leipzig (though he came back some months later for the notable "hundred days," and had to be crushed again at Waterloo), Britain sent over an army of veterans. This army entered Washington almost unopposed and burned the public buildings. Its effort to capture Baltimore was thwarted by the guns of Fort McHenry, so the principal result of that engagement was the writing of *The Star Spangled Banner*. The only major American victory in the war was the Battle of New Orleans, but that battle was fought a week after the peace treaty had been signed.

The Treaty of Ghent, which ended the war, was little more than an agreement to stop fighting. The British refused to give up their rights of search and impressment, though they had no further occasion to use them. The treaty did provide for four joint commissions to settle segments of the boundary between the United States and Canada. Two of these commissions, whose only task was to take depth soundings through the Great Lakes, did their work quietly and efficiently. We shall hear more about the other two later. One effect of the war was to create a brief wave of nationalism throughout the country which made possible the so called "era of good feeling." This was soon shattered on the rocks of sectionalism. A related effect was to cause the death of the Federalist Party. The beginning of industrialization was the result of conditions prevailing for several years before the war (and continuing during it) rather than of the war itself. The partial settlement of the Canadian boundary may be considered a by-product of the war. The commission to settle the Maine boundary bogged down, and this boundary was not finally settled until the Webster-Ashburton Treaty of 1842. The commission on the boundary west of Lake of the Woods agreed, in 1818, on the forty-ninth parallel as far west as the crest of the Rocky Mountains, with joint occupation of the region between the Rockies and the Pacific Ocean (the Oregon Country). A by-product of this negotiation was an executive agreement (the Rush-Bagot Agreement) for disarming the Great Lakes, later extended to the whole Canadian border.

Rise of Sectionalisms. In the period under consideration,

two sectionalisms, East *versus* West and North *versus* South, began to play a conspicuous part in the affairs of the country. Both had roots extending far back into the colonial period, but they became conspicuous only during and following the War of 1812. We have already noted that the Westernism of the "war hawks" was a factor in bringing on the war. After the war, it took the form of a clamor for a more liberal public land policy and hostility to the Bank of the United States. East-West sectionalism reached its political crescendo in the election of Andrew Jackson. It was a cross current during the period of the North-South sectional conflict. It flared up again after the Civil War, but never really threatened disunion.

The North-South sectionalism largely dominated the scene from Monroe's administration to the Civil War, as conflicting sectional interests, largely over tariff, drove a wedge between the North and the South. As industrialization proceeded apace in the Northeast, the industrialists demanded high protective tariff to shut out competitive imports, and also favored a bank of the United States to provide them with credit. At the same time, thanks to Eli Whitney's invention of the cotton gin during Washington's administration, the South was turning to the growing of cotton. This not only made slavery profitable again, but rendered the South bitterly hostile to protective tariff. The South joined the West in opposing the Bank, but the main concern of the planters was with tariff. High tariff would, of course, increase the cost of what the planters had to buy, but much more seriously, it would undermine the market for cotton. Almost all of the Southern cotton was sold in England. The way international exchange works, if the British could not acquire American credits by shipping manufactured goods to the United States, they would not have the means to pay for imported cotton. The higher the tariff, the more the cotton market was hurt, and if tariff protection were pushed far enough, that market might be destroyed entirely, to the ruination of Southern planters.

Slavery, because it stirred emotions, became the symbol of this sectionalism, rather than a major cause of it. At the time the sectionalism began to be acute, it so happened that there were an equal number of slaveholding and non-slaveholding states, or as it was usually expressed, slave states and free states, separated by the Mason-Dixon line and the Ohio River. Since the North was increasing in population much more rapidly than the South, it followed automatically that the North would dominate the House of Representatives, so it became a matter of supreme importance to the South to maintain an equal balance in the Senate. To this end, there came about a tacit agreement that, when a new free state was admitted, a slave state must be admitted before another free state.

The Missouri Compromise. The first crisis in the North-South sectionalism arose over the admission of Missouri. At the beginning of 1819, the Territory of Missouri applied for admission as a slave state. It was then the turn for a slave state. However, several Northern congressmen, considering that Missouri should be Northern, since most of it lay north of the mouth of the Ohio River, introduced an amendment to the Missouri bill to require the gradual abolition of slavery in Missouri. While the issue was pending in Congress, Northern congressmen voted enthusiastically for the admission of Alabama as a slave state. This would make it the turn for a free state and so, they thought, strengthen their position on Missouri.

The wrangle dragged on through the remainder of that session of Congress and carried over to the next. It became so heated that the aging Jefferson remarked that it startled him "like a firebell in the night." By 1820, Maine had gained permission from Massachusetts to separate and seek its own state-hood. By admitting Missouri as a slave state and Maine as a free state, the Senate balance was maintained. The important part of the Missouri Compromise, though, was the provision that, for the future, no other slave states should be admitted in the Louisiana Purchase north of the southern boundary of Missouri—the parallel 36°–30'. A superficial glance at the map makes one wonder why the South would agree to this provi-sion. The explanation is that misinformation brought back by Lewis and Clark had brought about the belief that the ter-ritory west of the western line of Missouri was not suitable for settlement, and should be left to the Indians forever. East of that line, there was room for two more free states, the areas that became Iowa and Michigan, and two more slave states, Arkansas, and Florida (which was just being acquired). That would freeze the Senate balance permanently. When it de-veloped, thirty-odd years later, that the area west of Missouri was suitable for settlement, the Missouri Compromise became a red hot issue in sectional politics.

Significance of the Monroe Doctrine. The Monroe Doc-trine of 1823 crystallized certain aspects of our foreign policy in terms that became part of our national tradition. It was fol-lowed with relative consistency until early in the present cen-tury. It was not entirely new. Two of its five points, non-inter-ference with existing colonies in the hemisphere and non-in-tervention in the internal affairs of European countries, had been stated clearly before. Other parts of it grew out of cur-rent situations. Russia was extending her Alaska claims south-ward into the Oregon Country and the statement that the Western Hemisphere was no longer open to colonization was intended as a warning to Russia. The part dealing with Latin America was prompted by a threat, real or imagined, of some of the continental European powers to intervene to reestablish

Spanish authority in the newly independent countries of Latin America. It was considered almost certain that, if Austria and Prussia should restore the power of Ferdinand VII in America, they would demand as compensation the cession of some of his territory in this hemisphere, and a foothold by these aggressive monarchical powers on our side of the Atlantic would constitute a threat to our security. Therefore, the "Doctrine" states, in diplomatic language, that any such intervention, or attempts to set up "their system" (absolute monarchy) in the Americas would be considered grounds for war.

The chain of developments started with a proposal by Prime Minister Canning of Great Britain that his country and ours issue a joint diplomatic warning in which both would renounce any territorial ambitions in the hemisphere. At first, President Monroe and most of his cabinet favored doing this, but John Quincy Adams, the Secretary of State, persuaded them that it would be much better to make our statement of policy separately, by embodying it in the President's message to Congress, without the pledge that we would not seek territorial expansion. It was Adams who penned the exact words of these parts of the message, so it would not be amiss to consider him, rather than Monroe, as the actual author of the Monroe Doctrine.

This statement of the Doctrine was as important for what it did not say as for what it did. Not only did it not pledge that the United States would seek no more territory in the hemisphere; neither did it promise that we should not interfere in the internal affairs of Latin American states. It was not, as many Latin Americans assumed at the time, nor was it ever intended to be, an unqualified guarantee of protection of other nations of the hemisphere. It was intended only to safeguard the security of the United States.

In view of the military weakness of the United States at the time, as compared with the great powers of Europe, it might seem audacious for us to have spoken out so boldly—a case of "making threats with an empty gun." The simple fact was that Adams knew that we could depend on the British navy to enforce the warning. Britain had the same interest we did in Oregon under the joint occupation agreement. In fact, a few years later, Russia, in separate treaties with the United States and Great Britain, agreed not to extend her claims south of 54°–40′, thus drawing a northern boundary for the Oregon Country. In regard to Latin America, Britain was not yet ready (from considerations of European diplomacy) to extend diplomatic recognition to the new countries, but could not afford, for economic reasons, to let them be restored to Spanish rule or to pass under the control of other European powers. Spanish and Portuguese mercantilism had barred the British almost completely from trade with any of the American mainland south of the United States. As soon as these colonies asserted their independence, they repudiated the old trade restrictions and opened their ports to world trade, which for them meant mainly British. This was a great boon to Britain. Coming just at the time when industrialization in the Unted States and on the European continent was shrinking her export markets, access to the new Latin American market meant the economic salvation of Britain. The Latin Americans not only bought British goods, but supplied the United Kingdom with foodstuffs and raw materials. For that reason, Britain could be depended upon to use any means at her disposal, including her navy if necessary, to retain this trade.

For the moment, the Monroe Doctrine had little, if any, effect, but as time went on, it became a major factor in our foreign relations until, during World War II, the most important part of it merged into the broader policy of hemispheric solidarity. Some have seen in the Monroe Doctrine the turning point in our retreat into isolationism. If so, it was only a land-mark, not a real cause, of this development.

Realignment of Political Parties. By the time of the War of 1812, the Federalist Party retained significant strength only in New England. In that section, the party virtually committed suicide by opposing the war and calling the Hartford Convention with a view to proposing secession from the Union. The Convention did not go that far, but the damage was done: the Federalists were branded as disloyal. In 1816, they nominated their last candidate for President, and after that the party disappeared. In 1820, Monroe was unopposed for reelection. By 1824, the Republicans had split into five factions, each formed around an outstanding leader. Four of these leaders ran for the presidency, nominated by state legislatures, and the fifth, John C. Calhoun, was "bought off" by putting him on all four tickets as candidate for Vice President and promising that he would be next in line for President. By 1828, these factions had combined into two new parties, each anxious to cling to the magical name Republican. The party led by Henry Clay and John Quincy Adams called itself National Republican. The other party, a motley coalition of three incongruous elements, took the name Democratic Republican. In that election, the Democratic Republicans nominated Andrew Jackson, as the most likely vote getter, for President, with Calhoun to continue as Vice President and still to be regarded as the "heir apparent." Their success in that election inaugurated "the age of Jackson."

The moral of this realignment would seem to be that, although our two-party system might break down temporarily, the two-party tradition is strong enough that we will always get back to it after an election or two. This was confirmed by a second realignment in the 1850's and 1860's.

TOPICS AND QUESTIONS FOR DISCUSSION

Chapter 7

1. What were the major problems that confronted Washington's administration as President, and how were they met?
2. Why was involvement in power politics unavoidable in Washington's administration?
3. Analyze all the ramifications and the real significance of the "X. Y. Z. Affair."
4. How did the conflicting views of Thomas Jefferson and John Marshall produce the beginnings of the "unwritten constitution"?
5. What was the relation of the War of 1812 to events in Europe? What other factors were involved in it? What were its short range and long range consequences? Why is it a mistake to call it, as some do, the Second War for Independence?
6. Summarize the origins of North-South sectionalism. How did it produce the Missouri Compromise?
7. What was the basic purpose and what was the real effect of the Monroe Doctrine?
8. How and why did political parties form? How did they change after the War of 1812?

8 | The Age of Jackson — Looking Backward and Forward

JACKSON AND HIS ERA

Andrew Jackson. Andrew Jackson was a strong—some would say headstrong—personality. He had deeply ingrained prejudices, including one against the British, based on his experiences as a teenager during the War for Independence. Still, he was capable of compromise when the occasion demanded it. He did not distinguish between personal and political enemies (or friends) as illustrated by his dealings with Calhoun and Van Buren. He was reputed to have an ungovernable temper, but some who have studied his career believe this was a sham; he staged his temper tantrums only when there was something to be accomplished by doing so, and was always able to restrain his temper when this seemed to be the better course. He was an old Indian fighter and had little respect for Indians in general. Largely a product of the frontier, he usually reflected frontier attitudes and ideas. He was an ardent nationalist, though his nationalism differed drastically from that of Henry Clay. He was the only President who ever openly defied the Supreme Court. He may not actually have said, "John Marshall has made his decision, now let him enforce it," but he did say in public documents that, when he swore to uphold the Constitution, he swore to uphold it as he understood it, not as it might be interpreted to him by others. His English, like his handwriting, was notoriously bad. In his public documents, the thought was undoubtedly his own, but the language was that of staff writers.

The "Age of Jackson." The twelve-year era, to which Jackson's name has been given, was distinctive, and was in sharp contrast both with the period which preceded it and the period which followed it. It brought rapid strides toward political democracy, a time when most states turned to universal manhood suffrage, and marked the end of aristocratic rule in Washington. For the first time, it gave the West an equal voice with the Northeast and Southeast. Jackson certainly impressed his own personality on his time, but, on balance, he was more a product and a symbol of the era than the creator of it.

EPILOGUE TO REVOLUTION

Delayed Completion of the Revolution. Each of the great revolutions of history (if it has, as yet, proceeded far enough) has been followed, after an interval of one or more decades, by what we may call an epilogue. This epilogue, which may or may not be accompanied by violence, brings about at least the more moderate demands of the revolutionary radicals, which were shunted aside in the stabilization which ended the revolution proper. Such were the "glorious Revolution" in England, which established the basic features of the British constitution, and the French Revolution of 1830, which ended forever the institution of divine right monarchy in France. The Age of Jackson may be considered a comparable epilogue to the American Revolution. It brought, at least in part, the democracy demanded by such Revolutionary Radicals as

Samuel Adams and Patrick Henry and, in the South, a return to the doctrine of state sovereignty upheld by the Anti-Federalists.

The Rise of the Common Man.   One of the biggest factors in bringing this about was the phenomenon we call "the rise of the common man." As we use the term "common man" in American history, it is virtually synonymous with the American concept of middle class. It refers to those people whose social and economic status contrasts with a wealthy aristocracy on the one hand, and an impoverished peasantry or unskilled labor force on the other. In the later colonial period and during the first decades of independence, this class had consisted mainly of the independent small farmers and the skilled craftsmen. They were seldom allowed to vote or hold public office, and were at an economic disadvantage in their relations with the merchant aristocrats of the North and the planter aristocrats of the South. The surviving class consciousness of those times put them in a social status that was definitely inferior to the aristocratic classes. The Revolutionary Radicals sought to push on to a social revolution that would give equality of status and opportunity to the common man, but they had made little headway.

The rise of the common man to a position of influence—sometimes of dominance—did not come about suddenly. The Age of Jackson marked its zenith, but neither its beginning nor its end. It began in the West, largely as a result of the influence of the frontier, and spread eastward. One of its demands was political democracy. By the time of Jackson's election, nearly all the states had granted universal white manhood suffrage, and the election of Jackson, who was regarded as personifying the common man, was largely a result of this new democracy.

The common man also expressed his aspirations and influence

in other ways. One was a demand for universal free public education. The creation of free public schools "without a taint of charity" proceeded unevenly in different areas, but progress continued until, by Civil War times, a free public school (too often of inferior quality, it must be admitted) was open to almost every white child in the country. As industrialization advanced, controlled by a new group of industrial capitalists, the formerly independent craftsmen found themselves pushed down toward the level of unskilled labor. After some futile attempts to meet the situation politically through "workingmen's parties," labor began to form unions which could put pressure on their employers for better pay and better working conditions. The rise of the common man also found expression in the launching of movements for prison reform, better care of the insane, care of the destitute, and temperance in the use of alcohol. Another aspect was the beginning of the woman's rights movement. The feminists of this period were not yet asking for the right to vote, but only for legal equality and equal educational opportunities. The woman suffrage movement came later.

Influence of Westward Migration. Westward migration, which began to cross the Appalachians during the Revolution and pushed on until it reached the Pacific Ocean, affected the development of the country in several ways. The most obvious was that the western areas acquired population and became new states. By Jackson's time, all of the region westward to the western boundary of Missouri had been organized into territories, and most of these territories had been admitted to statehood. This area made up "the West" which figured in the sectionalism of the time. It is well to bear in mind, though, that the West was constantly moving geographically. As a particular region became well established and the frontier moved on beyond it, it gradually lost the characteristics of a frontier community and took on the traits of older sections. In time, it ceased to be a part of the West and became a part of the North or South, while a "new West" developed farther westward. At first the West was settled from the East and did constitute a drain on the population of the older states, but as the frontier advanced and migration from the East became more difficult and costly, pioneers usually moved only a short distance from older sections of the West. Industrialists of the Northeast continued to worry about the West draining away their labor supply, and so opposed liberalizing the public land policy, but by the end of the Jacksonian era, this drain had ceased to be significant.

The West developed its own characteristics, largely as the result of frontier influences, but also out of its need for transportation and markets. Life on the frontier was hard and required great stamina for survival. The Indians were always a problem and a danger until the federal government succeeded in moving them to lands not yet wanted for settlement. At the same time, the Indians were useful for fur trade, by which the pioneer supplemented his income until his land became fully productive. Until the frontier reached the prairies, most of the land was heavily forested, so the timber had to be cleared before crops could be planted. Class lines broke down, and the settlers became highly individualistic. They did cooperate in such heavy work as clearing forest and building cabins. Few had much education and, if anyone had wealth, there was little he could do with it. In this environment there developed the spirit and practice of democracy. Any man was considered capable of holding any of the local public offices or serving in the legislature, and there was a feeling that these favors should be passed around.

All of the Westerners were in favor of making the public land easy to acquire and many of them, if they could borrow easily, speculated in land. Most of them accepted Henry Clay's tariff doctrine, and favored protective tariff in the belief that the expansion of Eastern industry behind a tariff wall would expand the market for their foodstuffs and raw materials. Practically all of them were hostile to the Bank of the United States, which they regarded as an Eastern monopoly that blocked the easy credit they desired. The outlet down the rivers to New Orleans was not entirely satisfactory, so most Westerners wanted roads and canals by which they could send their products to the Eastern seaboard. Since their states and territories lacked the financial means to construct these, Westerners generally favored internal improvements by the federal government. When Jackson vetoed the Maysville Road Bill, he was letting his hostility to Clay override his loyalty to the West. It was these characteristics and viewpoints that determined the position of the West in the East-West sectionalism.

Jacksonian Democrats Successors to Revolutionary Radicals. As already noted, the Democratic Republican Party that elected Jackson in 1828 was a coalition of three incongruous elements. One, headed by John C. Calhoun, was the voice of the plantation South. A second element, led by Martin Van Buren of New York, was made up of professional politicians, organized into "machines" in most of the Eastern cities, and was interested mainly in the spoils of office. The third element was the Jacksonian Democrats. For the most part, these were Westerners and represented the ideas prevalent in the West. At the same time, they may be considered successors to the Radicals of the Revolutionary period. They stood for real democracy and the elevation of the common man, just as had Samuel Adams and Patrick Henry. They no longer stressed state sovereignty as those men had. That doctrine had been taken up by the plantation South. The Jacksonian Democrats were nationalists, because the new states had been brought into existence by the federal government and looked to that government to get things done. Even so, this element accomplished much that the Revolutionary Radicals had advocated, but had failed to achieve.

When Jackson's administration began, Calhoun expected to dominate it. He dictated the selection of three of his followers for posts in the six-member cabinet. Van Buren received the top post of Secretary of State. There were only two Jackson men in the cabinet. Before long, though, Van Buren, "the little magician," was able to maneuver the Calhoun men out of the cabinet and virtually to expel Calhoun from the party. He also wormed his way into Jackson's good graces and became the "heir apparent" to the presidency. He had little difficulty in persuading Jackson that the Western concept of rotation in office fitted perfectly with his own spoilsmanship, and so committed Jackson's administration to what has been called ever since "the spoils system." From that point until the election of 1844, the Jacksonian Democrats and the Van Buren politicians made up the Democratic Party.

SECTIONALISM AND NATIONALISM

Sectional Crises. The Jackson Administration saw two major sectional crises: one between East and West over the Bank of the United States, and one between North and South over the tariff. There was also a crisis of sorts over Indian policy. Jackson, in defiance of a Supreme Court order, removed the Southeastern Indians beyond the Mississippi into what later became Oklahoma. He used the army to force the migration, and the troops inflicted great hardships on the Indians. One group of Seminoles escaped into the Florida Everglades, and their descendants are still there. In this action, Jackson was supported by the South, where the planters wanted to be rid of the Indians (mainly to get their lands), and by the West, which had little respect for Indians anyway and was glad to see them moved beyond its pale of development and expansion. The Northeast, however, for a combination of partisan, legalistic, and moral reasons, denounced the movement.

The Bank War—West versus East. The Second Bank of the United States was universally hated in the West and Jackson carried this hatred with him into the White House. However, it was Henry Clay, a supporter of the Bank, who precipitated the crisis. In 1832, the charter of the Bank still had four years to run. Clay, believing that making the Bank an issue in the approaching presidential campaign would enable him to defeat Jackson, persuaded the President of the Bank, Nicholas Biddle, to apply for a recharter at that time. Clay, with help from Daniel Webster, pushed the Charter Bill through Congress and, as expected, Jackson vetoed it. In spite of this veto (or perhaps, in part, because of it), Jackson was reelected, and interpreted his victory as a mandate from the people to destroy the Bank. After getting rid of two Secretaries of the Treasury who refused to do his bidding, he found the right one in Roger B. Taney, later rewarded with the Chief Justiceship of the Supreme Court. Taney stopped depositing federal funds in the Bank of the United States and deposited them, instead, in selected state banks, called by opponents of the administration "Jackson's pet banks." For this action, the Senate passed a vote of censure against President Jackson. This removal of the deposits, as it is often called, forced the Bank to curtail its activities to such an extent that, for the remaining three years of its legal life, it operated only as a local bank in Philadelphia.

Partly as a result of the killing of the Bank, there followed a chain of developments that culminated in the financial crash or so-called "panic" of 1837. In those days, the issuance of bank notes, which would circulate as currency, was considered as much a part of banking as receiving deposits and making loans. Any state or private bank could issue currency. Although the Bank of the United States had no direct control over state and private banks, as long as it was functioning normally it could exert a restraining influence on this issue of currency. If the soundness of a particular bank were questioned, the Bank of the United States would hoard up the notes of that bank, as they came to it in the regular course of business, until it had a large quantity. It then presented these notes to the bank of issue for redemption in hard money. If the local bank could not redeem these notes, it collapsed. This possibility influenced most local bankers not to issue more currency than they could redeem if called upon. With this restraint removed, and with a clamor for "easy money" for land speculation, especially in the West, many local banks began issuing currency far in excess of their resources. Many new and completely unsound banks sprang up, nicknamed "wildcat banks," for the sole purpose of issuing such "wildcat currency" for speculative loans. This flooding of the country with worthless or near-worthless money was bound to bring a crash sooner or later in any case. However, in the last days of his administration, President Jackson brought the matter to a head. At the behest of his friend Thomas Hart Benton, "Old Bullion," he had his Secretary of the Treasury issue the "Specie Circular" which required that all public land be paid for with gold or silver. This brought about the immediate collapse of all the wildcat banks and many sound banks, including the "pet" banks, were pulled down with them. Currency holders and depositors, including the federal government, lost enormous sums and the country was in financial chaos. Fortunately for Jackson's political popularity, Van Buren had succeeded him in the presidency when the crash came. There were, however, a couple of silver linings to the cloud. The states began reforming their banking laws and Van Buren was finally able to push through Congress the creation of the Independent Treasury.

The Tariff Issue—South versus North. An even more serious crisis between North and South arose over the tariff issue. Early in 1832, again with an eye on the approaching election, Clay pushed through Congress and President Jackson signed a genuine high tariff law to replace the "tariff of abominations" of 1828. Under the guidance of John C. Calhoun (who was still Vice President and so had to stay in the background), South Carolina reacted immediately. Its legislature issued a "South Carolina Manifesto," asserting the right of nullification, and called a state convention which declared the tariff act "null and void" in the State of South Carolina. In the presidential election, South Carolina (where the legislature still chose the electors) threw away its electoral vote on a Southerner who was not a serious candidate, rather than vote for either Clay or Jackson.

Jackson is usually credited with having slapped down nullification. To say the least, this is an overstatement. He talked vigorously, but all he actually did was to ask Congress to pass an enforcement act, the so-called "force bill," to authorize him to use the armed forces to collect the duties in South Carolina. He really needed no such authorization from Congress, since the Constitution gave him authority to see that the laws are "faithfully executed" and, as commander-in-chief of the armed forces, he could have ordered troops into South Carolina, but this might not have been good politics. After the election, a backstage deal was made. Clay was to sponsor, and Congress was to pass with the concurrence of all sectional elements, the "Force Bill," a drastic reduction in the tariff, and, as Clay's reward, a "distribution bill" which Clay had been advocating, to distribute the proceeds of land sales to the states. All three passed. Jackson, of course, signed the force bill which he wanted. He also signed the compromise tariff to end the crisis. But he vetoed the distribution bill, thus breaking his promise to Clay.

Thereupon, the South Carolina convention reassembled, revoked its nullification of the tariff, and nullified the force bill. Who won the nullification issue? Clearly, South Carolina. That state got what it wanted, drastic reduction of the tariff, and had the last word in nullifying the force bill. This fact is of great importance for the interpretation of our pre-Civil War history. Had South Carolina really been defeated on nullification, she might have been hesitant to rush into secession in 1860. It is also significant that this prelude to secession was over the tariff, not over slavery. Slavery became the symbol of the North-South sectionalism, but was not the most important reason for it.

The Webster-Hayne Debate.   While the nullification crisis was brewing, a significant debate occurred in the Senate between Daniel Webster and Robert Y. Hayne of South Carolina. It started over a resolution by Senator Foote of Connecticut to restrict Western land sales, and at least a part of Hayne's original motive seems to have been to win the West over to an alliance with the South against the tariff. Very quickly, however, the debate turned into an argument over the nature of the Union and the two men set forth, clearly and publicly for the first time, the conflicting doctrines of the South and the North as to what the federal union really was. Hayne proclaimed the "compact theory." According to this view, the United States was an association of sovereign states. The Constitution was a compact among the states by which they delegated certain functions to a joint agency, the federal government. If, in the judgment of any state, the federal government exceeded or violated the powers conferred upon it, that state, in the exercise of its sovereignty, could nullify such action within its own borders, or even secede from the Union.

Webster expounded the "national theory." This doctrine held that the United States is a sovereign union of people, not a union of sovereign states. The Constitution is, as it declares itself to be, "the supreme law of the land," and the federal government, so long as it adheres to the Constitution, has full power over the states. If there is a question of the constitutionality of an act of Congress or other federal action, it can be resolved by judicial review, by constitutional amendment, or by the regular elections. This debate drew the doctrinal battle lines of the Civil War.

Clay and Nationalism. Jackson was a nationalist in that he believed in the supremacy of the National government, except when it suited his purpose to act otherwise. Henry Clay was a nationalist of a different sort. He put the stress on holding the Union together, and this he believed could be done by sectional compromise. He was sometimes called "the great conciliator." He worked out a scheme, which he called the "American system," to hold the three sections in economic and political balance. Under tariff protection, the Northeast would develop the industries to supply the nation's needs. The South would grow the cotton for the Northern textile mills, and produce other raw materials. The West would grow the nation's food, and produce other raw materials. Clay's tariff of 1824, aimed at bringing this about, was called the "American System Tariff." The fallacy lay in the fact that, except under a totalitarian government, it would be impossible to hold the production of each section in such an equilibrium. Even so, Clay continued to the end of his life to strive to reconcile sectional differences by compromise, with the great object of preserving the Union.

Further Realignment of Political Parties. These developments, along with some others, produced a further realignment of political parties. In the election of 1832, a third
party appeared, the Anti-Masonic Party which was said to
be more anti-Jackson than anti-Mason. Its great contribution was the introduction of the national nominating convention. As the election of 1836 approached, Clay was able to
merge the Anti-Masons with his National Republican Party
and to absorb a large but unorganized group of anti-Jackson
Democrats. He named this coalition the Whig Party. About
all the three elements had in common was hostility to Jackson;
hence the name. Clay and his followers dubbed Jackson "King
Andrew," and referred to his administration as "the reign of
Andrew Jackson." While it did not quite fit the facts, Americans regarded the old British Whig Party (which had disappeared around the year 1800) as anti-royalist. So when Clay
called his party Whig, he was expressing hostility to the
alleged royalism of Jackson. From 1836 to the middle 1850's,
the alignment was Democrats versus Whigs. The Whigs were
quite effective in opposition, but, on the two occasions when
they won presidential elections, their elected presidents died
in office and the vice presidents who took over left much to
be desired. In the Democratic Party, the Southern element
gained control in the election of 1844, and retained that control until the eve of the Civil War.

JACKSONIAN DEMOCRACY AND
LATER TRENDS

A New Concept of the Presidency. The concept of the
presidency has changed with different presidents. As noted
earlier, Washington regarded the presidency as a kind of elective English kingship of the days of William III. Jefferson
introduced the new element of the President as party leader.

As *President*, Jefferson was self-effacing. He introduced the Cabinet as advisory council, and always deferred to the advice of the Cabinet. But as party leader, he virtually told his advisers what to advise him. Jackson introduced the concept of the "strong" president. He considered himself the supreme representative of the people and, so long as his actions had popular support, he felt that he could do anything that was not clearly unconstitutional. He sought advice, but, as President, he made the final decisions. Lincoln was the next "strong" president. Andrew Johnson tried unsuccessfully to be one, but from his time until Theodore Roosevelt's day, the idea lapsed. The first Roosevelt, Taft (to a less extent), and Woodrow Wilson were all "strong" presidents. The concept lapsed again during the 1920's, but was revived by Franklin D. Roosevelt and has prevailed ever since.

Growing Importance of Western Influence. Except briefly on the eve of the War of 1812, when the Western "War Hawks" made themselves heard, the West as a section had exerted little influence on federal government policy prior to Jackson's day. The national government had undertaken, not always successfully, to clear the Indians from the land in advance of settlement, and on three occasions, 1800, 1804 and 1820, Congress had liberalized somewhat the terms on which western settlers could buy lands, but that was about as far as Western influence went. True, William Henry Harrison exerted influence in Washington, especially in obtaining liberalization of the land laws, and Henry Clay rose to a position of influence in the 1820's. Clay, however, although his home was in Kentucky, spoke for a composite nationalism rather than for the West as a section.

With the election of Jackson to the presidency, the picture changed, and the West became a major force in national affairs. This was not only because Jackson was a Westerner and upheld Western views, but perhaps even more because the West as a section now had enough congressmen and presidential electors to make itself heard. Western influence and involvement in political issues continued to the end of the nineteenth century, though it must be borne in mind that the West itself was continually shifting westward as settlement advanced. As we shall note later, the rise of the Republican Party was a Western movement, and the post-Civil War currency movements, "greenbackism" and "free silver," centered in the West. The Populist movement of 1890–1892 was the last great upheaval of the West. By 1900, Western views had, for the most part, become national views, and the West as a section ceased to be significant.

Trend Toward Federal Centralization. The age of Jackson accentuated, rather than created, the trend toward centralization. By this is meant the shifting of power and authority from the states to the central government. It appears to be an inevitable tendency in all federal unions. Alexander Hamilton advocated it in Washington's day, and his "loose construction" of the Constitution was aimed primarily at making it possible. Centralization was pushed by several of John Marshall's Supreme Court decisions. Jackson's conduct of the presidency gave it a boost, and the growing spirit of nationalism won it popular support in the North and West. The outcome of the Civil War gave centralization a free hand, and it has gained momentum ever since.

TOPICS AND QUESTIONS FOR DISCUSSION

Chapter 8

1. How and why did Jackson's presidency inaugurate a new era?

2. In what sense was Jacksonian Democracy an epilogue to the Revolution?

3. How was the "Bank war" a reflection of East-West sectionalism? Was Jackson wrong in killing the Second Bank of the United States?

4. In what ways did the nullification crisis affect the growing North-South sectionalism? What did it show about basic issues between North and South?

5. How and why were political parties realigned in Jackson's time?

6. How important was the role of Henry Clay in both sectionalisms?

7. What influence has Jackson's concept of the Presidency had on later times?

8. How important was the impact of Jacksonian Democracy on federal centralization?

9

The Inevitable Sectional Conflict

THE PERIOD OF "MANIFEST DESTINY"

Westward Expansion. Superficially, it may appear that there was little if any connection between the westward expansion of the 1840's and the growing sectional conflict between North and South. Actually, the connection was very real and very important. Each of the old sections wanted westward expansion, but on its own terms. Each wanted as many new states as possible to be created in its own image for the sake of the Senate balance. Beyond this, though, each section was impelled by economic motives. The merchants and industrialists of the Northeast sought an expanding market for their wares, and they had learned by experience that free states and territories provided a much better market than slaveholding areas. The Southern planters wanted places to establish new plantations. As the soil of an old plantation became exhausted by one-crop cultivation, a process that went on very rapidly, the usual thing was for the planter to sell off his land for what he could get, move westward with his entire retinue (including slaves), and start a new plantation on virgin soil. By about 1840, room for such migration of plantations was exhausted.

144

Politicians naturally catered to these urges, and it was they who coined the term "manifest destiny" to win popular support for expansionism.

Influence of the Opening of China. Great Britain's "Opium War" in China may seem a far cry from either westward expansion or the sectional conflict in the United States, but it had a direct bearing on both. In 1842, Britain imposed a treaty which opened several Chinese ports to British trade and granted extraterritoriality to British subjects in China. Two years later, an American representative, by persuading the Chinese Emperor that granting concessions to Britain alone would risk subjugation by that country, was able to obtain the same privileges for the United States. This gave rise to the idea in America that enormous wealth could be amassed from the China trade, if we could only beat the British to the punch. This, in turn, led to the projecting of a railroad to the Pacific coast. Such a railroad would eliminate the long ocean shipping route around South America, and so would enable the United States to bring in Chinese goods and to ship our exports to China at a lower cost than the British would face. Before the railroad could be built, United States territory would have to be expanded westward to the Pacific. Each section wanted the railroad routed to bring the Chinese trade its way. Northeastern merchants and industrialists clamored for more profit, but the South felt that it had a bigger stake. If the China trade, expected to reach astronomical proportions, could be funneled into the South, it might create an equilibrium of wealth and population with the North, and so give the South an even break in the House of Representatives. Although overshadowed by other matters in all public discussion, the Pacific railroad issue was a potent factor in shaping the course of events from 1844 until the eve of the Civil War. It is significant that, as soon as the North gained full control of Congress by the secession of the Southern states, Congress provided for the building of the railroad by a northern route.

Oregon, Texas, and the Mexican War. The Democratic convention of 1844 was dominated by the Southern element of the party, which maneuvered the nomination of James K. Polk of Tennessee as the first "dark horse." As an old disciple of Jackson, Polk would attract the votes of Jacksonian Democrats, though actually, as was known to those who engineered his nomination, he agreed with the position of the South. The platform declared for "the reoccupation of Oregon and the reannexation of Texas." The "re-," in both cases, was political hocum. We had never had a valid claim to more than the southern half of the Oregon Country, and the contention that we had bought Texas as part of the Louisiana Purchase had no real foundation. Campaigners put the stress on Oregon to attract Northern votes, although the real interest of the party insiders was in Texas, shouting the slogan "Fifty-four-forty or fight." Polk, though he proclaimed his intention to get "all of Oregon," never mentioned fifty-four-forty, and probably had in mind only the forty-ninth parallel.

Eastern Texas, previously unoccupied except by native Indian tribes and a few mission stations, had been settled by Southern Americans, who had introduced cotton culture and the plantation system. Texas was a part of Mexico, but in 1836 it achieved *de facto* independence and, since then, had operated as an independent republic. The transplanted Americans there, with the support of Andrew Jackson, wanted annexation to the United States, but this had been blocked by Northern opposition. In 1844, the Southern leadership was determined to achieve the annexation, and linking Texas with Oregon appeared to be the way to do it. It would not only give the South two more Senators, but would open up new lands for plantation migration. Actually, John Tyler put over annexation, by somewhat devious means (a joint resolution of Congress when a two-thirds majority of the Senate could not be mustered to approve the treaty), before he turned over the presidency to Polk. After his inauguration, Polk had little difficulty in negotiating a settlement of the Oregon boundary along a line much more favorable to the United States than to Great Britain.

The Texas boundary was the excuse, but not the reason, for the Mexican War. Polk had his heart set on getting California and the intervening area to tap the China trade and build the Pacific railroad by a southern route. He first tried to accomplish this through the Slidell mission. Mexico had agreed several years before to pay a certain sum of money to the United States as compensation for damage to American persons and property in the successive Mexican "revolutions." When Texas was annexed, two annual payments had been made, with a small installment on the third. In protest against the annexation (Mexico had never acknowledged the independence of Texas), the Mexican government stopped the payments and broke off diplomatic relations. Polk sent John Slidell as a personal envoy, ostensibly to negotiate a resumption of diplomatic relations, and equipped him with credentials as minister of Mexico, to be presented when diplomatic relations should be restored. He was to offer cancellation of the remaining payments due from Mexico if that country would restore diplomatic relations and recognize the Rio Grande boundary. But this was only on the surface. Slidell's real goal was to secure the cession of California and New Mexico and he was to offer any amount of money necessary to achieve this. When the Mexican government discovered what his real purpose was, he was ordered out of the country.

Polk then entered into a secret deal with General Santa

Anna, several times dictator of Mexico, but then in exile. Santa Anna was smuggled back into Mexico on an American naval vessel and was given funds to finance his seizure of power. In return, he agreed to cede California and New Mexico, but warned that the United States would have to make a "show of force" so it would appear that he was compelled to make the cession. That was why General Taylor was ordered, first across the Nueces, and then across the Rio Grande. When, instead of living up to the agreement, Santa Anna resisted the invasion with all his strength, Polk decided to send General Winfield Scott to attack Mexico City.

Meanwhile, Polk was doing several things to get possession of California. First, he sent John C. Frémont with a commando party disguised as surveyors. Frémont left his men north of the forty-second parallel in Oregon, and went to the San Francisco area to deliver a message from President Polk to the few thousand American settlers there. The gist of the message was that, if these settlers should see fit to declare their independence from Mexico and seek annexation to the United States, the President would look with favor upon their petition. This gave rise to the abortive "Bear Flag Republic." A naval flotilla under Admiral Stockton was sent to San Francisco Bay with orders to go ashore and take control when word was received that war had been declared.

Immediately after the declaration of war, two regiments of dragoons were dispatched on an overland march from Fort Leavenworth to California under the command of General Stephen Kearny. Soon after the column had passed Albuquerque, a dispatch rider overtook it with an order to detach most of the force to go to the aid of Taylor in Northern Mexico. Kearny continued on with only a token force, following the Gila River. As he advanced, a party of army engineers made a preliminary survey for the Pacific railroad. When these engineers got back to Washington after the war, they reported that there was no feasible route for the railroad north of the Gila, which became the boundary under the peace treaty that ended the war. It was this fact that led to the negotiation of the Gadsden Purchase in 1853.

The "Five Bleeding Wounds." At the first session of the Congress elected in 1848, Henry Clay enumerated what he called the "five bleeding wounds of the Republic." These were highly controversial sectional issues regarding California, Texas, slavery in the territories, the District of Columbia, and the Southern demand for a stringent fugitive slave law.

Southern planters had expected that California, along with its railroad value, would provide a large area for new plantations and become another slave state to hold the Senate balance. However, the gold rush of 1849 had carried in an influx of gold seekers who, at the beginning of 1850, were demanding admission as a free state. Under these circumstances, the best the South could hope to do was to deny immediate statehood, and organize California as a territory open to slavery. This would open it up to planters and might, eventually, make it a slave state.

Texas was demanding that the United States assume the old national debt of the Republic of Texas, on the ground that statehood had transferred the power to levy import duties, which might have been used to pay the debt, to the federal government. On the other hand, since the settled area of New Mexico lay within the boundary claimed by Texas, it would be necessary for Texas to give up some territory to permit the organization of a Territory of New Mexico.

The question of slavery in the territories, though it generated much heat, was not, in the long run, very important. It was generally agreed that territorial governments should be set up for the Mormon settlers in Utah (though the Mormons themselves would have preferred to be left to their own devices) and for the Spanish Mexican population of New Mexico. The climate and soil of these areas being what they were, there was never a chance that a plantation system could develop or that slaveholding could ever take root. As Daniel Webster expressed it in his famous Seventh of March Speech, he "would not take the trouble to reenact a law of nature or to reaffirm the will of God." Even so, Southerners insisted that the territories be created with slavery legalized, while Northerners, harking back to the Wilmot Proviso, demanded that slavery be barred.

Abolitionists in the North, appealing to the national conscience, had raised a demand that slavery be abolished in the District of Columbia, where Congress clearly had the power to act. Southerners, fearing that this might be an entering wedge to push abolition into the deep South, objected strenuously.

The old fugitive slave law having been rendered ineffective by court interpretation, Southerners were demanding, as a matter of right, a new and more stringent law with federal enforcement. This was opposed by the entire North.

Clay introduced an "omnibus" bill to deal with all of these issues in a single package. Except that Stephen A. Douglas's popular sovereignty formula (later called "squatter sovereignty" in Kansas) was substituted for a slightly different formula proposed by Clay to deal with slavery in the territories, all of Clay's proposals were finally enacted separately. California was admitted as a free state, an outright concession to the North. Texas was reduced to its present boundaries and, in return, the federal government assumed its old national debt. Utah and New Mexico were organized as territories open to slavery, with the provision that, when ready for statehood, their voters should decide, in adopting state constitutions, whether each should be a free state or a slave state. In the District of Columbia, slave auctions were prohibited, but neither slavery itself nor private slave trade. The South got its fugitive slave law as compensation for the loss of California.

Failure of Compromise of 1850 to Resolve Sectional Conflict. In some ways, the Compromise of 1850 was a turning point. It was the end of the road for the old political giants, Webster, Clay, and Calhoun, and marked the debut of such new leaders as Stephen A. Douglas, William H. Seward, and Jefferson Davis. It shifted the public emphasis from expansion to the question of preserving the Union, symbolized by the slavery issue. However, rather than resolving the sectional conflict, the Compromise only aggravated it. It may be considered the first in that chain of events of the 1850's that led up to the Civil War. The fugitive slave law was bitterly opposed throughout the North, and Northern states, while shunning the hated word *nullification*, virtually nullified it with their "personal liberty laws." The South could not reconcile itself to the loss of California because there was no place where another slave state could be created to restore the Senate balance.

The public reaction was shown clearly in the election of 1852. The Democrats nominated Franklin Pierce of New Hampshire, who was practically unknown outside his own small state. The Whigs nominated the Mexican War hero, General Winfield Scott. Pierce was elected by such a landslide that the Whigs never recovered. It is obvious that the voters were voting neither *for* Pierce *nor against* Scott. They were voting against the Compromise of 1850. A Whig, Millard Fillmore, had been President when the Compromise was enacted so that, although the legislation was the work of both parties, the Whigs received the blame. By the next presidential election, the Whig Party had disappeared.

DOMINATING FACTORS OF THE
CONFLICT IN THE 1850's

The Senate Balance. The admission of California as a free state upset the Senate balance in favor of the North. Until or unless a way could be found to add another slave state, and so restore the balance, the only safeguard the South had left was to keep a President in office who would use his veto, if necessary, in the interest of the South. However, since control of the presidency was tenuous at best, every effort must be made to bring in another slave state. The Missouri Compromise stood in the way, so the South must strive to get that enactment either repealed or declared unconstitutional, or both. If this could be accomplished, the South would have to get a slave state north of thirty-six-thirty, even if violence were required to do it. Hence, the Kansas Conflict. Even if the South could win in Kansas, though, there would still be room for more free states. More slave states would be needed, so a project was launched to seize Cuba from Spain and admit it as a slave state. Some toyed with the idea of dividing Texas to obtain more pro-Southern Senators, but Texas would not agree and, under the Constitution, a state can not be divided without the consent of its legislature.

"Doughface" Presidents. During the 1850's, Southern politicians were convinced that, until or unless the Senate balance could be restored, the survival of the South within the Union depended on keeping a pro-Southern President in the White House. In order to be elected, such a President must live in the North and, in his campaign, must stress other issues than those that were clearly sectional. Once in office, though, Southerners must be able to rely upon him to veto any legislation detrimental to the South, especially protective tariff. Many

Northern politicians dubbed these men "doughface" Presidents. Both Pierce and Buchanan fitted this pattern. They not only used the veto in the Southern interest, but threw the prestige of their office to the support of all measures desired by the South. In fact, Pierce's administration was dominated almost completely by Jefferson Davis, who held the post of Secretary of War.

The Pacific Railroad Issue. There was not much public discussion of the Pacific Railroad issue in the 1850's, possibly because neither Northern nor Southern politicians wanted to admit publicly that they were scheming to get the railroad away from the other section. Even so, it was lurking in the background and exerted considerable influence on the course of events. It was the main reason for the Kansas-Nebraska Bill. When Senator Dodge of Iowa introduced the original Nebraska Bill, he made no secret of the fact that his concern was to get the territory west of the Missouri River organized so that the railroad could be built westward from Council Bluffs along the Platte River, to connect with a line already being built across Iowa. When Senator Stephen A. Douglas of Illinois, to whose Committee on Territories the Dodge bill was referred, took up the sponsorship, it was not so much to advance his presidential hopes, as was often assumed, as because he, too, was interested in that route for the railroad. It would funnel the China trade into his home town of Chicago, where he owned a large amount of undeveloped real estate. Since some Northern Senators would not support the Dodge-Douglas Bill, because they wanted the railroad to follow a route still farther north, it was necessary to gain Southern votes to get the bill passed. Partly for this purpose, and partly because it had become a kind of fetish with him, Douglas introduced the "squatter sovereignty" feature. This would open the territory to slavery. His dividing the territory into Kansas and

Nebraska was also a bid for Senate votes. It would attract the powerful support of Thomas Hart Benton of Missouri (then still in the Senate, though destined soon to be defeated for reelection), who wanted the railroad built along the Kansas River to connect with the state-subsidized Pacific Railroad of Missouri (later Missouri Pacific) already being built across Missouri. Dividing the territory also gave the South a chance to get Kansas, and so to restore the Senate balance, at least temporarily. When confronted by some Southern Senators with the fact that "squatter sovereignty" in effect repealed the Missouri Compromise, Douglas had to agree to include a specific repeal or risk losing the votes of these Senators.

Growth of Southern Nationalism. Although it began to germinate earlier, Southern nationalism reached its full fruition in the 1850's. This was a widely held feeling in the Southern section that the South really constituted a distinct nationality, linked in an unnatural union with a separate and antagonistic nation in the North. The public talk was about states rights, because it fitted in with the compact theory of the Union which implied the right of an individual state to secede. This was really little more than a pretext. It is significant that when the Southern states did secede, they immediately formed a federal union of their own, the Confederate States of America, and during the Civil War, patriotism in the South was given to the Confederacy, far more than to individual states. This feeling in the South increased enormously the difficulty of finding peaceful solutions to the sectional differences.

CHAIN OF DEVELOPMENT OF THE 1850'S

The Kansas Conflict. The Kansas Conflict, which became a small scale civil war in the summer of 1856 was the result of several factors. Most immediate was the scheming of Senator David R. Atchison of Missouri, first to retain his seat in the Senate and, when he lost that, to create a new Senatorship for himself in Kansas. He aroused western Missouri to a state of panic by picturing the New England Emigrant Aid Company as a "powerful moneyed corporation" that intended not only to seize Kansas with "armies of hirelings," but to invade and "abolitionize" Missouri. On several occasions, he led armed bands of Missourians into the territory to vote fraudulently or to fight. The Emigrant Aid Company, and other organizations in the North formed in imitation of it, did seek to promote anti-slavery migration to Kansas, and supported the Free State movement which was led by one of its agents, Dr. Charles Robinson. The conflict was carried into the halls of Congress, where it provided the rallying point to consolidate the nebulous Republican Party, and it gave the Republicans the slogan "Bleeding Kansas" for the campaign of 1856. When the Free State Cause triumphed in Kansas, the South was driven to desperation because the last hope of restoring the Senate balance was gone.

The Ostend Manifesto. In the summer of 1854, Southerners generally assumed that Missourians would flow into Kansas and take it over, so little effort was made in the South to support the pro-slavery cause in Kansas. Part of the reason was that the Southern leadership, at that time, was pinning its hopes for another slave state on the scheme to take over Cuba. Early in the fall, on instructions from Washington, the American ministers to Great Britain, France and Spain met in Belgium to consider the matter, and drew up a document which came to be called the Ostend Manifesto. Ostensibly this was a very secret report to the President recommending that, if Spain refused to sell Cuba, the United States should seize it by force. The real purpose, though, was to feel out Britain and France, so the report was deliberately "leaked." The response of the British and French foreign offices was emphatic. If the United States should attempt to seize Cuba by force, those countries would go to Spain's assistance. That settled it. With the North hostile to the project, the administration could not undertake a major war for Cuba. With that hope gone, the South began to concentrate in earnest on Kansas.

Rise of the Republican Party. The beginnings of the Republican Party in the summer of 1854 were a "grassroots" reaction to the Kansas-Nebraska Act. Throughout what was then the West as a section, "schoolhouse" meetings were called by local politicians, attended by "Conscience" Whigs, "Anti-Nebraska" Democrats, and members of the Free Soil Party. These meetings adopted resolutions condemning the Kansas-Nebraska Act and demanding the repeal of the Fugitive Slave Law, and elected delegates to state conventions. These conventions, held later in the summer, formed state party organizations and nominated candidates for state offices and members of Congress. Some of these party organizations, at the suggestion of Horace Greeley, adopted the old Jeffersonian name Republican. Others called themselves Whig, Free Soil, or merely Independent. In the November election, they swept the West. Northeastern Whigs, however, considered this movement too radical and feared it might threaten the Union. They took up what had originated as an extreme nativist movement and, around it as a nucleus, formed the Native American Party, nicknamed "Know-Nothing." This party was generally successful in 1854 in the Northeastern states.

The Kansas Conflict and the debates over it in Congress, consolidated these state parties into a unity. By the fall of 1856, they were ready to hold a national convention and nominate a candidate for President—John C. Frémont. "Bleeding Kansas" was a perfect campaign slogan. The platform called for a homestead law to please Western farmers, and protective tariff to attract Eastern industrialists. It also declared against the extension of slavery into any more territories. The "Know Nothings" nominated former Whig President Millard Fillmore, and their platform centered on the conciliation of sectional differences through compromise. In the election, the Republicans came in a strong second, and the "Know Nothings" a poor third. This determined that the Republicans would be the new major party to replace the Whigs.

To Southerners, this in itself meant a new peril. The Republicans were strictly a Northern sectional party. They stood for everything the North wanted, and opposed any concessions to the South. Most Southerners felt that, if the Republicans should ever win a national election, their future within the Union would be hopeless.

The Dred Scott Case. This case began as a *bona fide* effort to secure Scott's freedom. Scott lived in St. Louis, where his former master had died. His present master, Sanford, lived in New York and had virtually abandoned Scott, except that he always turned up to collect his wages whenever Scott had a job. Taylor Blow, a not-very-successful St. Louis lawyer, was a son of Scott's original owner and felt a moral obligation to aid Scott and his family financially. To escape this responsibility, he brought suit, in Scott's name, in a St. Louis court. Had Blow based the suit on abandonment, he could have won hands down, but for some reason he based it on the fact that Scott had been taken by a former owner into the free state of Illinois. It was perfectly good law for the court to deny freedom on this basis, and for the state Supreme Court of Missouri to deny it on appeal. At this point, when Blow, unwilling to throw more good money after bad, was ready to drop the matter, three prominent political lawyers, with offices both in St. Louis and in Washington, proposed to take over the case. Nominally these were Scott's lawyers, but they

wanted to lose the case for political reasons, and they promised
Scott his freedom whatever the final decision. They could have
appealed from the Supreme Court of Missouri to the Supreme
Court of the United States. Instead, they started a new suit in
federal court in order to inject a new issue: the constitutionality of the Missouri Compromise.

The Supreme Court decision, written by Roger B. Taney
and delivered a few days after Buchanan's inauguration, not
only declared the Missouri Compromise unconstitutional (it
had been repealed three years before by the Kansas-Nebraska
Act), but went on to rule that Congress did not have power to
prohibit slavery in any territory. This was expected to wreck
the Republican Party, whose main plank was non-extension of
slavery, by making that party stand for something that was
unconstitutional. Actually, it had the opposite effect. The
Republicans invoked the doctrine of *obiter dicta* (extraneous
pronouncement). Since the court had first ruled that Scott was
not a citizen, and so had no standing in court, the Republican
politicians argued that the rest of the decision was not binding
law, but only represented an illegal scheme to foist slavery
upon the whole country. The Dred Scott decision turned out
to be a great boon to the Republicans.

The "Panic of 1857". Republican prospects received another boost from the relatively severe depression, the "panic
of 1857," which afflicted the country during Buchanan's administration. Economic difficulties always produce a political
reaction against the party of the President. In addition to this
general advantage, Republicans in Congress sought to capitalize
the situation in other ways. The depressed conditions were
particularly hard on Western farmers, who were unable to
make the payment for their preempted land. The Republicans
were able, in 1857, to maneuver a homestead bill through the
House of Representatives, giving 160 acres free to each frontier

farmer. The Senate finally agreed to a compromise which reduced the price of the land to twenty-five cents an acre. The planters, however, objected to any concession on the public land so, when the act reached the President's desk, it met with a veto. Since the bill had been pushed by the Republicans and vetoed by a Democratic President, most Western farmers were convinced that their interests lay with the Republican Party.

The Northeastern industrialists were asking for higher tariff, in the belief that this would alleviate the depressed condition of their business. The Republicans made a futile effort to push an increase in rates through Congress. In the spring of 1860, they were not even able to block a further reduction in the already low rates, largely because those Western farmers who were still Douglas Democrats thought that tariff reduction would help them by reducing the cost of items they had to buy, and their representatives in Congress voted accordingly. Even so, this all reacted to the benefit of the Republicans with the business community. The Democrats had cut the tariff when the business men thought that they needed an increase, while the Republicans had battled for higher rates.

The Emergence of Lincoln. Abraham Lincoln in 1858, when he emerged on the national scene through his debates with Douglas, was by no means the obscure backwoodsman that many believed. Although he had been born and had grown up on the backwoods frontier, he had, for many years, been a highly successful practicing lawyer in Springfield, and was a leader in Whig (later Republican) politics in Illinois. While he had little formal education, he had educated himself broadly through his reading. When, in 1858, the Illinois Republicans nominated him for Senator to oppose Stephen A. Douglas, they were not, as sometimes supposed, picking an obscure figure as a sacrificial candidate in a contest they knew they could not win, but were naming the most promising man they had available. Lincoln is reputed to have said, on that occasion, that he knew he could not defeat Douglas for the Senate, but that he was "out for bigger game." This is usually interpreted to mean that, even then, he had his eye on the Presidency. True enough, he was probably thinking of the Presidency, but for his party, not for himself.

Lincoln must have figured that if, in the campaign, he could maneuver Douglas into saying something that would make him unacceptable to the South, that would split the Democratic Party in the election of 1860 and make Republican victory almost certain. Douglas would have the full support of Northern Democrats for the presidential nomination. If the Northern and Southern wings of that party could not unite on Douglas as a candidate, it seemed most unlikely that they could unite at all. That was why Lincoln challenged Douglas to the famous debates. Douglas accepted the challenge because he recognized in Lincoln an opponent worthy of his best efforts. When, at Freeport, Lincoln put Douglas into such a dilemma that any answer Douglas might give to his question would be wrong, he had accomplished his purpose. The South almost certainly would not accept Douglas as the Democratic nominee in 1860.

The Election of 1860.   When the time came for presidential nominations, the Democrats split as was to be expected. The Southern delegates twice bolted the party convention, and finally nominated a separate ticket of their own with John C. Breckinridge of Kentucky as nominee for President. As expected, the Northern Democrats nominated Douglas. There were several Republican hopefuls, with Lincoln prominent among them. His national stature had grown rapidly since the Lincoln-Douglas debates. He had spoken in many parts of the North, most notably at Cooper Union in New York, with excellent effect. At the party convention, held in Chicago to promote Lincoln's candidacy, his supporters finally secured his nomination by arguing publicly that a Western man was needed to carry the West against Douglas, and by privately promising cabinet posts to all of his rivals. Lincoln was not consulted in the making of these promises, but he felt bound to honor them.

A "third" party appeared, the Constitutional Union, which nominated John Bell of Tennessee. It was made up chiefly of old middle-of-the-road Whigs who still believed that the sectional crisis could be resolved by compromise. This party was a forlorn hope. It ran strong in the border states, where the people feared being caught in the middle in case of civil war, but it had no chance of real success.

When the votes were in, Lincoln had carried the entire North and Breckinridge all the states of the deep South. Douglas carried only Missouri, though his popular vote was almost as large as Lincoln's. Bell carried Virginia, Kentucky and Tennessee. Lincoln's electoral vote exceeded that of all three of his rivals. The die was cast.

TOPICS AND QUESTIONS FOR DISCUSSION

Chapter 9

1. How was "manifest destiny" expansion related to the sectional conflict?
2. What was President Polk's real purpose in the Mexican War?
3. Why did the Compromise of 1850 fail to resolve the sectional conflict? What effect did it have on the presidential election of 1852?

4. Why was the Senate balance so important to the South? Why did the South need "doughface" Presidents in the 1850's?

5. How and why was the Kansas Conflict a major step in leading to the Civil War?

6. Why did the Republican Party arise and what effect did it have on the sectional conflict?

7. What other developments of the 1850's helped to set the stage for the Civil War? How and why?

8. Why did Lincoln's election precipitate secession?

10 | The Broader Meaning of the Civil War

AN ATTEMPTED REVOLUTION

Comparison with the American Revolution. The American Civil War, or War Between the States as Southerners often prefer to call it, was an attempted revolution. In many respects it resembled the American Revolution of the 1770's. In both cases, a portion of a country, feeling that its vital interests were threatened, undertook to secede and establish its independence. True, the colonies were separated from Great Britain by an ocean, but the colonists were essentially Englishmen, with English language, institutions, and traditions. In both instances, the revolt, at least in its incipient stages, was prompted, not so much by any harm actually suffered by the revolting section, as by the fear that the policies of the central government, over which the rebellious section lacked (or soon would lack) any effective restraint, would damage the economy and undermine the institutions of the disgruntled area.

In both situations, the rebels held some initial advantages. In both, the old government was unprepared to cope with a major rebellion, was hampered by political spoilsmanship, and lacked the full support of its people. In both, the rebels were fighting on their own soil and, apart from any enthusiasm (or lack of it) for their cause, felt that they were fighting in defense of their homes and families. In addition, in the 1770's, Britain was at the disadvantage of having to conduct military operations across an ocean from her base of supplies, with communication slow and uncertain. Furthermore, the rebels of the 1860's had some initial advantages that colonists had lacked. They had most of the country's trained military officers, and the aristocratic structure of their society made it much easier to train and discipline raw recruits into effective soldiers.

In both cases, though, the long-range advantages lay with the loyal area. Both Britain in the 1770's and the Union in the 1860's, had well established governments with foreign recognition and established credit. Both had much greater populations than the rebellious sections, and both were far ahead in industrial development. Both were much better prepared than the rebels to supply their own wartime needs. In both cases, the hope for eventual success of the revolt depended on the ability to get effective foreign aid. In this, the colonists succeeded, where the Southerners failed.

Some historians object to calling the revolt of the South an attempted revolution, though its parallel with the revolt of the colonies in the 1770's is obvious and, for purposes of analysis, significant. One of these historians states that, after the war aims of the North changed in 1863 from saving the Union to abolishing human slavery, the Union cause became the revolutionary one. This observation is pertinent as far as it goes. However, it should be borne in mind that President Lincoln introduced the emancipation issue only to aid in suppressing the rebellion and saving the Union. It is probably true that, in the minds of most Northerners, this changed the basis of the war, but to Lincoln and most of the statesmen who surrounded him, saving the Union remained the paramount issue right down to the end of the war. Certainly, the prime aim of the South did not change from achieving independence to preserving slavery.

The Immediate Reason for Secession. It is obvious that the immediate occasion for secession was the election of Lincoln, but why should the mere fact of the election of a President who was unpopular in the South have triggered so momentous a step? The usual explanation is that, because of Lincoln's hostility to slavery, his election was regarded in the South as a threat to the "peculiar institution." Some Southerners, in their excited state of mind, may have felt that way, but this can hardly have been the controlling factor with responsible Southern leaders. Lincoln was not an extreme abolitionist. He opposed any further *extension* of slavery, but both he and his political party had stated emphatically that they had no intention of interfering with slavery where it existed.

The more likely explanation is that control of both Congress and the Presidency by a Northern sectional party posed an immediate threat to Southern economic interests, and a long-range threat to the entire economic and social structure of the South. The Republicans were pushing for a homestead law which, by giving free 160-acre farms to western settlers, would hamper any westward expansion of the plantation system. They planned to build the Pacific Railroad by a northern route, thus denying its benefits to the South. Most significant of all, though, the Republicans were committed to high protective tariff for the benefit of the rapidly growing Northern industries. High tariff, of course, would raise the price of what the Southern planter had to buy, but that was not the most serious aspect. If the British could not sell their manufactures in the United States, they could not obtain the foreign exchange with which to pay for Southern cotton, and the sale of cotton to Great Britain was the mainstay of the Southern economy. Pushed far enough, protective tariff could destroy the British market for American cotton, and with it, the entire economy and social structure of the South. Tariff played at least as large a part as slavery in bringing on the Civil War.

The reason Lincoln's election was so decisive ties in with the old matter of the sectional balance in the Senate. So long as this balance could be maintained, the South felt protected against unfriendly legislation. But this balance had been lost by the admission of California as a free state, and the two attempts of the South to restore it had both failed. The failure to win the Kansas Conflict ended forever any hope of restoring the balance. With the Senate balance gone, the only way the South could feel protected was to keep a "doughface" President in the White House. A Pierce or a Buchanan could be depended upon to veto any legislation favorable to the North and detrimental to the South. With a Northern sectional President like Lincoln in office, however, it appeared to the Southern leadership that the only way to preserve the South's economy and way of life was to withdraw from the Union.

Probably most Southerners regarded secession as definitive and final. Some (but by no means all) of their leaders, though, felt that it would put the South into a bargaining position to secure some kind of constitutional amendment to safeguard Southern interests. As some of them expressed it, they could "get better terms outside the Union than in it." Actually, several attempts at compromise were made in Congress, including the much discussed Crittenden Compromise which would have extended the Missouri Compromise line across the continent, and would have frozen it by a constitutional amendment. A "Peace Convention," called by the legislature of Virginia and presided over by former President John Tyler, met in Washington in February. There were delegates from twenty-one states, many of them eminent political leaders, but none from the deep South. The convention presented an elaborate program of seven amendments, but these were not even submitted to the states by Congress. Secession would have to see it through.

Southern Dependence on British Aid. In view of the long-range advantages of the North, it was obvious that, unless the South could win a quick decisive victory, the Confederacy's only hope of survival lay in getting foreign aid, and Great Britain was the only country from which this aid could come. British naval supremacy would prevent Napoleon III of France—always ready to fish in troubled waters—from intervening without British collaboration. This same naval supremacy would enable the British, if they should intervene, to keep the sea lanes open and to get supplies to the Confederacy. British textile mill owners were as dependent on the supply of Southern cotton for raw material as the Southern planters were dependent on the British market for their crop. These same mill owners dominated British politics, and could usually control government policy. It was not unnatural, then, for the Southern leadership to assume that, even if the British should not intervene with full military aid, they at least would use their naval power to keep the sea lanes open to supply Confederate war needs.

Early in the war there were two diplomatic crises between the United States and British governments which might have brought about active British intervention. The first of these occurred when an American naval vessel forcibly removed from a British passenger ship, the *Trent*, two Confederate diplomatic agents, James Mason and John Slidell, bound for Europe to seek diplomatic recognition for the Confederacy. At the urging of Queen Victoria and her husband, the Prince Consort, the British government toned down its ultimatum, and Lincoln, against the advice of his cabinet, accepted the

British demand for the release of Mason and Slidell. The other situation arose a little later when it was learned that Confederate sea raiders were being built in Britain. President Lincoln demanded that the British government either prevent these vessels from going to sea or accept full responsibility for any damage they might do to United States shipping. Wisely, however, he avoided pushing the matter to a showdown, and it was settled by arbitration after the war.

Emancipation as a Diplomatic Move. Lincoln's master stroke in keeping Britain neutral was the Emancipation Proclamation. From the beginning of the war, many prominent Northerners had tried to introduce the slavery issue. Lincoln, however, fearing that raising the slavery issue would drive the border slave states into secession, resisted all such efforts until the border slave states were all safely in Union hands. Military possession of the border states was complete by the late summer of 1862. By that time, too, British mill owners were exhausting their reserves of cotton and were putting pressure on their government to intervene. Lincoln knew that both the Queen and the working population of Britain held strong antislavery sentiments. The workers could not vote, but they could strike or riot, and this, with the Queen's blessing, they would be apt to do if their government should intervene on behalf of the slaveholders in what could be made to appear a war over slavery. Hence, introducing the slavery issue would make it impractical, if not impossible, for the British government to come to the aid of the Confedercy. To that end, Lincoln issued his preliminary proclamation on September 22, 1862. From that moment on, slavery became an issue in the Civil War though, to Lincoln's mind, a less important one than the restoration of the Union.

It should also be noted that, in part, President Lincoln acted in response to a growing wave of public opinion in the North, spearheaded by Horace Greeley. Another consideration of the President was rallying the support of Negroes to the Union cause, and making possible the enlistment of Negro soldiers. There can be little question, though, that the diplomatic purpose was the main one.

DEVELOPMENTS IN THE NORTH

Relation to the Broader Meaning of the War. Developments that took place in the North during and immediately following the Civil War had much to do with making that war the turning point in our history that it was. True, many of these developments would probably have come anyway, but without the stimulation of the war, they certainly would have come much more slowly and, in some significant ways, probably would not have taken the form they did. Undoubtedly, railroads would have been built across the continent. The trans-Missouri West would have been settled, and would have given rise to new problems. Industry would have expanded and consolidated, bringing labor problems and a swarm of new inventions. The powers of the federal government, as compared with those of the states, would have grown in any case. Even so, because the war speeded the process, and crowded these developments into a few short years, economic, social, and political conditions were created which have shaped the course of the country's history ever since.

The New West. Almost as soon as Southern Senators and Representatives withdrew, Congress enacted several measures to serve the Northern interests. The long disputed Pacific railway, with parallel lines along the Kansas and along the Platte, was authorized and subsidized, and construction began. It was named the Union Pacific, on the theory that it would help preserve the Union. After the war, several other railroads to the Pacific coast were similarly subsidized. The ways in which the matter was handled left much room for graft and corruption on the part of the railroad promoters, but the roads did get built, opening the great plains and the mountain area to trade and settlement. The first industry to profit was the range cattle business, which gave rise to our traditions of the wild west. However, Congress also passed the Homestead Law which gave free 160-acre farms to settlers. Soon after the war settlers streamed westward and, within a quarter of a century, they had occupied all usable land all the way to the Pacific. Since they could produce wealth almost immediately from their farms and mines, this westward migration meant an expanding market for Eastern industry. This new West did raise problems and political issues, usually taking the form of demands for currency inflation, but it was part of the rapid development of the country after the Civil War.

The Rise of Big Business. The by-product of the war that had the greatest impact on the future of the country was the rise of large-scale industry or, as it was usually called, "big business." A trend in this direction probably would have come anyway, but war demands for production crowded into a few years developments that otherwise would have spread over a much longer time, and might have taken a very different form, as happened in Europe.

The distinctive feature of what happened in the United States was the formation of the so-called trusts. These were business combinations, each usually dominated by a single financial manipulator, which were able to create monopolies or near monopolies of whole sectors of production, such as steel, sugar, and petroleum. Smaller competitors were driven out of business by "cutthroat competition," and this permitted the charging of monopoly prices. In most instances, the "tycoons" amassed vast fortunes. It was to their interest to control government. They wanted high protective tariff and, sometimes, subsidies, and they wanted to make sure that no legislation was passed to restrict their activities. They were willing to spend large sums of money, either as outright bribes or as contributions to political campaign funds, to influence politicians. At the same time they were able, thanks largely to an influx of immigrants in the decades right after the war, to exploit labor through low wages, long hours, and inadequate working conditions. This, too, required a friendly government.

Development of Political "Vested Interests." It was probably inevitable that these developments should give a large proportion of the political leaders in the North a vested interest in supporting big business. The "captains of industry" paid their campaign expenses, entertained them lavishly, gave them valuable "presents," and cut them in on the ownership of corporation stock. These politicians were able to dominate the Republican Party and to keep it in office most of the time by "waving the bloody shirt" (appealing to Union patriotism) in their campaigns. Even many of the political leaders who, for one reason or another, called themselves Democrats, were as willing to ally themselves with big business as were their Republican rivals. This situation conditioned the political life of the country for several decades.

THE REAL REASON FOR RADICAL RECONSTRUCTION

Why Called "Radical" Reconstruction. Lincoln had favored a moderate, conciliatory policy toward the defeated South, and had shown this in a number of things he had done before the end of the war. His successor, Andrew Johnson, a "Union" Democrat from Tennessee, elected Vice President with Lincoln in 1864 on a "Union" ticket, tried, with only minor modifications, to carry out Lincoln's policy. Before he had to confront Congress, he actually had carried through his plan of "Presidential" reconstructions, and had "loyal" governments in operation in all of the seceded states. It remained for Congress, however, to seat the Senators and Representatives from these states.

When Congress met, it took the bit into its teeth and undid all that President Johnson had done. Step by step, Congress imposed its own scheme, called "Radical" reconstruction in contrast with the Lincoln-Johnson moderate plan. Nearly all Southern whites were disfranchised and the vote was given to all "freedmen"—the former slaves. "Union leagues" were set up in the South, manned by Northern politicians, to organize the freedmen politically and to direct their voting. The upshot was the so-called "carpet bag" regimes. But what was the purpose of it all? It was simply to keep the South under Northern control for reasons to be discussed presently.

It is true, as argued by several contemporary historians, that the "carpet bag" governments were not entirely bad. They enacted laws intended to create a democratic society in the South, and they made a beginning of mass education in their states. The fact remains, however, that for the most part, they were corrupt, extravagant and inefficient. They were dominated by men who had moved down from the North after the end of hostilities. Some of these men, largely inexperienced in the ways of politics, had a real missionary zeal to remake the South. Most of them, though, were small-fry politicans who were concerned primarily with furthering their own fortunes, political and financial. Good or bad, they embittered most of the Southern Whites, and so intensified the later Southern reaction against the Negro.

Rivalry of President and Congress. To some degree, Radical reconstruction was an outcropping of the historic rivalry between President and Congress. Whenever there has been a strong or active President, Congress has been jealous of growing presidential power. During a war or other national crisis, Congress usually defers to presidential leadership, but when the crisis has passed, Congress sets about to regain the power and influence that has slipped away to the President. This factor might have made Congress somewhat obstructive, but it would not, alone, have produced the drastic program that Congress imposed.

Influence of the "Vindictives." There were, among the leaders of Congress several genuine "vindictives"—men who felt that the North should take revenge on the South. These were of two types. One type, represented by Charles Sumner in the Senate, had some concern for the freedmen, but mainly felt that Southern whites should be punished for rebelling and causing the war. The other group, typified by Thaddeus Stevens in the House of Representatives, were racial egalitarians and regarded it as poetic justice to make the ex-slaves rulers over their former masters. These "vindictives" were the real Radicals. It was they who worked out the plans and plotted the strategy of Radical reconstruction. But they would not have had the votes in Congress to carry out their ideas had it not been for another all-important factor.

Close Alliance of the Radicals and the Business Tycoons. The factor that turned the trick was the close alliance between the bulk of Northern political leaders and the tycoons of big business. From the point of view of this alliance, the old Southern leadership must be kept out of Congress and out of the governments of their own states, where votes of legislatures might be needed to ratify or defeat constitutional amendments. The planters hoped to restore their plantations, in a somewhat modified form, and to regain the British market for their cotton. They were as bitter against protective tariff and other government aids to Northern industry as they had been before secession. They had shown by the "Black Codes," enacted by the "Johnson governments," that they intended to control the freedmen and compel them to work on the plantations. If they were allowed to retain their old predominance in the South, they would control the state legislatures and send Senators and Representatives to Congress. If they could then pick up support in the West and the border states, where the move to industrial combination was unpopular and where there was indignation at the growing political corruption, they might gather enough votes in Congress to wreck the whole big business scheme and, as a result, turn many Northern politicians out of office. Pondering these considerations, a majority of each House of Congress became "Radicals" on reconstruction, though most of them were ultra-conservative on other issues. They would vote for any scheme that would keep the South "Republican."

The Freedmen as Pawns. It is obvious, then, that, except in the thinking of people like Thaddeus Stevens, the freedmen were merely being used as pawns, much to their long-range detriment and that of their descendants. It was largely the excesses of "carpet bag" government, in which the Negroes played a conspicuous, though not very decisive role, that led to the repression of the Southern Negro and to the various schemes to evade the Fifteenth Amendment, and thereby to deprive him of his right to vote. It was mainly reaction to the "carpet bag" regimes, which called themselves "Republican," that created the Democratic "solid South," which finally broke down only in 1964.

"Re-Reconstruction" by the South an Inevitable Reaction. Such a situation, of course, could not last indefinitely. It was inevitable that, sooner or later, the Southern whites should regain control in their section. Actually, with the help of

liberal elements in the North, they achieved this within a decade after the passage of the Reconstruction Acts. Some of the devices to which they resorted, such as the terrorism of hooded night riders, were reprehensible, and probably accomplished nothing. It was political pressure in the North that led to the withdrawal of federal troops and the collapse of the "carpet bag" governments. Even so, Radical reconstruction lasted long enough to accomplish its real purpose. By the time it ended, the conservative coalition of big business and the "Radical" politicians was so firmly entrenched that it could not be dislodged until after the turn of the century.

LONG-RANGE CONSEQUENCES
OF THE CIVIL WAR

A Turning Point. What has already been said here should make it obvious that, in several important ways, the Civil War was a major turning point in our national history. Developments took a different turn. It is fitting, therefore, that we examine some of the long range consequences of the conflict, and try to tie them together to show their impact on the United States of the twentieth century.

Problems Raised by the Abolition of Slavery. The most obvious, but by no means the most important consequences were those which followed from the abolition of slavery. The end of slavery created the problems of educating the ex-slaves and their descendants, adapting them to a role in a free society, and transforming them into responsible citizens. There would, in any case, have been problems of race relations, which would have taken time to solve, but these were complicated and embittered by "Radical" reconstruction. The elimination of slavery brought an end to the old plantation system, despite the efforts of many planters to preserve or restore it. Much of the plantation land passed into the hands of independent small farmers, as the planters were forced to sell off acreage to meet expenses. Much of it came under a scheme of sharecropping, which was inefficient and, in many cases, led to virtual abandonment of the land. The old social structure of the South could not survive these economic changes. The old class distinctions did not disappear suddenly, but they broke down gradually, so that economic opulence, rather than family, has become the basis of social status in the South as elsewhere in the country. Gradually, there developed a "new South," with its economy based on business and industry. The problem of race relations has persisted, and has now taken a new turn with the Negroes demanding full political equality and full equality of opportunity in education, employment, and housing.

Stimulation of Economic Development. As already noted, the process of industrialization was already well under way in the North before the Civil War, and undoubtedly would have continued if the war had not occurred. However, the war and its immediate aftermath influenced the process in several ways. First, war demands speeded up both industrialization and mechanization. Mechanization affected agriculture also. With manpower being withdrawn from the farms to the army, and with spiraling needs for agricultural products bringing very high prices, farmers began the extensive use of farm machinery, which had been invented before the war, but had been used only sparingly. As this agricultural mechanization continued at an increasing tempo, it contributed to the general industrialization of the country. As an ever shrinking proportion of the population was needed on the farms, an ever increasing proportion moved into the cities seeking work in industry. This brought that rapid growth of cities, with all of its attendant problems, which has changed us from a rural to an urban nation.

The Civil War not only speeded industrialization but, along with reconstruction (which may properly be considered a part of the war), it modified the process. It permitted a comparatively few individuals to create vast business combinations which virtually monopolized whole sectors of the economy, and dominated the government for a third of a century. This committed the government to policies favorable to business, such as high tariff, "sound" money, and restrictions on labor. Naturally, such policies were considered detrimental by farmers and industrial workers. The close alliance between big business and politics, along with the psychological let down which followed the war, opened the way for political corruption.

There was reaction against this state of affairs, coupled at first with reaction against "Radical" reconstruction, as early as 1870. In the next chapter we shall trace the rise of this protest movement which, after the turn of the century, brought about drastic changes in government policy. However, the positive values remained. By 1900, the country had achieved industrial maturity and had developed resources that were soon to make us a world power.

Labor Problems. It was inevitable that these developments should create labor problems. Expanding enterprise needed labor and wanted cheap labor. At first there was a shortage. The rapid migration to the new West drained off the surplus farmers displaced by agricultural mechanization. The former slaves were not fitted by background or education to become industrial laborers, and anyway they were in the wrong place. The formation of labor organizations put the available workers into a position to bargain hard for higher wages and better working conditions, despite laws to restrict their activity. To offset this situation, industrialists, with the blessing of the government, encouraged immigration from Europe. When the immigrants were no longer needed to augment the labor force, the huge influx posed new problems of government policy. In all major labor disputes, the weight of the government was thrown on the side of the employers.

Federal Centralization. One of the most important long range consequences of the Civil War was the centralizing of power in the federal government. This centralizing trend always exists in federal unions, and it definitely was operating in the North before the firing on Fort Sumter. However, the outcome of the war intensified it enormously. Since the South had based its right to secede on the sovereignty of the states, the crushing of the Confederacy destroyed the old concept of "states' rights." The reconstruction amendments subordinated the states to the federal government in matters of civil rights and suffrage. In "Radical" reconstruction, Congress assumed complete control over the formerly seceded states. As time went on, the federal government, through ever broader interpretation of the grants of power in the Constitution, especially the interstate commerce clause, was able to extend its control over many matters which the founding fathers had intended to leave to the separate states. An important factor in making this possible was the growing feeling of American nationalism, itself helped along by the Civil War, which came to look upon the federal government as *the* government, and to regard the states as little more than local government units. Equally important, or even more so, was the fact that, as life became more complex and most business became nationwide in scope, situations developed with which the individual states could not cope, so that more and more matters, by common consent, passed under federal control.

Today, scarcely a shred of the old concept of state sovereignty remains. This centralizing trend certainly would have existed anyway, but probably would have moved much more slowly without the impetus given to it by the Civil War. That struggle determined that we were to be a nation, not just a federation of states. In short, the war cleared the way for the development of a real feeling of national unity.

TOPICS AND QUESTIONS FOR DISCUSSION

Chapter 10

1. In what ways was the Civil War like the American Revolution and in what ways was it different?
2. What were the fundamental reasons for the Civil War?
3. What was the actual relation of the slavery question to the Civil War? Why did Lincoln try to keep the issue from being raised at first?
4. Evaluate the various factors that produced "Radical" reconstruction.
5. Try to form an unbiased evaluation of President Andrew Johnson.
6. What was Southern "re-reconstruction," and why was it inevitable?
7. What were the direct consequences of "Radical" reconstruction in the South and in the North?
8. What were its long range or permanent consequences?

11

An Age of Conservative Reaction, 1865–1901

FACTORS PRODUCING IT

Basis for This Caption. The period 1865 to 1901 was an era of conservative reaction in the sense that conservative elements were able to maintain control of the federal government and the governments of most of the states, and were able to combat successfully most of the efforts to turn national policy into a different direction. There were, it must be noted, other characteristics of the period, some of which we shall discuss a bit later. There was also a growing protest movement. This movement was able to exert enough pressure to secure the enactment of three major reform laws: the Civil Service Reform Act of 1883, the Interstate Commerce Act of 1887, and the Sherman Anti-Trust Act of 1890. However, these had little effect until after 1901. Only a small beginning was made in introducing the merit system into the civil service. In the case of the other two laws, efforts at enforcement were lax, judicial interpretation rendered the legislation almost meaningless, and, there is good reason to believe, the acts were drafted with a view to minimum effectiveness. On balance, the conservatives were able to have their way until the presidency of Theodore Roosevelt.

There were several factors that made this conservative dominance possible. A few of them deserve special mention.

Psychological Reaction to the Civil War. In the first decade or so of the period, the psychological letdown from the Civil War was an important factor. A major war or other great crisis puts people on a strain and their nerves on edge. When the war ends or the crisis passes, there is a feeling of exhaustion and a desire to get as far away as possible from the recent tension. The voters, so long as they are getting along individually, become indifferent to conditions. Only a comparative few react strongly to a prevalence of public corruption or to the unwillingness of government authorities to correct inequities. There is more than a grain of truth in the statement, often made, that war produces a general moral letdown.

Strong Position of Corporate Business. We have already noted the close alliance between the business monopolists and most of the politicians. However, it was not only the promoters of monopolies who were interested. A host of new industries, growing out of the flood of inventions, was springing up and growing to large proportions. Even if these did not have monopolistic trends (some did and some did not), their corporate managers wanted "friendly" legislation and abhorred government regulation. Besides influencing the votes of their own employees, these corporations contributed to the campaign funds of conservative politicians, and used their advertising and propaganda resources to lull public opinion into apathy.

Free Land in the West as an Outlet. With the Homestead Law providing free land and the new railroads providing accessibility, hundreds of thousands of voters and their families, who would have joined in the protest movement had they remained in their old homes, migrated into the new West. So long as they could sell their produce and build new communities to their own liking, these people could not have cared less about conditions in the older sections. Only when they began to feel the pinch of railroad discrimination did they raise their voices to demand reform.

General (Though Interrupted) Prosperity.   Although there were two economic recessions during the period, the so-called "panics" of 1873 and 1893, which spurred demands in the Middle West for currency inflation, the era, in general, was one of prosperity. When times are prosperous, the prevailing feeling is to "let well enough alone," and not "rock the boat" by agitating for reform. The conservatives took full advantage of this attitude to keep themselves in power.

CHANGING WAY OF LIFE

Factors Involved.   During the period under discussion, the prevailing way of life in the United States was changing, as was also happening in Europe, and this change was destined, eventually, to undermine the conservative reaction. We were changing over from a predominantly rural and agricultural society to a predominantly urban and industrial one. As cities grew, slums and poverty developed within them, while more and more new conveniences were available to the more prosperous. As is usually the case, a number of factors were involved in producing the changes.

Inventions.   One writer called this period "the age of invention." Some inventions that had been made before the Civil War, such as the reaper and the sewing machine, came into general use. Additional farm machinery soon appeared. The sewing machine was adapted to factory use and made possible a whole new industry of ready-made clothing. The typewriter was invented and revolutionized office practice. Thomas A. Edison's incandescent electric light changed the pattern of illumination, first in the cities and eventually everywhere. Edison's phonograph and motion picture machine foreshadowed great developments in the future. Alexander Graham Bell's telephone provided instant communication. The electric trolley car solved, for the moment, the problem of urban transportation and enabled the cities to spread out over large areas. Many factory machines made their appearance, and speeded up the mechanization of industry. Toward the end of the period, the internal combustion engine and the automobile were in the experimental stage, but their impact was to come later.

New Industries. We have already noted that many new industries, most of them growing out of the new inventions, came into being during this period. They affected the life of the people in many ways. They employed a large number of both skilled and unskilled workers. This employment not only expanded the market for consumer goods, but stimulated greater activity on the part of organized labor. For a time, it was an attraction to immigrants. The development of new products raised the standard of living of all who could afford the new items. The new industries were also a major factor in the growth of cities, and hence in the rise of such urban problems as housing, sanitation, water supply, and control of crime. The industrial expansion was moving the country along the road to economic maturity which was reached in the 1890's.

Immigration. The growing influx of immigrants has been mentioned several times. Not only did the number of persons migrating to the United States increase rapidly from year to year, but the source and quality of the immigrants was changing. In the 1850's, the largest groups came from Ireland and Germany, and these people were assimilated into the American population easily and rapidly. After the Civil War, sizable numbers came from the Scandinavian countries, and these posed no great problem of assimilation. The greatest number of post-war immigrants, however, came from Southern and Eastern Europe. Most of them were illiterate. They tended to cluster in slum areas of the cities in a "Little Italy" or "Little Hungary." They had great difficulty learning English, and most of them could be employed only as unskilled laborers. Only in about the third generation do we find significant numbers of these people rising to responsible positions. Organized labor protested and demanded restrictions on immigration. Except a ban on immigration from China, though, nothing was done until the 1900's.

Education.   Education at all levels made great progress during this period. Tax-supported elementary schools, of varying quality, were established almost everywhere. Public high schools became common in the Middle West and in the South, though the East continued to depend mainly on private academies for secondary education. Every state had a land grant college, provided for by the Morrill Land Grant Act passed during the Civil War. These were devoted mainly to agricultural and engineering training. All of the Western and Southern states established state universities. Many of the old "independent" colleges of the East expanded into universities. New private colleges, many too feeble to last long, sprang up everywhere. In the South, and to a less extent elsewhere, education at all levels was racially segregated. Too often, this meant that Negroes received a poorer quality of instruction than white children.

Relation to the Period.   These and other changes were slowly broadening and improving the life of most Americans, though very unevenly. Gradually, they brought about a change in the prevailing attitude, and foreshadowed the end of the reign of conservatism.

THE RISING TIDE OF PROTEST

The Greenback Movement. During the Civil War, a large proportion of Middle Western farmers, in order to take advantage of the high prices of agricultural products, had borrowed beyond their depth to buy new machinery and to improve their land. After the war, farm prices dropped sharply and farmers had difficulty making payments on their mortgages. The real reason was overproduction, but the farmers blamed the declining prices on contraction of the currency. As greenbacks came into the treasury, they were destroyed, thus shrinking their volume. At the same time, the war bonds were being redeemed in gold, to the great profit of Eastern investors, many of whom had bought the bonds with depreciated greenbacks. This was undoubtedly good for the national credit, but to many Westerners it looked like a conspiracy to exploit the many for the benefit of the few.

There had been objection to reducing the volume of the greenbacks as early as 1865. In 1868, George Pendleton of Ohio, who narrowly missed getting the Democratic nomination for President that year, advanced what he called the "Ohio idea." This was a proposal to redeem the bonds with greenbacks, and to maintain the volume of that currency. Eight years later, a group of Western farmers launched the Greenback Party. At no time did the party receive enough votes to be a major factor in politics, but reforms demanded in its platform foreshadowed the future. It may have had some influence in getting a law passed in 1878 which froze the volume of the greenbacks by providing that they should be reissued as they came into the treasury. Eventually, the Greenbackers were absorbed into the Populist movement and their presidential candidate of 1876, James B. Weaver, became the Populist candidate in 1892. The real significance of the Greenback movement was that it was the first in a series in the rising tide of protest.

The Liberal Republican Bolt of 1872. While the Greenback movement was getting under way, there was another development of a very different character, with both converging toward the same goal. This was the Liberal Republican bolt of 1872. The Liberal Republican movement started in Missouri in 1868 under the leadership of Carl Schurz and B. Gratz Brown, to overthrow the corrupt regime that held control of that state. Succeeding in Missouri, the leaders determined to enter the national campaign of 1872 in an effort to overthrow "Grantism," by which they meant the corrupt group that controlled the Grant administration. They could not work within the Republican Party because the element they opposed was too firmly entrenched and was determined to renominate Grant. Accordingly, they organized a separate Liberal Republican Party. They were able to make a deal with the Democratic leadership that the Democratic convention would endorse their ticket and not nominate rival candidates. Besides protesting corruption in government, their platform demanded civil service reform, an end to Radical reconstruction, and a liberal attitude toward the South, and hinted at reduction of the tariff.

Had the Liberal Republicans carried out their original intention of nominating Charles Francis Adams of Massachusetts, they would have had an excellent chance to win the election. Adams, the son of one President and the grandson of another, was not a glamorous figure, but he was universally respected and most Democrats would have voted for him. However, the party convention was stampeded into nominating the erratic Horace Greeley, powerful editor of the *New York Tribune,* who had fought the Democrats all his life, was an avowed protectionist, and was lukewarm on civil service reform. The Democratic convention carried out the commitment to endorse the Liberal Republican nominees and platform, but on election day most Democrats did not vote at all. As a political movement, Liberal Republicanism was a failure, but fear of its potential did influence Congress to pass an Amnesty Act for the South and to make a slight gesture toward tariff reduction. Most important of all, though, it foreshadowed future developments as a step in the rising tide of protest.

The "Mugwump" Defection of 1884. In 1884, James G. Blaine had become "Mr. Republican," and was assured of his party's presidential nomination. The Democrats nominated Governor Grover Cleveland of New York, a moderate liberal (though conservative on many issues) with a reputation for rigid honesty. In the course of the campaign, facts came to light linking Blaine, as a Congressman several years earlier, with shady deals in connection with an Arkansas railroad project. Shocked by these implications of corruption, a large number of Republicans, who called themselves independents but were nicknamed "Mugwumps," announced publicly that they would not vote for Blaine, but would support Cleveland. Many of them had been Liberal Republicans in 1872. The campaign was hot and bitter, punctuated with such incidents as the Mulligan letter revelations and the "Rum, Romanism and Rebellion" episode. These incidents undoubtedly affected the outcome of the election, but the main factor in Cleveland's victory appears to have been the support of the Mugwumps. Many of the Mugwumps were still conservative on most issues, but they were all against public corruption. Their defection was another important step in the rising tide of protest.

The Free Silver Movement. Prior to 1873, the United

States, like most other countries, had based its monetary structure on bimetallism. Both gold and silver were standard money, at a legal ratio of approximately sixteen to one; that is, there were sixteen times as many grains of silver in a silver dollar as grains of gold in a gold dollar. Under an economic principle known as Gresham's Law, sometimes phrased as "bad money drives out good," the metal that was cheaper in terms of the coinage ratio tended to drive the more valuable out of circulation. Since the California gold discovery, gold, in this sense, had been the cheaper metal and silver had ceased to be presented at the mint for coinage. In 1873, the silver dollar had been dropped from the list of authorized coins. Soon thereafter, though, due to the opening of new mines in the West, the supply of silver increased and it became the cheaper metal. Immediately, various interests that wanted cheaper money, along with owners of the silver mines, began to demand a restoration of the free and unlimited coinage of silver or, as the popular phrase had it, "free silver."

Twice, in the Bland-Allison Act of 1878 and the Sherman Silver Act of 1890, Congress authorized the purchase and coinage of limited quantities of silver, but this did not satisfy the "silverites." They continued to demand free and unlimited coinage. Free silver was a major plank in the platform of the Populists in 1892. In 1896, William Jennings Bryan, who was a Populist in all but name, was able to commit the Democratic Party to free silver in the famous "free silver campaign." By 1900, the issue had died a natural death with the influx of new gold supplies from the Klondike which made it once more the cheaper metal. In that year, Congress passed the Gold Standard Law which made gold alone the standard of value for American money.

The importance of the free silver movement, which was never really organized, lay not so much in the issue itself as in those who supported it. With the exception of the mine owners, the "silverites" were the same people who were advocating other reforms and were working for an end to conservative rule.

The Populist Revolt. The People's Party, usually called Populist, was what politicians would refer to as a genuine "grass roots" movement. It grew out of a widespread agrarian organization, the Farmers' Alliance. It swept several Western states and, in 1892, was a significant "third" party in the national election. In 1896, most of the Populists supported Bryan and eventually merged into the Democratic Party. The remnant continued on as a minor party into the early 1900's.

The man who has written the best book on the Populist movement interprets it as the last dying gasp of American agrarianism: the last effort of the farmers to control the government and its policies in the face of the upsurge of industrialism and urbanism. Although there have been some minor agrarian political movements since, some of which attained importance in limited areas, this interpretation is correct as far as it goes. But this was only one side of the coin. On the other side, Populism portrayed the shape of things to come. In addition to free silver, its platform advocated: the abolition of national bank notes as currency, expansion of the currency to fifty dollars per capita, government loans to farmers, parcel post, postal savings banks, direct election of Senators, government ownership of railroads and telephone and telegraph lines, a graduated income tax, and initiative and referendum in the states. With the exception of free silver, which became a dead issue, and government ownership of railroads and other public utilities, for which strict regulation was substituted, all of these things came to pass during the Progressive Era or under the New Deal. The Populist Revolt may well be regarded as the climax of the rising tide of protest.

TOPICS AND QUESTIONS FOR DISCUSSION

Chapter 11

1. Analyze the conservative reaction that followed the Civil War. How does this compare with what happened after other wars?
2. What were the various manifestations of the conservative reaction?
3. Was corruption in public office a cause or a result?
4. How did the rapid development of the West affect the course of events in older parts of the country?
5. Why did the agrarian protest take the form of demands for currency inflation?
6. Did the Liberal Republican movement really have a chance of succeeding? What killed it? Did it have any permanent results?
7. Analyze the reasons for the Populist revolt. Was its greatest significance looking backward or looking forward?
8. What concessions were made to these protest movements by those who controlled the federal government?

12 | Imperialism and World Power

MOTIVATION

The New Imperialism. Around the turn of the century, the United States caught a mild case of the fever of imperialism that was sweeping most of the countries of Western Europe. The background and buildup went back almost to Civil War times, but it became a conspicuous national policy only in the 1890's. It was very different from the "manifest destiny" expansionism of the 1840's. We were not acquiring contiguous territory into which a growing population could expand. This time we were seeking to dominate certain areas that either were believed to be valuable economically or would provide strong strategic positions for a role in world politics. We limited our activities to the Western Hemisphere and the Pacific Ocean, and did not compete in the partition of Africa which was then going on. The motivation may have been, partly, a desire to do what other important countries were doing, but this was not the whole story.

Coming of Age Industrially. By the mid-1890's, the United States had reached what may be called industrial maturity. At least in terms of dollar values, our industries were out-producing the home market (even though that market was guarded by a high tariff wall), and were beginning to reach out for export markets. To be sure, there were still many items that we imported: items that we either could not produce at all, such as tin and rubber, or could not produce as economically or of as good quality as some other country. These items, of course, we paid for with our exports. Even so, industrialists saw a glaring need for expanding export markets. In keeping with the imperialistic spirit of the time, it seemed that the way to provide such an expanding market was to establish national hegemony over potential market areas that had not yet been preempted by other industrial nations.

Power Politics.   Partly a result of this economic motivation, but also a contributing motive in itself, was a growing feeling that the United States should begin to play an active role in world power politics. Our country had attained the size and strength to consider itself a world power, though most European governments did not accord us this status until after the Spanish War. We were beginning to recognize that we were affected by happenings everywhere in the world, and to see American national interests involved in the international maneuvering of governments for advantage. This led the government to push what it regarded as our national interests abroad, especially in the Western Hemisphere, the Pacific Ocean and, very soon, the Far East.

The "White Man's Burden" Theme.   An ideological element, which probably had little to do with the desire of industrialists and politicians to push American influence beyond our shores, but was a powerful propaganda force in winning popular approval for this policy, was Rudyard Kipling's plea to "take up the white man's burden." Kipling was speaking to his fellow Britishers, but he was heard in America. Many idealists accepted the notion that the United States, along with Western Europe, had a natural mission to carry the blessings of

Western civilization to what they regarded as "backward" areas. Some Protestant religious groups saw an opportunity to expand their missionary activities, especially in Catholic and largely non-white Latin America. Public opinion generally was ready to rally to the idea that we were carrying freedom and democracy to oppressed peoples.

EARLY BEGINNINGS

Alaska. One of the first moves in the pushing of American power beyond the United States proper was the purchase of Alaska from Russia in 1867, through the efforts of Secretary of State William H. Seward. People talked about "Seward's folly" and "Seward's ice box," but the Senate was finally persuaded to ratify the treaty. At the time, no one knew of the great wealth of natural resources we were acquiring, and certainly no one, including Seward, saw in the vast wilderness of Alaska a future state of the Union. With the wisdom of hindsight, we can now understand what Seward's real purpose was, and so how the purchase of Alaska fits into the picture of the later imperialism. Seward must have foreseen that, in time, American national interests must push across the Pacific and that naval power (he probably did not foresee air power) would be needed to protect those interests. A glance at the Pacific area on a globe will make the point clear. A naval base in the Aleutian Islands would be almost equidistant from San Francisco, from the Pacific islands that stretch in a broken chain from Hawaii to the Asian mainland, and from Japan. The shortest distance from San Francisco to Tokyo skirts the Aleutian Islands very closely. This provided the "great circle" air route in World War II. In a word, Seward's concern was strategic.

Samoa. The protracted and complicated Samoan affair,

which we can not go into in detail, lasted from 1872, when
a local chieftain offered the United States the privilege of
establishing a naval base at Pago-Pago, until a final settlement in
1899. Germany coveted the islands, and the British did not
want to be left out. At one point, in 1889, a three-way naval
engagement was averted only when a hurricane destroyed
most of the ships involved. Following this incident, a triple
protectorate was established over the island group, but it was
unable to keep down native insurrections. Finally, in 1899,
the islands were partitioned between Germany and the United
States, with the United States getting the largest island, Tu-
tuila, with the strategic harbor of Pago-Pago. Despite much
discussion along the way about "entangling alliances" and the
unwisdom of American involvement, the Samoan affair marked
another step in our penetration of the Pacific.

Hawaii. American infiltration of Hawaii was begun by religious missionaries in the mid nineteenth century. The sons of
these missionaries established great sugar and pineapple plantations, cultivated by imported Chinese and Japanese laborers.
The old king, Kalakaua, in return for being permitted to enjoy
the frills of royalty, let these American-Hawaiian planters manage the country in their own interest. In 1875, a reciprocity
treaty was made giving Hawaiian products unrestricted access
to the American market. In 1884, Kalakaua granted the United
States a naval base at Pearl Harbor. When he died in 1891, he
was succeeded by his niece, Liliuokalani. "Queen Lil," as she
was popularly called, soon revoked the old constitution, which
vested all real power in the planter class, and announced her
intention to issue a new one under which she would rule somewhat arbitrarily in the interest of the aboriginal Hawaiians.
This spurred the leaders of the planters, with the connivance
of the American minister, J. L. Stevens, and the tacit support
of the American naval force at Pearl Harbor, to plot a revolu-

tion to overthrow the monarchy. In January, 1893, they proclaimed the revolution and set up a provisional government headed by S. B. Dole of pineapple fame. This regime at once signed with Stevens a treaty of annexation to the United States, which President Benjamin Harrison, at the very end of his administration, submitted to the Senate.

However, when Cleveland reentered the Presidency a few days later, he would have none of it. He promptly withdrew the treaty and sent a personal envoy to investigate the whole matter. When he received the report of this envoy, he undertook to undo the Hawaiian revolution and restore the Queen. When he found that he could not do this without military intervention, he gave up and the situation rested until the Spanish-American War in 1898. At that time, the McKinley administration signed a new treaty of annexation. When the necessary two-thirds majority could not be mustered in the Senate to approve the treaty, annexation was carried out by the dubious means of a joint resolution of Congress, which required only a simple majority in each house. The precedent of Texas was cited, but the parallel was faulty. In 1845, Congress had admitted the Republic of Texas as a state of the Union, something the Constitution clearly gave it power to do. In 1898, Hawaii was annexed as territory, and there is no grant of power in the Constitution for Congress to annex territory. At that time, it was part and parcel of the flowering of the new imperialism.

Beginning of Pan-Americanism. Early in 1889, James G. Blaine, as Secretary of State under President Benjamin Harrison, invited all of the then independent nations of the Western Hemisphere to attend an international "Congress" in Washington later that year. The first Pan-American Congress (it might better have been called a conference) convened in October, 1889, and continued until the following April. Blaine's motives smacked strongly of the growing economic imperialism. What he sought was the creation of a hemispheric customs union, the effect of which would have been to give the United States a virtual monopoly of Latin America's foreign trade. The Latin American delegates would have none of this. Their countries had developed important commercial ties with Great Britain and Germany, which they were unwilling to sacrifice. Even more serious, they feared that a customs union dominated by the "colossus of the North" would threaten their independence. What they worked for in the meeting was a firm pledge that the United States would never intervene in their internal affairs. Such a pledge, Blaine was unwilling to give.

Even though neither side got what it wanted, this first Pan-American Congress was important in two ways. It set a precedent which was followed by the holding of Pan-American congresses, usually at five-year intervals, right down to the time of World War II. Also, it created a Bureau of American Republics, a name later changed to the Pan-American Union, to work for cooperation among the member countries. The Pan-American Union grew in importance until it became a hemispheric alliance on the eve of World War II, and the Organization of American States shortly after the end of that conflict. Inherently, Pan-Americanism is cooperative, not imperialistic. However, in its beginning and early stages, it bore a taint of United States economic imperialism.

Involvement in Chile. In 1891, Chile had a short but bitter civil war between the followers of the President, José Manuel Balmaceda, and supporters of the Congress. Balmaceda had been striving for reforms to benefit the underprivileged and insisted on maintaining strong executive power. Members and supporters of the Congress were of the privileged aristocracy, determined to maintain their privileges. They undertook to reduce the President to a mere figurehead by imposing a European type of cabinet government. It is understandable that Blaine should have sympathized with Balmaceda, but he did not stop with sympathizing. The American minister to Chile, a Blaine selection, with the full backing of Secretary Blaine, grossly violated international propriety by openly supporting the Presidential Party in the civil war. In the midst of the conflict, the Congress Party sent a ship, the *Itata*, to San Diego, California, to buy war supplies. When the ship left port without clearance papers, an American naval vessel was sent in pursuit, and captured the *Itata*. Although the *Itata* was soon released, when a United States court ruled that the pursuit had been illegal, the incident aroused bitter hostility in Chile, and in some other parts of Latin America.

A United States naval vessel, the *Baltimore*, was dispatched to Valparaiso, Chile "to protect American lives and property." By the time the *Baltimore* arrived, the civil war had ended in the defeat and suicide of Balmaceda. Anti-American feeling was intense, especially in the Chilean navy which had supported the Congress Party. Under the circumstances, it was a mistake, to say the least, for the commander of the *Baltimore* to give shore leave to some of his sailors, who promptly got into a brawl with Chilean sailors in a saloon. One American was killed. Instead of treating the incident as what it was, a typical sailors' brawl, Blaine declared it to have been an attack on the American uniform, and threatened war unless the new Chilean government should make amends. In view of the great disparity in power between the two countries, Chile capitulated, but most Latin Americans regarded the "*Baltimore* Affair" as an act of aggression by the United States.

The Venezuela Boundary Case. The Venezuela boundary case was too protracted and involved to be traced here in any detail, but some of its implications and consequences need to be noted. Briefly, the boundary between Venezuela and British Guiana had never been defined, and both countries made extravagant claims based on old Spanish and Dutch grants. In 1840, a British commissioner, Sir Robert Schomburgk, had proposed a line approximating the present boundary. On several occasions, Britain offered to settle for the Schomburgk line, but Venezuela refused. Venezuela, in turn, insisted that the whole question be submitted to international arbitration, but the British, for reasons that seemed valid to them, refused to arbitrate. Around 1890, a few gold nuggets were found near the mouth of the Orinoco River, and Britain proclaimed a new boundary which would give the river mouth to British Guiana. The Venezuelans became panicky and appealed to the United States. The Orinoco was the outlet for the cattle and forest products industries of the Venezuelan interior and, until the later discovery of oil in the Lake Maracaibo region, these industries were the basis of Venezuela's economy. If Britain held the river mouth, Venezuela would be at her mercy.

This occurred just as Cleveland was beginning his second Presidency. He protested to Britain, and his Secretary of State, Richard Olney, carried on a heated diplomatic correspondence with Lord Salisbury, British Prime Minister and Foreign Minister. On one occasion, Olney used the provocative expression, "Today the United States is practically sovereign on this continent." Needless to say, this did not sit well with the stronger Latin American countries. Congress took a hand by creating a United States commission to determine the true boundary, virtually threatening war if such boundary should not be accepted by Britain.

When matters seemed to have reached a crisis, Lord Salisbury made a sudden about face, agreed to arbitrate, and invited the American commission to use the British archives in investigating the proper boundary. A contributing factor in

Salisbury's change of front may have been the fact that the gold deposit turned out to be almost negligible. The main reason, though, was a matter of world politics.

On the continent of Europe there were two antagonistic alliances: the Dual Alliance of France and Russia, and the Triple Alliance of Germany, Austria-Hungary, and Italy. Great Britain had serious clashes of interest or policy with members of both groups. In the circumstances, she decided that her "splendid isolation" was not so splendid, and the possibility was explored of working out an understanding with either alliance. Thwarted in this, an idea occurred to Lord Salisbury or his advisers. Two new world powers were looming on the horizon: the United States and Japan, both with strong navies. If these could be brought into a triple naval alliance with Britain, a world balance of power would be created which probably could preserve peace. With a view to attracting the United States into such an arrangement, Salisbury reversed his stand on Venezuela and made other moves to win American favor. Out of the effort, continued by King Edward VII and Theodore Roosevelt, there developed an Anglo-American *entente*, or informal understanding, which has persisted to the present day and is now a key factor in world relations. The triple naval alliance never quite materialized. In 1902, Britain signed a naval alliance treaty with Japan, only to regret it later, but relations between Japan and the United States remained strained. In the early 1900's, Britain patched up her differences with France and Russia and entered into an informal understanding with them. Thus the Dual Alliance became the Triple Entente of World War I.

Building the New Navy. In keeping with this expanding role in power politics, the United States had begun, in the 1880's, to build a powerful all-steel navy. The inspiration came largely from the writings of Captain (later Admiral) A. T.

Mahan, preaching the doctrine of the supremacy of sea power. Naval construction received a great boost in 1890 when, for one of the few times in our history, there was a large surplus in the treasury. Much of this was poured into ship building. By the time of the Spanish-American war, the United States navy, with warcraft of every type then in existence, was second in size and strength only to the navy of Great Britain.

INTERVENTION IN CUBA AND THE SPANISH WAR

Cuba. The Cubans had revolted against Spain in 1868 in an effort to win independence. After five years, the revolt was put down and Spain promised reforms, a promise that was never carried out. In 1895, the Cubans rebelled again, and sought to involve the United States in their support. There were atrocities on both sides, but a Cuban *junta* in New York, calling itself a revolutionary government-in-exile, ignoring the misdeeds of the rebels, issued heartrending stories of Spanish cruelty. These were spread abroad by the "yellow press," just appearing on the American scene, as sensational news. This propaganda did much to prepare American public opinion to support intervention.

Reasons Behind American Intervention. The excuse for the demand in high places for American intervention in Cuba was the suffering of the Cubans and the desire to free them from Spanish tyranny. This excuse, however, was exploited to the full by several special interests whose motives were far from altruistic. Economic conditions in the United States were depressed (the so-called "Panic" of 1893), and the "regular" Republican politicians hoped that a war, which we could win easily, would not only divert attention from "hard times" at home, but would produce an artificial boom of prosperity. President McKinley was opposed to war, but was pushed by the politicians of his party.

Another special interest involved was the sugar refining industry which hoped that intervention would bring duty-free access to Cuban raw sugar. The sugar refiners were willing to spend a sizable amount of money to promote intervention.

Still another potent factor was a small but influential group of younger politicians, who operated quite independently of the party regulars. They wanted war for a combination of reasons. Some were outright imperialists, hoping that war would bring new territory to the United States. Others, while not averse to territorial gains, stressed the theme that war would bring a great upsurge of national patriotism. Probably an undercurrent with each individual was the expectation that war could be made to further his own political aspirations. Prominent among these men were Henry Cabot Lodge and Theodore Roosevelt. On one occasion, Lodge wrote to Roosevelt, "What this country needs is a short but glorious war." Roosevelt, as an Undersecretary of the Navy, laid the plans for Admiral Dewey's conquest of Manila.

"Remember the Maine." The battleship *Maine* had been dispatched to Havana Harbor "to protect American lives and property" (the standard phrase). The Spanish authorities had mined the harbor against the rebels, but they conducted the *Maine* along a secret passage through the minefield to a supposedly safe anchorage. They did all they could to make the officers and crew of the vessel feel welcome. Then one night the ship blew up. No one ever knew exactly what happened, and the usual investigations revealed nothing significant. The most likely explanation is that one of the floating mines broke loose from its moorings, drifted against the ship, and exploded.

To the excited American mind, though, it appeared that the Spanish had deliberately destroyed the vessel, and "Remember the Maine" became the battle cry of the war.

The "Short But Glorious" War.   It is known with certainty that the Spanish government did all it could to avert war. It even offered to surrender Cuba, but the diplomatic note containing the offer was suppressed in Washington. Admiral Cevera, commander of the Spanish fleet, was defeated before he left Spain, and warned his government that it would be suicidal to dispatch the fleet. But Congress declared war. On land, we were utterly unprepared, but, fortunately, the navy was strong enough to win the war. Hopelessly defeated, Spain "relinquished" Cuba to the United States, ceded Puerto Rico as war indemnity, and ceded the Philippine Islands, ostensibly as a sale. We were launched on a new career of imperialism and world power.

EMERGENCE AS A WORLD POWER

Acquisition of the Philippines.   Our new foothold in the Caribbean was only advancing a process that had begun with the Venezuela Boundary Case. Acquiring the Philippines put us into a new position in world affairs as a power in Southeast Asia. It was said, perhaps not truly, that when President McKinley received the news of Manila Bay he had to look in an atlas to find out where it was. When the peace commission had been dispatched to Paris to meet the Spaniards, something had moved the President to instruct them to demand the cession of the Island of Luzon. Negotiations had barely started when a cablegram was sent to the American commission to demand the cession of all of the Philippines. Why this sudden demand?

The answer seems to lie in a situation that was developing in

Southeast Asia. Spurred by the demand of Germany for the control of Shantung Province, the powers of Europe began a process of partitioning China into "spheres of influence." This was of concern to the United States. We did not want to be shut out of the Chinese trade. American public opinion would not have tolerated our entrance into the scramble to partition China. Just at that point, the fortunes of war virtually tossed the Philippines into our lap. Possession of these islands would give us a military and naval base within striking distance of China and entitle us to a voice in any decisions regarding the Celestial Empire. Hence, our insistence on acquiring the islands from Spain.

Boxer Intervention in China. In 1900, a fanatical anti-foreign society in China, known to the Western world as the Boxers, launched a terror campaign to expel all foreigners. They even attacked missionaries and besieged the foreign legations in Peking. The United States joined with the European powers and Japan in a joint military intervention. The Boxers were soon crushed, and the Europeans insisted on imposing a punitive treaty on China with a large money indemnity. In the negotiations, the British favored moderation and the United States sought to commit the powers to the "open door" policy. Finally, in return for Britain's and the United States' agreement to the indemnity, the other powers made a vague promise to respect the "open door." A little later, the United States first, and then Britain, committed all of their indemnity money, beyond the actual cost of their intervention, to funds for the education of Chinese students in the schools and universities of their respective countries. Many of the leaders of the Chinese revolution of 1911 had been "indemnity" students in the United States or Britain.

The "Open Door" Policy. The "open door" policy meant that the trade of all China should be open to all nations on

equal terms. Secretary of State John Hay proposed the first
version of it in a note to the powers in 1899. This only urged
them not to discriminate against the trade of other nations in
their respective spheres of influence. During the Boxer negotiations, Hay expanded this to an effort to get a general treaty that
the trade of all of China would be open to all countries on
equal terms. He did not get the treaty, and the half-hearted
promise he did get probably would not have been observed but
for the fact that growing tensions among the powers in Europe prevented all of them except Russia, who was infiltrating
Manchuria, from following an aggressive policy in China. Even
so, the United States was now fully involved in the power
politics of the Far East.

CREEPING DOWN THE CARIBBEAN

A Heritage of War. The aggressive American policy in
and around the Caribbean Sea in the early 1900's grew out of
the developments of the Spanish-American War. Not only did
the outcome of that war give us full possession of Puerto Rico
and responsibility for Cuba, but a development during the war
conditioned our whole Caribbean policy. A new battleship,
the *Oregon,* had just been completed on the Pacific coast
when the war began. It was considered highly desirable, if not
absolutely necessary, to get this ship to the Caribbean before
the battle with the Spanish fleet. Accordingly, the *Oregon*
began a race against time and events around the southern tip
of South America. She did reach Cuba in time for the battle,
but the experience convinced many Americans, most notably
Theodore Roosevelt, that the United States must cut a canal
through Central America.

The Panama Canal. As soon as Roosevelt became President,
he began to cope with the problems that must be solved before

a canal could be started. We can not trace all the devious diplomacy involved. A French company had started a canal across Panama years before, but had abandoned it because of engineering difficulties and lack of funds. This company now wanted to sell out to the United States at an exorbitant price and, to get the price down we had to threaten to build the canal across Nicaragua. We had an old treaty with Britain under which neither country was to build a canal across Central America without taking the other into full partnership. The British had to be persuaded to agree to an abrogation of that treaty. When Colombia rejected a treaty giving us a right-of-way across Panama, President Roosevelt connived at and supported, if he did not instigate, the secession of Panama from Colombia. The resulting treaty with Panama not only gave the United States the right to build and fortify the canal, but made that little republic a virtual protectorate of the United States.

The bearing of the Panama Canal on the general Caribbean policy of the United States was that, once we were committed to building the canal, we had to be in a position to defend it. This meant that no potentially hostile power could be permitted to gain a foothold within striking distance of the canal. When conditions developed in any Caribbean country which might give a pretext for intervention by an old world power, it appeared necessary that the United States should step in and bring that country under our domination. This was the real explanation of that succession of interventions which constituted the process of creeping down the Caribbean.

The Roosevelt Corollary of the Monroe Doctrine. Realizing this situation, especially the proclivity of some of these countries to change their governments by "revolution," and their habit of defaulting on their debts to European bankers,

President Roosevelt, in 1904, stated what came to be known as the Roosevelt corollary of the Monroe Doctrine. This was that, in order to maintain the Monroe Doctrine principle of preventing intervention in the Western Hemisphere by European powers, it would become necessary in some cases for the United States to "exercise an international police power." In other words, we should have to intervene to prevent intervention by a European power. This may only have been facing facts but, when applied in Central America a little later, it aroused bitter hostility in most Latin American countries.

Successive Interventions. In 1905, we intervened in the Dominican Republic, when European bankers were putting pressure on their governments to collect debts by force, and set up a receivership of customs. When the Senate rejected the treaty, President Roosevelt put it into effect by executive agreement. Later, the United States intervened with armed force in Haiti and Nicaragua, and financial control was established over the other Central American countries. The last step in this creeping down the Caribbean came in 1915 with the purchase of the Danish West Indies or Virgin Islands to keep Germany from acquiring them. Possession of these islands by Germany would have put a potential enemy within striking distance of the canal. By that time, our fever of imperialism had run its course and we were shifting to a "good neighbor policy" toward Latin America.

INVOLVEMENT IN WORLD
POWER POLITICS

The Hague Conferences. As the United States emerged into the status of a world power, it became almost inevitable that we should take an increasingly active part in world affairs. Generally speaking, the older powers did not accord us equal rank with them until after the Spanish-American War. Immediately following that conflict, our government took a first step by sending delegates to the First Hague Peace Conference in 1899. This meeting was called by the Tsar of Russia to try to work out a general disarmament agreement. The conference failed in this purpose, but it did create the Hague Tribunal, an international court of arbitration.

By the time the Second Hague Conference met in 1907, the United States was already deeply involved in power relations and our participation was a matter of course. About all that this conference accomplished was to draft a number of conventions (multilateral treaties) to make war less cruel and inhuman, such as prohibiting the use of explosive bullets and poison gas, and requiring the humane treatment of prisoners of war. It did draft a broad convention for the peaceful settlement of international disputes, but most ratifying agencies, including the United States Senate, attached reservations that made it almost meaningless.

The Peace of Portsmouth.   By the spring of 1905, the Russo-Japanese War had reached a point where peace negotiations were feasible. The Japanese were everywhere victorious, but were nearing the point of exhaustion of their financial resources and manpower. The Russians, confronted with the Revolution of 1905 at home, were anxious to end the war on any basis that would save face. After some diplomatic feelers, President Theodore Roosevelt offered his "good offices" as mediator, and both countries sent peace delegations to Portsmouth, New Hampshire. At first, President Roosevelt was inclined to favor Japan, but as negotiations progressed, he became convinced that Japan posed a greater threat to American interests, especially the "open door" in China, than did Russia. After that, he used his influence to obtain more moderate terms for Russia.

There was great resentment of Roosevelt's attitude in Japan and, as the Japanese pushed their aggressions on the Asian mainland, relations between the United States and Japan worsened progressively until the climax at Pearl Harbor. At the moment, though, by being a successful peacemaker, President Roosevelt greatly enhanced the prestige of the United States among the great powers.

The Algeciras Conference. The "First Morocco Crisis," precipitated when the Kaiser made a blustering speech in Tangier in 1905, hinting that Germany intended to seize control of Morocco from France, gave President Roosevelt another opportunity to play a dramatic role in world affairs. When it appeared that the crisis might explode into a general European war, for which nobody was ready, the Kaiser dropped a diplomatic hint that he would welcome a move by the American President to bring about a conference of the powers to settle the matter peaceably. Although he had some misgivings about American involvement, Roosevelt arranged a meeting of the powers at Algeciras, Spain, early in 1906. The settlement reached was a defeat for Germany, and it undoubtedly strengthened both the Anglo-French and the Anglo-American *ententes*. More importantly, it was a strong factor in postponing World War I for almost a decade. It certainly enhanced the prestige of the United States.

TOPICS AND QUESTIONS FOR DISCUSSION

Chapter 12

1. What factors combined to produce the wave of imperialism around the end of the nineteenth century? Was it inevitable? Why or why not?

2. Review early incidents (prior to mid-1890's) that showed a rising interest in the Far East and Latin America. Were there solid reasons for this growing interest? If so, what were they?

3. Could or should the Spanish-American War have been averted? Justify your opinion.

4. Summarize the direct and indirect effects of the Spanish-American War.

5. Why did the American government decide to build the Panama Canal? What were the obstacles and how were they overcome?

6. Summarize the process of "creeping down the Caribbean," and explain why each step occurred.

7. How did the United States become involved in the power politics of the Far East? Were our actions wise or otherwise?

8. How did our new position as a world power in the early 1900's involve us in world power politics?

13 | The Progressive Era

THE PERIOD

The Span. The span usually called the Progressive Era extended from the fall of 1901 to the spring of 1917. It covered the presidential administrations of Theodore Roosevelt and Taft, and the first administration of Woodrow Wilson. It came to an end when involvements with World War I, culminating in our entry into that war, shifted attention from domestic reform to international affairs.

Characteristics. The Progressive Era was a distinct reaction against the conservatism which had been predominant ever since the Civil War. The attitude and policies of government at all levels shifted over from protecting special interests to serving the welfare of the common man. There was a similar change in the direction of public opinion. What had formerly been the viewpoint only of protest groups became the prevailing point of view of the general public. A new leadership took over in public life, not only in politics but also in other activities. Most, but not all, of these new leaders, took the "progressive" attitude, at least in some measure, though they differed as to the amount of innovation they were ready to accept.

Was the Period Really Progressive? There may be room to argue whether the innovations of the period represented true progress. Some of them, such as the recall of judges, proved unworkable and were later abandoned. On the whole, though, they were in line with trends that were taking hold, not only in the United States, but in Western Europe as well. Appropriately or not, the name "progressive" has become attached both to the period and to the measures which it produced.

BEGINNINGS

Foreshadowing Developments. Several things during the conservative period foreshadowed the Progressive Era. The Civil Service Reform Law of 1883, the Interstate Commerce Act of 1887, and the Sherman Anti-Trust Law of 1890, were all, on the surface, steps in this direction. As previously noted, though, Congress passed these measures with tongue in cheek, and they were hampered by judicial interpretation and lax enforcement, so that they had little real effect until the early 1900's. The Populist movement also foreshadowed the new era by calling for many enactments that became law during the progressive years.

Bryan and the Campaign of 1896. The real beginning of the movement that flowered into the Progressive Era may be seen in William Jennings Bryan's first campaign for the Presidency in 1896—the famous "Free Silver Campaign." Bryan, just barely old enough at the time to be eligible for the Presidency, was one of the most aggressive of the new leaders. In this campaign, he put the emphasis on free silver, soon to become a dead issue, but he stood for almost everything in the Populist program. He had stampeded the Democratic Convention with his great "Cross of Gold" speech, and had secured not only that party's nomination, but a "progressive" platform. For the first time, one of the major political parties was committed to extensive reform. Bryan, as everyone knows, was defeated in 1896, as he was later in 1900 and 1908, but he remained a power in public life until World War I. Although he never achieved the Presidency, many of his ideas triumphed.

Theodore Roosevelt and the Campaign of 1900. Theodore Roosevelt, another of the younger new leaders, was a complex personality. Personally ambitious, he was something of a political opportunist and a clever political manipulator. He was a genius at advertising himself by making news (which he sometimes distorted) and getting it printed. After the Spanish-American War, he created the impression that his regiment, the "Rough Riders," was primarily responsible for the victory. With it all, though, he was a genuine progressive. Hurrying home from Cuba in the fall of 1898, he used his genius for publicity to get himself elected Governor of New York. In that office, he became a thorn in the side of the machine politicians.

In 1900, it was virtually inevitable that the Republicans should renominate McKinley, who had been President during the "short but glorious war." The New York politicians, who wanted to get Roosevelt out of state politics, decided it would be a good idea to "bury" him in the Vice Presidency. Knowing that this position had usually been the end of the road in political careers, "Teddy" hesitated. He finally decided, though, that he could use the Vice Presidency to keep himself in the limelight and have a chance at the Presidency in 1904.

During the campaign, Roosevelt, unlike earlier Vice Presidential candidates, campaigned vigorously. Without openly challenging the relatively conservative platform of his party, he hinted strongly at the "progressive" ideas for which he stood. As we know, the McKinley and Roosevelt ticket was victorious over Bryan, and it appeared that the Progressive Era had been postponed for four years. An assassin's bullet was destined to change the picture. When, in September of 1901, Roosevelt stepped into the Presidency upon the death of Mc-Kinley, he announced that he intended to carry out McKinley's policies. Someone wisecracked that "he carried them out —and buried them."

State Movements: La Follette in Wisconsin. Mention should be made of the reform movements in several of the states in the mid and later 1890's. In those years, a sizable sprinkling of states adopted some of the Populist proposals that required state action. Among these were the direct primary for the nomination of party candidates, and the initiative and referendum for direct legislation. Just a bit later, the elder Robert M. La Follette, as Governor of Wisconsin, secured the creation of the first state commission to regulate railroad rates. Because of his national prominence, La Follette's reform program attracted particular attention.

REFORMS AND EVENTS

Presidents and Reforms. It is not necessary for present purposes to elaborate the reforms of the period in detail, but it seems desirable to sketch the main lines of development. Since, to a greater extent than had been usual since Lincoln's day, leadership came from the Presidents, we shall sketch the reforms by Presidential administrations.

Roosevelt. Early in 1902, President Roosevelt had his attorney general bring suit to dissolve the Northern Securities Company as a violation of the Sherman Anti-Trust Law. Northern Securities was a holding company formed to combine the management of three railroads, the Northern Pacific, the Great Northern, and the Burlington. The Supreme Court decision dissolving the company did not accomplish its ostensible purpose of restoring competition, since the owners of the three railroads continued to combine management under a "gentlemen's agreement." It was of great importance, though, in bringing the anti-trust law back to life and so in opening the way for suits to dissolve the Standard Oil Company, the American Tobacco Company, and the meat trust.

In the spring of 1902 a strike occurred in the anthracite coal mines of Pennsylvania. The operators urged the President to do as Cleveland had done in the Pullman strike, use the power of the federal government to break the strike. Instead, Roosevelt used all his powers to force the issue to arbitration. This was the beginning of a drastic change in the attitude of government toward labor.

After his reelection in 1904, when Roosevelt spoke of being "President in his own right," he became more aggressive in his reform attitude. In 1906, he secured the enactment of three reform laws: the Pure Food and Drugs Act, the Meat Inspection Act, and the Hepburn Act which, though it proved inadequate, made a beginning of enlarging the powers of the Interstate Commerce Commission to regulate railroad rates.

Roosevelt also made a beginning in the conservation of natural resources. Very early in his first administration, taking advantage of an old unused statute, he began withdrawing forest and mineral lands from public entry. Prior to that time, lumbering and mining companies had been allowed to acquire these lands and to exploit them ruthlessly, with no thought to future needs. In 1902, the Newlands Act provided the first federal funds for irrigation projects. At the same time, individual states were taking up conservation and were passing their own conservation laws.

Taft. As Roosevelt's second term drew toward its end, it became obvious that William Howard Taft was the "crown prince." Nominated and elected mainly on the basis of "Teddy's" popularity, he was generally expected to be a carbon copy of his predecessor. Though destined to acquire the reputation of being a conservative, Taft actually was an authentic progressive, even though he was more cautious and deliberate than Roosevelt had been. Despite the controversy that developed out of it, he was an ardent conservationist, and pushed through several new conservation laws. He carried forward the anti-trust movement vigorously. His attorney general prosecuted successfully the cases started under Roosevelt, and instituted nearly a hundred new suits to dissolve monopolies. In 1910, Congress passed the Mann-Elkins Act which took up where the Hepburn Law had left off in increasing the power of the Interstate Commerce Commission to regulate railroad rates.

Two constitutional amendments which the Populists had urged were submitted during Taft's administration. The sixteenth, in 1909, authorized the income tax, and the seventeenth, in 1912, provided for direct election of United States Senators. Other reform laws, also foreshadowed by the Populists, created postal savings banks in 1910, and the parcel post in 1912. However, Taft damaged his reputation for progressivism by vetoing a provision for the recall of judges in the constitutions of New Mexico and Arizona, then up for admission as states.

Wilson. Woodrow Wilson called his reform program "The New Freedom," and it marked the culmination of the Progressive Era. Several of its enactments were of more far reaching consequences than any that had come before. Within a few months after his inauguration, Wilson secured the passage of the Underwood Tariff. Although this law did not abandon the doctrine of protectionism entirely, it brought the first general reduction in tariff rates since the Civil War. Taking advantage of the new Sixteenth Amendment, which had just been ratified, the Underwood Act also levied the first graduated income tax.

One of the most important of the Wilson reforms was the creation of the Federal Reserve System at the end of 1913. The President took a personal hand in the drafting of the legislation. The law undertook to systematize our entire banking and currency system. Besides setting up the ten Federal Reserve Banks to take the control of credit away from the big New York banks, it provided for Federal Reserve notes to replace the national bank notes as the basic currency. It also set up the Federal Reserve Board, not only to direct the management of the Federal Reserve Banks, but to exercise considerable control over private credit by fixing the interest rate on loans by the Federal Reserve Banks to private banks. The system has been modified only slightly in the years since.

A new turn was given to the anti-trust movement. The Clayton Anti-Trust Law of 1914, in form an amendment to the Sherman Law, further increased the powers of the Interstate Commerce Commission, and spelled out specific practices of business corporations which should be illegal. It specifically exempted labor organizations from the anti-trust law. A companion measure created the Federal Trade Commission to police the operation of interstate commercial business in much the same fashion that the Interstate Commerce Commission policed the railroads.

Other Wilsonian reforms included the Federal Farm Loan Act of 1916, which set up Federal Land Banks to make capital loans to farmers. Another law set up the agricultural extension service, with a farm agent in each county, to advise farmers. There were several items of legislation to aid labor, including the Child Labor Act of 1916. A law to impose a literacy test on immigrants, demanded by the labor organizations, was passed over President Wilson's veto.

Background of the "Bull Moose" Movement. From the very beginning of Taft's administration there was friction between the new President and his predecessor. Roosevelt was disappointed when Taft did not retain most of his cabinet, and he was displeased that his successor did not operate the way he had. Taft, having been a judge most of his life, had a judicial and legalistic attitude toward Presidential action, whereas Roosevelt was inclined to act impulsively and not worry about questions of legality. Soon things began to happen which, despite his essential progressivism, pushed President Taft into the arms of the conservative element of his party.

One of the most decisive of these was controversy over tariff. The Republican platform of 1908 had promised "revision" of the tariff, and this was generally understood to mean revision downward. Soon after his inauguration, President Taft called Congress into special session to revise the tariff. After much wrangling in both Houses, the Paine-Aldrich Tariff, which finally emerged, raised more rates than it reduced. During the fight in the Senate, ten Republican Senators, called "insurgents," voted with Democrats in a futile effort to defeat the bill. Later, during the mid-term election of 1910, they carried the fight to the country in fiery campaign speeches. The President, out of a sense of party loyalty, signed the bill, and later defended it in a public speech. This began to brand him as a conservative.

At about the same time another group of "insurgents" in the House of Representatives was battling against the arbitrary rule of Speaker Joseph G. Cannon. This was prompted in part, but only in part, by Cannon's handling of the tariff issue. These "insurgents" also carried their fight to the country in the election of 1910. When that election gave the Democrats control of the House, the insurgent Republicans joined with the Democrats in forcing a revision of the rules of the House to deprive the Speaker of much of his power. The President neither supported nor opposed this "revolution," but it was assumed that he favored Cannon and this seemed to align him with the conservatives.

Another occurrence that damaged Taft's reputation as a progressive was the Pinchot-Ballinger controversy. Richard A. Ballinger, Secretary of the Interior, was, like Taft, a real conservationist, but a cautious and legalistic one. Because of his scruples about legality, he took some steps which appeared to some of his subordinates, notably Gifford Pinchot, Chief of the Bureau of Forestry, to be undoing some of Roosevelt's conservation measures. Pinchot attacked his chief publicly, even writing magazine articles denouncing him. The President, very naturally, supported Ballinger. The wrangle dragged on until Ballinger resigned. The public airing of the affair branded Taft, very unjustly, as an enemy of conservation.

Taft was also made to suffer from the failure of a reciprocity treaty he negotiated with Canada. He worked hard, even soliciting the support of Democrats, to get the treaty ratified over the opposition of both the ultra-conservatives and the Western progressives of his own party. He finally secured ratification, but the treaty was rejected by Canada, and Taft was blamed for the failure.

Rise of the Progressive Republican Movement. Out of these developments, a "Progressive Republican" movement began to take shape in 1910. Its aim was to gain control of the Republican Party and replace Taft with one of their own group in the election of 1912. The prime mover was Senator Robert M. La Follette of Wisconsin, and a "La Follette for President" boom soon took form. At first unorganized, the leaders of the movement formed the National Progressive Republican League in January, 1911. In June, 1910, Theodore Roosevelt returned from more than a year's absence from the country, hunting big game in Africa and being wined and dined by European royalty. Two months later, in a speech at Osawatomie, Kansas, he proclaimed "the Square Deal," and was highly critical of the Taft administration. After that, many of the Progressive Republican leaders decided that they would stand a better chance of success in 1912 with Roosevelt as a candidate rather than La Follette, and they began to beseech him to enter the race. In February, 1912, he used the expression "My hat is in the ring," and a few days later he announced that he would accept the nomination if it should be offered him.

The Election of 1912. The 1912 Republican convention was definitely maneuvered by the conservative-dominated National Committee, which was determined to renominate Taft. There were enough contesting Roosevelt delegates to control the convention, had they all been seated. However, the packed Credentials Committee seated all the Taft contestants, assuring the President's renomination on the first ballot. At that point, all of the Roosevelt delegates, including the few uncontested ones, withdrew from the convention. They held a separate meeting of their own and called a convention of the Progressive Party for August.

At the Progressive convention, Roosevelt nicknamed the new party by saying, when asked how he felt, that he felt "like a bull moose." Needless to say, he was nominated without opposition.

The Democrats were prepared to nominate Speaker Champ Clark, a moderate conservative, but once again, Bryan upset all plans. First, he pushed through a resolution declaring the convention opposed to the nomination of a candidate who was under obligation to the tycoons of big business. On the second day of balloting, when the Tammany delegation switched to Clark, Bryan announced to the convention that this showed that the Speaker was accepting help from big business. That sealed Clark's doom. Bryan then threw his powerful support to Governor Woodrow Wilson of New Jersey, who had made a reputation as a progressive, and finally secured his nomina-

THE "BULL MOOSE" ELECTION OF 1912

As Roosevelt envisioned it

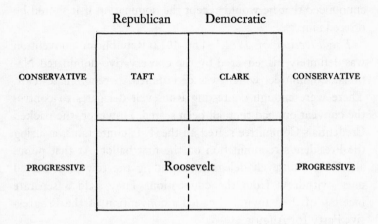

	Republican	Democratic	
CONSERVATIVE	TAFT	CLARK	CONSERVATIVE
PROGRESSIVE	Roosevelt		PROGRESSIVE

As Bryan maneuvered it

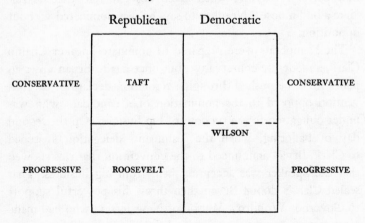

	Republican	Democratic	
CONSERVATIVE	TAFT		CONSERVATIVE
		WILSON	
PROGRESSIVE	ROOSEVELT		PROGRESSIVE

tion. Bryan did not like Wilson personally, but he disliked Roosevelt more, and this looked like the best way to defeat the Rough Rider.

Roosevelt's hope of election depended upon the Democrats nominating a conservative. That, presumably, would drive most of the progressive Democrats to vote for the Progressive Party. With the conservative vote divided between Taft and Clark, the "Bull Moose" would stand a good chance of wining. As it was, practically all Democrats voted for Wilson, with the normally Republican vote split between Taft and Roosevelt. This virtually assured Wilson's election.

Effects of the Outbreak of World War I. Late in President Wilson's second summer in office, World War I broke out in Europe. From the very beginning, it created diplomatic problems, at first with both sides, but more and more with Germany. The reform program did not grind to a halt suddenly, but as the war progressed and grew more intense, both the attention of the administration and the interest of the public shifted away from domestic problems to problems of our relations to the war. When the United States entered the war in April of 1917, the Progressive Era came to an end.

SIGNIFICANCE OF THE PROGRESSIVE ERA

Direct Effects. The direct effects of the Progressive Era are quite obvious. The institutional changes it brought have remained permanent. The policy of regulating private business has continued, though some of the techniques have been changed. Such policies as conservation and a benevolent attitude toward labor have continued, though different administrations have followed them with varying degrees of enthusiasm. The public attitude of demanding governmental response to its wishes has changed little since Theodore Roosevelt's day.

Long Range Significance.   Looked at from the long range point of view, the Progressive Era is even more significant. It marked a major turning point in the course of our national development. It changed that course from corporate domination to the attitude of the welfare state. Development toward the welfare state has not been steady. It suffered a setback during World War I, and it stagnated during the 1920's. It bounced back with a vengeance in Franklin D. Roosevelt's "New Deal," and has advanced continuously, if not steadily, ever since. Although industry has expanded enormously, both in size and in scope, there could be no turning back to "the age of big business" and domination by multi-millionaire tycoons.

TOPICS AND QUESTIONS FOR DISCUSSION

Chapter 13

1. Review developments prior to 1900 that led up to the Progressive Era. Was there a consistent build-up?
2. Who was the principal author of Progressivism: Bryan, Roosevelt or LaFollette?
3. To what extent did state movements prepare the way for a national movement?
4. What were the major "Progressive" reforms before 1912? After 1912? To what extent were they permanent?
5. How did Bryan's political maneuvering upset Roosevelt's calculations in the "Bull Moose" campaign of 1912?
6. How did the outbreak of war in Europe in 1914 affect Progressivism?
7. What was the relation of the "New Deal" and the "Great Society" to the Progressive Era?
8. How would you evaluate the permanent effects of Progressivism on the United States?

14 The Impact of World War I

BACKGROUND OF THE WAR

Relation to Power Politics. World War I grew out of a clash of interests and ambitions among the great powers of Europe, particularly a conflict of Russian and German aspirations in the Balkans. Ever since the time of Catherine II (Empress at the time the United States gained independence), Russia had sought to dominate the Balkans in order to carry Russian power directly to the Mediterranean. After the Second Balkan War, which had enlarged Serbia as well as several other Balkan states, a scheme was concocted, with Russian backing, to create a "greater Serbia" by annexing the South Slav portions of Austria-Hungary. Rumania, also with Russian support, sought to acquire the Transylvania area from the Dual Monarchy. Success of these schemes would have meant the complete disintegration of Austria-Hungary, already a German satellite.

Besides her obligation to protect her "ally" Austria, Germany had an ambitious scheme to create a *"Mitteleuropa"*: domination of a broad band of territory stretching from the North Sea to the Indian Ocean, and including Germany, Austria-Hungary, the Balkans, and the Turkish Empire, which then included most of the Arab lands of the Middle East. There was much talk of a "Berlin to Bagdad Railroad." Many segments of this road were already in operation and all that would be needed to complete the project would be to build some connecting links. Germany had already acquired so many concessions in Turkey, for trade and the development of resources, that she was virtually a suzerain over that decrepit empire.

France also figured in the situation. Anxious to avenge her defeat in 1871 and to regain Alsace-Lorraine, France was ready to push the Balkan crisis into a general European war if the chance appeared good of winning it. The French felt that Britain, though not formally committed to an alliance, could be brought to a war to support France. Raymond Poincaré, President and former Premier of France, hastened to St. Petersburg when trouble started in the Balkans and urged upon the Tsar's ministers the full mobilization which made war inevitable. He argued that Germany could not stand up under a three-front war.

The British were anxious to avert war. They tried in vain to bring together an international conference to resolve the crisis peaceably, as several earlier ones had been resolved. However, most British statesmen felt that, if war should come, Britain could not stand aloof. They were apprehensive of Germany on three major scores: they knew full well that Germany coveted some of Britain's colonial possessions; the growing strength of the German navy challenged Britain's control of the seas, deemed necessary to defend the wide-flung British Empire; finally, Germany was undercutting Britain's foreign markets which were considered necessary to British survival. British public opinion was won over by the German invasion of neutralized Belgium.

The Balance of Power Aspect. Although statesmen of the day may have been only dimly conscious of it, the balance of power question was a potent factor in producing the war. Early complete success by either side would have upset the delicate and fragile equilibrium of power. Russian control of the Balkans would have strengthened that country's influence in world affairs enormously and, with Russia's long record of aggression, would have constituted a threat to the security of western Europe. Even more serious would have been the success of Germany's *Mitteleuropa* project. This would have made Germany, with her militaristic regime of those days, the strongest power in the world. Such a Germany would undoubtedly have seized much of Britain's colonial empire and, by dominating world markets, would have undermined Britain's economy. Such a Germany could, and probably would, have exercised a virtual hegemony over France, the Low Countries, and Italy. Even the economic and diplomatic interests of the United States would have been placed in jeopardy. It was highly important that the other powers prevent this from happening.

Effects on the United States before American Entry. Effects of the war were felt almost immediately in the United States. Britain and France, but especially Britain, were in desperate need for supplies which only the United States could furnish. The American economy boomed. Besides stepping up the production of food and other basic necessities, war industries sprang up to supply all kinds of military equipment. At first, there was some diplomatic conflict with Great Britain over her definitions of contraband and her seizure of American ships and cargo bound for Germany. Very soon, though, Germany's adoption of unrestricted submarine warfare shifted the emphasis completely.

The German high command, realizing that the British could not carry on war, or even exist, without importing supplies from overseas, decided that Britain could be starved into submission by using submarines to sink cargo ships. This brought heated protests from the United States. President Wilson contended that the sinking of non-military ships without warning and without providing for the safety of passengers and crew was a violation of international law. The Germans retorted that rules of international law made to regulate the conduct of surface war vessels could not be applied to submarines. The crisis came when the liner *Lusitania* was torpedoed with the loss of more than a hundred American lives. The President sent an ultimatum to Germany, hinting strongly that the United States would enter the war unless the unrestricted submarine warfare stopped, and it was stopped for the time being.

Could the United States Have Stayed Out? Since the United States was not attacked directly, as happened at Pearl Harbor in World War II, presumably we could have stayed out of the first World War. However, German submarine warfare was a strong provocation. After the second *Lusitania* note, we were virtually committed to enter the war if unrestricted submarine activity was resumed, and it was resumed shortly after President Wilson's reelection in 1916. At that point, we could have backed down only with severe loss of face and damage to our international stature.

Another important factor was the very efficient British propaganda, which exaggerated and even invented German atrocities. This propaganda convinced American public opinion that the Germans were barbarians, and that we had a moral obligation to help suppress them. Besides wanting to present their own country in the best possible light, the British propagandists were anxious to bring the United States into the war for three major reasons. First, the British needed military help, especially early in 1917 when the collapse of Russia enabled the Germans to transfer large numbers of troops from the Eastern to the Western Front. Equally important, Britain needed government credit in the United States to enable her to go on buying war supplies. By the end of 1916, the British had used up all available foreign exchange and had liquidated almost all of their investments in America to pay for war materials. Only an American loan, not available from private banks, could enable them to keep on going. Finally, when Germany announced the resumption of submarine warfare, the British navy told the government that it could not combat the submarine adequately without help from the American navy. The propaganda influenced the American public, but it was the facts behind the propaganda that influenced the President and his advisers.

The Real Reason for American Entry. Undercutting all other considerations was the balance of power question. A victorious imperial Germany would have been such an aggressive super-power that it would have imperiled the vital interests, if not the actual security, of the rest of the world. With Russia in the throes of revolution, it appeared that it would be a long time, if ever, before that country could again serve as a counterweight to Germany in world relations. Under these conditions, the United States could not afford to stand by and let Germany triumph. It is not at all certain that President Wilson, although he was a noted political scientist, understood this very clearly. The nearest he ever came to explaining it to the American people was his statement that we entered the war to "make the world safe for democracy." Not only democracy was at stake, though, but the whole position of the United States in the world.

PROBLEMS POSED BY
AMERICAN PARTICIPATION

Military. As in all earlier wars, the United States entered
the conflict almost completely unprepared. The regular army
was almost negligible in size, and there was a constitutional
question as to whether national guard units could be sent outside the country. This was resolved by drafting the guards-
men, in their military units, into the United States Army. A
draft law was passed immediately, but it took all summer to
set up the machinery (which did not work entirely satisfac-
torily), to register and classify the men, to hold the drawing,
and to permit local draft boards to consider claims for exemp-
tion. The first draftees were inducted early in September, but
it was the following spring before "National Army" units
could be sent overseas. Then, however, the pressure became
so great that whole divisions were sent across with almost no
training. By the time of the armistice, around two million men
had been inducted, and about half of these had been sent to
France, though not all were in the lines.

Equipping the forces was an even greater problem. New and
improved weapons were devised, but getting them into production was so slow that none reached the troops in the field
until the last days of the war. Our men had to get along with
older equipment, designed for the British or the French. It
was remarkable that the American units, many of them under-
trained and all of them ill-equipped, made such a good showing at the battle front.

Economic. The nation was not as well equipped as in
World War II to cope with economic problems, and was not
as effective. With Americans balking at rationing and retail
price controls, the efforts of Herbert Hoover to handle the

problem by persuasion met with some success, but not enough. The war created a need for expanded production in all fields, but there were shortages both of labor and of raw materials. Price inflation became inevitable, and this, in turn, produced labor troubles. Had the war lasted another year, we might have attained something like the wartime economic proficiency that we did in the Second World War but, as it was, we were just beginning to catch up with needs when the fighting stopped.

Finance and War Loans. Financing the war was a problem. Taxes were increased, but the chief reliance was on successive "Liberty loans." It was necessary to finance not only our own war efforts but, to a large extent, the efforts of our Allies. As soon as we declared war, commissions from all the Allies descended on Washington seeking loans. The loans were all granted, but not always in as large amounts or on as easy terms as the Allies hoped for. These war loans, which were to cause serious international problems in the 1920's, were in the form of Treasury credits which the borrowing country could use to buy war supplies in the United States. Except for a comparatively small amount of gold shipped to Britain to stabilize the currency, none of the money ever left the United States.

Propaganda and Witch Hunting. A Committee of Public Information was set up, with George Creel as chairman, as an American propaganda agency. This agency did good work in undermining German morale. In his releases to the American press, although there was much news he had to withhold for security reasons, Creel leaned over backward to report only the truth. However, Allied propaganda in the United States, which continued after our entry into the war, was less scrupulous. Partly because of this, but also due to a high fervor of patriotism, anti-Germanism was carried to ridiculous lengths. The teaching of the German language in the schools was stopped, and even the playing of the music of German composers of decades earlier was forbidden by state and local authorities. All German property was sequestered and placed in the hands of an Alien Property Custodian.

EFFECTS OF AMERICAN PARTICIPATION

Economic. The immediate economic effects have already been indicated, but there were long range effects also. The price inflation continued through the 1920's. The expanded productive capacity remained and, in general, was converted successfully to peace time production after the war. The end of the war brought a superficial prosperity, except to the farmers. They had geared themselves to maximum production. When the war demand for their products dropped off, they began to suffer from depressed conditions which continued until they blended into the Great Depression. There were speculative booms which contributed to the crash of 1929.

Psychological. During the war, the first major war in which the United States had been engaged since the Civil War, Americans generally became worked up to a high pitch of emotional tension. When the fighting stopped, there was the same kind of emotional let-down that followed the Civil War, with similar consequences. Warren G. Harding summed up the prevailing attitude in his bad-English campaign slogan, "Back to normalcy." Most people wanted to turn their backs on the war and everything they associated with it: strong government, foreign commitments and personal sacrifice. This attitude goes far to explain the popular rejection of the League of Nations, the election of a weak President in 1920, and the let-down in public morals which once more, as after the Civil War, brought corruption in high places in Washington. It also goes a long way toward explaining the weakening of private morals and the almost irrational gaiety of the 1920's.

Relations with Latin America. Early in his first term, President Wilson had begun trying to improve relations with Latin America. It remained for Franklin D. Roosevelt to coin the term "Good Neighbor Policy," but Wilson tried to move in that direction. The state of affairs in Mexico and our purchase of the Danish West Indies (the Virgin Islands) seemed to some to negate his other actions, but he assured the Latin Americans that we should never take another foot of territory in the Western Hemisphere by conquest, he encouraged American banks to make development loans, and he sent diplomats who were instructed to emphasize our neighborly attitude. All of this produced good effects in Brazil and around the Caribbean. When war came, several Latin American nations declared war on Germany in support of the United States. Brazil and Cuba took a small but active part in the war, and most of the other governments broke off diplomatic relations with Germany. Only Mexico, embittered by Pershing's pursuit of Villa into her territory, remained on good terms with Germany, and this inspired the Zimmermann Note, suggesting that Mexico cooperate with Germany in an attack on the United States. On balance, though, the war served to improve relations with Latin America and helped to prepare the way for such later developments as the formation of the Organization of American States and the Alliance for Progress.

Tipping the Balance. Unlike World War II, when the United States had to throw in enough weight to turn worldwide defeat into victory, it was necessary in World War I to provide only enough strength to offset Germany's advantage from the collapse of Russia and to tip the military balance in favor of the Allies. Prior to the Russian breakdown at the beginning of 1917, the war on the Western Front had been a stalemate for two years. The German advantage was not as great as might appear. Not all the forces could be removed from the Eastern Front, lest the Russians rally, as they did briefly under Kerensky. The German railroads were in disrepair, and German army trucks were without rubber tires. There were many other problems of shifting troops from one front to the other. Even so, the advantage might well have given the Germans victory in the West had the Allies not had American help. When the Anglo-American North Sea blockade had rendered the submarine useless, German morale began to break. In the spring of 1918, the German army launched a last desperate drive to break through in the West, but when this drive was blunted by the Americans at Chateau-Thierry, the Kaiser's generals began to think only of saving their army. Italy had bounded back to recover her lost ground in the North, and Austria-Hungary had broken to pieces. In September, the Allies, under the unified command of Marshal Foch at last began a pincer drive to nip off all German forces in France, with the British driving down from the north, the Americans up from the south, and the weakened French holding the center of the line. When it appeared that this movement was likely to succeed, the German High Command told the Kaiser he must leave the country, and approached President Wilson for an armistice based on the "Fourteen Points."

THE PEACE SETTLEMENT

Versailles. When a conference of the Allies to draft a peace settlement was called to meet in Versailles, the old royal suburb of Paris, President Wilson felt that he must attend in person. This was contrary to American tradition and brought heated criticism. However, the delegations of the other Western Powers were to be led by their prime ministers (heads of government) so it seemed to the President that, if the United

States were to meet these powers on equal terms, our head of government must be there also. The man who sought to dominate the gathering was Premier Georges Clemenceau, "the tiger of France." He wanted to impose an extremely vindictive peace on Germany, with a crushing war indemnity (the euphemism "reparations" was used to sugar coat the pill) that would paralyze the German economy for generations. Wilson had to yield ground on most of the "Fourteen Points," but he did succeed in toning down Clemenceau's extremism. What he considered his greatest achievement was getting the Covenant of the League of Nations written into the treaty. He recognized that there were inequities in the treaty, but he believed that these could be worked out in the world organization. The Germans had no representation in the Versailles Conference, but were only permitted to send two delegates to sign the treaty when it was completed. These delegates objected strenuously to the war guilt clause, upon which Clemenceau had insisted over Wilson's objections, but they had no choice. This clause, by which Germany acknowledged full responsibility for starting the war, was a mistake. Not only was it untrue historically, but it produced a bitterness in Germany which Hitler was able to exploit to repudiate the whole settlement.

Failure of the United States to Face Responsibilities. Due partly to the "back to normalcy" reaction of American public opinion, but mainly to the fact that Wilson's opponents saw the opportunity to play politics with the situation, the United States failed completely to live up to its responsibilities. The League was made an issue in the presidential election of 1929, and the outcome of that election was interpreted as a popular mandate to reject the League. The Senate refused to ratify the treaty and instituted, instead, a separate peace with Germany. During the 1920's, the nation relapsed into an attitude of isolationism. We could not avoid all international activity, as witnessed by the Washington Conference on the Pacific and the Far East, but the government largely ignored our world responsibilities as a great power and centered on an ingrown negative nationalism.

TOPICS AND QUESTIONS FOR DISCUSSION

Chapter 14

1. What was the relation of the outbreak of World War I to the old "balance of power" problem?
2. What effects did the war have on the United States before American entry?
3. Compare the real reasons and the propaganda reasons for United States entry into World War I.
4. How much, militarily and economically, did the United States contribute to the outcome?
5. Why did President Wilson attend the Versailles Peace Conference? Was he justified in attending in the face of extensive opposition at home?
6. What were the good and bad features of the Versailles Peace Treaty? Why do you think so in each case?
7. What effects did World War I have on the United States, including relations with Latin America?
8. Would the course of major events since World War I probably have been different if the United States had joined the League of Nations? Justify your opinion.

15 | The Irresponsible Twenties

CHARACTER OF THE DECADE

Post-War Reaction.   The decade of the 1920's was a time of post-war reaction, which took several different forms. As noted in the last chapter, the prevailing attitude of people was to turn their backs on the war and on everything they associated with it: strong government, international commitments, and personal sacrifice. There was a general apathy toward government and toward personal responsibility. There was a general feeling of "devil may care."

Conservatism.   In the realms of politics and government policy, the reaction was one of conservatism. All three Presidents elected during the period were of definite conservative leanings, and both Congress and the Supreme Court expressed conservative views. The controls and regulations enacted during the Progressive Era were not repealed, but neither were they enforced, and no new progressive measures were enacted.

Laxity.   In the fields of ethics and morals, the reaction may be described as laxity. When the oil scandal broke, reaching into the President's cabinet, there was only mild public indignation. Highly dubious business practices were winked at. The public behavior of many individuals, which would have been shocking a few years earlier, was taken for granted. Not all people, of course, were either unscrupulous or immoral, but enough were to set the tone of the times.

PROBLEMS AND ISSUES OF WORLD RELATIONS

The Washington Conference.   The war had left a threatening situation in the Pacific Ocean and the Far East. Japan had obvious aggressive aims against China. Before the World War had spread beyond Europe, she had made "twenty-one demands" on that country which, had they all been acceded to, would have made all of China a Japanese dependency. The United States had advised the Chinese government to stall on the demands—conceding some of the more innocuous and asking for more time to consider the others. While this matter was still pending, and after the United States had entered the war, Japan declared war on Germany, but limited her activities to seizing German colonial territory in the Pacific Islands and in China's Shantung Province. The United States then persuaded China to enter the war in the hope that this would deter Japanese aggression on the Chinese mainland. At Versailles, Japan insisted on retaining Shantung, with only a vague promise to return it to China.

In the face of this Shantung question, coupled with Japan's known aggressive aims against other parts of China, it was obviously desirable to try to stabilize the situation through diplomatic means. There were other problems too. Japan was building a powerful navy, which might soon become strong enough to dominate the Pacific Ocean. This would be detrimental to the interests of all other countries with interests in the Pacific and, in the days before effective air power, might be a threat to the security of the Philippines and Hawaii. The

British were anxious to extricate themselves from their alliance with Japan, and it seemed highly desirable to create an international mechanism to preserve peace in the Pacific.

Charles Evans Hughes, Secretary of State and the most able man in the Harding Administration, with help in Congress from Senator Borah, took the lead in calling an international conference to cope with these problems. He had no difficulty in persuading Britain to join in the call. The conference convened in Washington in November, 1921, and continued into February, 1922. Besides the United States, Britain and Japan, France, Italy, the Netherlands, Portugal, Belgium, and China were represented. The major powers all included some of their outstanding national leaders in their delegations. Publicity centered on the limitation of naval armaments; at the time and since, the gathering has often been referred to as a "limitation of armaments" conference. A Five-Power Pact was agreed upon fixing the battleship tonnage of the naval powers: the famous 5-5-3 ratio. The United States and Britain were each to have 500,000 tons; Japan, 300,000, and France and Italy 175,000 each. Agreement proved impossible on limiting the tonnage of lesser warcraft.

Two other agreements carried even greater potential for preserving peace. The Four-Power Pact of Great Britain, France, Japan, and the United States provided for consultation among these powers on any situation that might arise which should seem to threaten peace in the Pacific. This pact also dissolved the Anglo-Japanese Alliance. The Nine-Power Pact, signed by all the countries represented, had as its purpose the stabilization of the Far East. The independence and territorial integrity of China were to be respected and the "Open Door" maintained. In other agreements, Japan promised to restore Shantung to China, and Britain, Japan, and the United States agreed to build no new fortifications on any of their islands in the Pacific, with a few specified exceptions, such as Hawaii.

The term which Herbert Hoover was later to apply to national prohibition, "a noble experiment," would apply even better to the Washington Conference. At the time, its achievements were hailed as epoch making, but in the end they accomplished little. About the only practical effect of the Five-Power Pact was to save British and American taxpayers a few millions a year for several years on battleship construction. When a conference was called by President Coolidge in Geneva in 1927 to revise and extend the pact, the whole project broke down. Italy and France did not even attend. Japan would extend the pact only if given full battleship equality with the United States and Britain, and Britain and the United States deadlocked on a basis for extending the limitation to cruisers. The Four-Power Pact and the Nine-Power Pact were never called into operation.

The War Debt Question.   Almost as soon as the shooting stopped, the Allied governments began to clamor for cancellation, or at least reduction, of their war debts to the American government. Despite the argument that we should write off the loans as a part of our contribution to winning the war, and the special argument of France that we should cancel to reciprocate for the loans made to the United States during the War for Independence, and never repaid, the real problem was strictly practical. The debtor governments could not pay in gold because, before our entry into the war, practically all of their gold reserves had been shipped to the United States to pay for war supplies. They could not pay in international exchange acquired through favorable trade balance with other countries, because existing conditions of world trade did not permit them to maintain such balances. They could and would have paid in goods exported to the United States, but the American tariff wall made this impossible. They could pay only with loans from American banks, which the state of their credit would not justify, or with the proceeds of German reparations, but the American government refused to recognize any connection between reparations and war debts.

In 1922, Congress created a War Debt Commission, authorized to negotiate settlements with individual countries. During the next few years, such agreements were negotiated with most of the debtor countries, scaling down the debts somewhat and reducing the rates of interest. What happened under these agreements was that American banks made loans, in international exchange, to Germany to pay reparations, and the Allied governments used this exchange to pay their installments on their war debts. The Dawes Plan of 1924 and the Young Plan of 1928, which scaled down reparations payments, made it increasingly difficult for the Allies to keep up payments on their war debts. They resumed their efforts to secure cancellation of their balances, but nothing came of this until the Hoover Moratorium of 1931. This suspended all intergovernmental payments for a year—the first time we had recognized a connection between reparations and war debts. At the end of the year, a few countries made token payments for a while, but the others defaulted. Only Finland, whose debt was very small, paid up in full. For all practical purposes, the Hoover Moratorium marked the end of both reparations and war debts. It was the American banks which took the bulk of the loss, and this fact hampered American recovery from the depression.

The World Court Issue. Although the League of Nations was flatly rejected by the United States, there was considerable sentiment in the 1920's in favor of joining the Permanent Court of International Justice (or World Court, as it was commonly called), membership in which was open to countries not members of the League. Presidents Harding and Coolidge both urged the Senate to ratify a covenant of membership. In December of 1925, the Senate finally did so, but it attached such crippling reservations that the League Council rejected the application and urged a conference to work out a compromise. A year later, a compromise was agreed upon which would merely have deleted the most damaging sentence in one of the reservations. This the Senate refused to approve. Later President Hoover tried again to get Senate approval of membership on the basis of a new compromise formula, but did not succeed.

Whether United States membership in the World Court would have had any significant influence on the course of world international relations, it is impossible to say. It is very obvious, though, that our rejection of the Court, after we had already rejected the League proper, was one of many manifestations of the feeling of isolationism and narrow nationalism which prevailed in this country during the 1920's. There can be little doubt that this attitude on the part of the United States as one of the world's major powers, and policies based on this attitude, did have an adverse effect on international efforts to stabilize peace.

World Economic Conditions. Just about everywhere in the world, except very superficially in the United States, the decade of the 1920's was a time of economic dislocation. European countries that had taken part in the war found recovery from the war dislocations slow and difficult, and recovery was still far from complete when the great depression struck. In Belgium, northeastern France, and Northern Italy, there had been great physical destruction, and much of the reparations money that might have been available for rebuilding was diverted to war debt payments. Almost all of the countries of continental Europe suffered from run-away currency inflation. In Russia, the Communists were trying to build a completely new economy along Marxist lines and they virtually starved the people in order to acquire the necessary capital. Except in Russia, there was no actual famine, but everywhere there was a shortage of consumer goods. The older channels of world trade had all been disrupted. Britain, which was more dependent than other countries on foreign trade, was in a bad way. Before the war, her foreign investments, particularly in the United States, had been an important source of what the British called "invisible exports," but these were gone. Her efforts to regain her pre-war markets around the world met with only very limited success in the face of competition from the United States, Germany, and Japan. Her once prosperous coal mining industry collapsed, and most of the miners were living on a government "dole." In the Asian countries, which had never been very prosperous, economic problems were complicated by political instability or revolutionary activity. The Japanese war lords justified their new aggression by the fact that the population of Japan had outgrown the productive capacity of the home islands. In the "have not" countries, those either without basic resources or whose resources were undeveloped, resentment developed against the "haves," and the United States appeared to be the wealthiest of the "haves."

The United States can not be held responsible for these conditions, though our isolationism and our "Uncle Shylock" position on war debts, probably contributed to them. Other than private contributions to Russian Relief, we did little to alleviate distress elsewhere. In the end, these conditions helped to work our own undoing by setting the stage for the great depression and the rise of Hitler.

DOMESTIC POLITICS

"Back to Normalcy." Mr. Harding's campaign slogan of 1920, "Back to normalcy," set the tone of the politics of the

decade. It implied both conservatism and isolationism. Most voters wanted only to be let alone. They were not much interested in international matters, beyond opposing any commitment that, by the widest stretch of imagination, might lead us into another war. They were not concerned with domestic policies, except that they were against anything that might "rock the boat." They were always willing to vote for candidates who promised to "let well enough alone."

The election of 1920 is readily explained as a direct reaction to the war. The Republican convention, passing up all more colorful presidential possibilities, nominated Harding just because he was colorless; he was the antithesis of a wartime "strong" president. It would have seemed that the oil scandals of Harding's presidency would have produced a strong reaction in the election of 1924, but they did not. It was virtually inevitable that the Republicans would renominate Calvin Coolidge, who had succeeded to the Presidency upon the death of Harding in 1923. Coolidge's reputation for rigid honesty was expected to counteract any political effect of the Harding scandals. The Democratic convention deadlocked between two outstanding leaders, William Gibbs McAdoo and Governor Alfred E. Smith of New York. On the hundred and third ballot (an all-time record) the delegates settled for the colorless but conservative dark horse, John W. Davis. Senator La Follette tried to reverse the prevailing conservatism by a liberal movement. After failing to make any headway in the Republican convention, he launched a third party, the second "Progressive Party." When the votes were in, the Republican slogan, "Keep cool with Coolidge," had triumphed. Davis carried only the "solid South," and La Follette only his own Wisconsin.

In 1928, President Coolidge, though urged by party stalwarts to accept another term, did "not choose to run," and threw his support to Herbert Hoover. Hoover, now considered a "safe" conservative (though a decade earlier he had been regarded as a liberal) was nominated by the Republicans on the first ballot. The Democrats nominated the colorful Governor Smith. The issue most discussed in the campaign was repeal of national prohibition, but the planks in the party platforms were so nearly alike that only the views of the candidates made a difference. It was a heated campaign, in which much was made of the fact that Smith was a Catholic. How much influence this had on the outcome no one can say, but Hoover won handily. It took the great depression to jar American politics loose from conservatism.

Prosperity. Economically, this was a time of great prosperity, and the party in office made the most of this for campaign purposes. Most lines of business were thriving. There were some labor troubles, particularly in the coal mines, but in general organized labor was prospering too. There were, however, some danger signals. Agriculture was in a depressed condition. There were wild speculative booms in real estate and corporation securities. Foreign trade had declined sharply.

THE SOCIAL AND CULTURAL SCENE

Frivolity. Social life, especially among younger people, was characterized by frivolity, though the young people probably regarded it as new freedom. Styles, which were extreme as compared with those of a decade earlier, prevailed in the attire of both men and women. Dancing to jazz music, usually accompanied by surreptitious drinking, was the favorite recreation. It seemed that no one was willing to think about anything serious.

Disrespect for Law. Disrespect for law became all too common. Business men followed prohibited practices with impunity. Gangsters thrived in all the big cities, corrupting law enforcement officers and acquiring vast wealth by the illegal sale of liquor. Even highly respectable people winked at many known illegalities such as bootlegging.

Prohibition.   Probably the most violated law of all was the prohibition law. The Eighteenth Amendment was put through Congress during the war on the grounds that grain, diverted into the manufacture of intoxicants, should be used to win the war. It was ratified by enough state legislatures to make it a part of the Constitution in October, 1919, and took effect one year later. It contained two important mistakes. The most immediately evident was that it granted concurrent enforcement powers to the federal government and the states. Several states refused to pass enforcement legislation, and even deliberately hampered federal enforcement. The other mistake showed up as public opinion against prohibition gained momentum. Had the amendment merely granted *power* to Congress to enact prohibition, only an act of Congress would have been needed to repeal it. As it was, it took a long struggle to repeal it by the Twenty-first Amendment.

Technology.   In technology, the 1920's were a time of great advance. New machinery was invented and came into use in almost every line of production. The radio appeared and became common. Talking motion pictures replaced the silent movies. The airplane was improved to the point of making commercial air lines possible, and this called for the building of air ports. Swarms of improved automobiles were turned out, and they created a demand for hard surfaced roads. New electrical appliances made housework easier.

Literature and the Arts.   To a considerable extent, but not entirely, literature and the arts reflected the temper of the times. There were a number of outstanding writers, but much of their writing tended toward the cynical or the sordid. There continued to be some serious music, but most of the music composed and performed was of the jazz variety. Painting and sculpture became more impressionistic than realistic.

Summary. Not everything, and certainly not everybody was off beat in the 1920's. Many of the old amenities and much of the older culture pattern survived, especially among middle aged and older people. Many of these people retained their interest in good literature, and in the better music and art. Unfortunately, there was enough of the other sort of thing to impress its image on the decade.

TOPICS AND QUESTIONS FOR DISCUSSION

Chapter 15

1. What world problems did the United States face in the 1920's? How effectively were they handled?
2. What did the Washington Conference appear to accomplish and what did it really accomplish?
3. Analyze the pro's and con's of the war debt question of the 1920's.
4. What did Mr. Harding mean by "back to normalcy"? Was it a sound idea? Why or why not?
5. Was national prohibition a justifiable experiment? What was wrong with the Eighteenth Amendment?
6. How much influence on the course of events did the Nineteenth Amendment (woman suffrage) have?
7. Compare the social and moral let down of the 1920's with the similar situation that followed the Civil War. Is any generalization justified?
8. How many positive gains (scientific, cultural, economic, etc.) can you list for the 1920's?

16 | The Great Depression: Causes and Consequences

FACTORS THAT COMBINED TO PRODUCE IT

International. To understand the Great Depression, that reached its peak in 1932 and gradually tapered off until it was submerged in World War II, we must bear in mind that it was not a strictly American phenomenon, due to strictly American causes. It was international in causes, in scope, and in effect. All countries of Western Europe and North America were involved directly, and most of the rest of the world indirectly. The sharp decline in international trade, though a consequence of depressed conditions, was itself an aggravating element in making the depression worse.

The Stock Market Crash. The stock market crash of 1929 seems to have been due primarily to American causes: overspeculation at a time when foreign trade and industrial production were declining. However, it was conditions in Europe which were chiefly responsible for the decline in trade and production. In its turn, the crash aggravated conditions in Europe. Private American investment in Europe ground to an almost complete stop. The large American banks, which suffered severe losses in the crash, stopped making loans in Europe, and this put a greater strain on reparation and war debt payments. Depression conditions gained momentum rapidly on both sides of the Atlantic.

Conditions in Europe. In many ways, post-war conditions in Europe combined to set the stage for a major economic breakdown. War-disrupted industries lacked both the resources and the markets for a speedy recovery and conversion to a peacetime basis. The rebuilding of devastated areas put a heavy drain on the resources of the countries involved. New boundaries and the appearance of new states, especially in what had formerly been Austria-Hungary, created new tariff barriers which disrupted old commercial patterns. Runaway currency inflation in most of the continental countries hampered still further all efforts at economic stabilization.

Reparations and War Debts. Except for purposes of discussion, it is impossible to separate the reparation and war debt situation from other conditions in Europe. They were all part and parcel of the same condition. Enough has been said already about the reparation and war debt matter, but we must note that its complete collapse in 1931 plunged both Europe and the United States deeper into depression. Early in that year, France, ostensibly to prevent an *anschluss*, or union of Austria with Germany, cut off credit to the Central Bank of Austria and so forced the closing of that bank. That started a chain reaction of bank failures throughout Austria and Germany, and made a continuation of reparations payments impossible. This rash of bank failures also dragged Germany and Austria deeper into the quagmire of depression. President Hoover tried to remedy the situation with his one-year moratorium on intergovernmental payments, but it was too late; the mischief was done.

IMMEDIATE EFFECTS

Disrupted Economy. Both in the United States and in Europe, the economy was completely disrupted. Industrial production and construction of housing and business plants dwindled to a trickle. There was vast unemployment, calling for relief of some kind. Crime increased. There were shortages of food and other types of consumer goods. In America, about the only business that flourished was bootlegging.

Most of the countries of continental Europe had long since stopped redeeming their inflated currencies in gold. Once the depression got well under way, first Britain and then the United States also found it necessary to stop gold redemption of paper currency and to withdraw gold from circulation. This was usually spoken of as "going off the gold standard," though the expression is inaccurate. The value of units of currency was still defined in terms of gold content, so that gold still (legally, at least) set the standard of values. A little later, both Britain and the United States devalued their currency by reducing the gold content of the pound and the dollar.

Some effort was made during the Hoover administration to cope with the depression. The President obtained pledges both from industrialists and from labor leaders to do all they could to stabilize prices, wages and employment. Although the pledges were kept faithfully for about two years, they produced no permanent improvement. Congress passed the Smoot-Hawley Tariff, which increased rates generally. This was intended to ease the depression, by shutting out foreign competition, but it actually made things worse by stifling what little foreign trade still survived.

Political Reaction. As always happens, people were antagonized by the hard times. Where they had a chance to ex-

press themselves, they acted to turn the "ins" out, possibly on
the theory that any change would be for the better. In Germany, this popular reaction to the depression, coupled with
deep resentment against the Treaty of Versailles, made it
possible for Hitler to rise to power. In the United States, it
was a foregone conclusion that Hoover could not be reelected
in 1932 (though his party felt obligated to renominate him),
and it was no surprise that Franklin D. Roosevelt swept the
election with his promise of a "New Deal." It may be significant that, in this election, the Socialist Party, headed by Norman Thomas, received more popular votes than were ever
given to it before or since.

THE NEW DEAL

The Term and Its Application. The term *new deal* is usually applied to all of the emergency and reform measures of
F. D. Roosevelt's first two terms in office. It falls naturally
into periods. What is called the "First New Deal," devoted
almost exclusively to emergency and relief measures, covers
the time from President Roosevelt's inauguration on March 4,
1933, through the congressional election of 1934. With some
overlap (for example the enactment of the Reciprocal Trade
Agreements Act in the summer before the election), the "Second New Deal" covered the last two years of the first administration, and consisted mainly of longer range reforms. The
further reforms and revamping of some earlier reform projects
during the first part of the second administration are sometimes called the "Third New Deal." However, compared with
what had already been done, these measures were few and not
very important. By 1936, a measure of prosperity had returned,
and outbreaks of trouble overseas—the Italian attack on Ethiopia, the Spanish Civil War, the Chaco War in South America,

and the menacing attitude of Japan toward China—diverted public attention away from domestic innovation. During the second Roosevelt administration, the New Deal became submerged under our involvement in world affairs.

The Bank Panic. On March 4, 1933, when Roosevelt was inaugurated for the first time, the country was in the throes of a bank panic. Depositors all over the country had become fearful for the safety of their money and were making "runs" on banks, trying to withdraw all of their deposits at once. By inauguration day, a number of banks had already been forced to close. Several states had ordered "bank holidays" for banks under their jurisdiction. The new President lost no time doing something about the situation. Under the dubious authority of an old statute, which was considered obsolete but had never been repealed, he proclaimed a national bank "holiday." The proclamation ordered all banks that were members of the Federal Reserve System to close until confidence could be restored and the financial condition of the banks shored up by loans from the federal treasury. When Congress met five days later, it ratified the proclamation and voted new powers to the President to deal with the banks. The scheme worked. Within a week, most of the banks were permitted to reopen, in most cases with no loss to depositors.

The "Hundred Days." On the very afternoon of his inauguration, President Roosevelt issued a call for the new Congress to meet in special session. It convened on March 9 and remained in session a bit less than a hundred days, until June 16. This session enacted a number of emergency measures that were intended to cope with the immediate situation and to restore public confidence.

A Civilian Conservation Corps was created to provide temporary work for young men. A Federal Emergency Relief

Administration was set up. A Public Works Administration was established to carry on public works projects that would have permanent value. This was intended to provide both work for unemployed and an outlet for the products of many industries. Federal Land Banks were authorized to make more liberal loans to farmers and the Home Owners Loan Corporation was created to stimulate the building of homes. The Reconstruction Finance Corporation, established during the Hoover administration, was given additional powers to make loans to business enterprises. The National Industrial Recovery Act and the first Agricultural Adjustment Act were passed. Neither worked out as planned, and both were later declared unconstitutional by the Supreme Court, but they served the temporary purpose of tiding business and agriculture over the immediate crisis. The Glass-Steagall Banking Act, passed on the last day of the session, increased the regulatory powers of the Federal Reserve Board and established the Federal Deposit Insurance Corporation. The most controversial enactment of the "hundred days" session was the chartering of the Tennessee Valley Authority.

The First New Deal. The enactments of the "hundred days" were, of course, a part of the "First New Deal." It is now necessary only to note a few other measures passed during the first regular session of the new Congress which began in December, 1933. One of these was the creation of the Civil Works Administration, on a temporary basis, to construct public buildings and other projects in local communities. This was intended both to provide employment for men in their own communities and to "prime the pump" by making more money available for the purchase of consumer goods. This operation continued only a few months, and opinions differ as to what extent, if at all, it accomplished its purposes.

Another development was a drastic change in monetary policy. Congress passed legislation authorizing the President to issue emergency currency if he should consider it necessary, and also to stop permanently the redemption of paper currency with gold, to withdraw gold from circulation as money, to reduce the theoretical gold content of the dollar by forty to fifty percent, and to acquire all existing monetary gold and hold it in the treasury as a reserve to protect the currency. The President did devalue the dollar to sixty percent of its former level, primarily to stimulate foreign trade.

Another drastic enactment of this session of Congress was the Reciprocal Trade Agreements Act, sponsored by Secretary of State Cordell Hull. Abandoning the time honored procedure of Congress fixing tariff rates at its own discretion, this law authorized the President to enter into executive agreements with individual countries to reduce our tariff rates (or increase them), by as much as fifty percent of the Smoot-Hawley rates, on commodities we import from the particular country, in return for the other country's making comparable changes in its duties on commodities bought from the United States. The Fordney-McCumber Tariff Act of 1921 had permitted the President, on recommendation of the Tariff Commission, to make minor adjustments in rates, but little use had been made of this power. The immediate purpose of the Reciprocal Trade Agreements Act was to increase our foreign trade as a stimulus to business recovery. Apparently it achieved this purpose, since trade did increase and there was an upturn in American business, though some have argued that this would have happened anyway. Be that as it may, the Act marked a sharp change in our traditional tariff policy. This has continued ever since and, on the whole, has worked well.

The Second New Deal. For present purposes, it is not

necessary to go into detail about the measures of the second New Deal which, in point of time, overlapped the first. Only a few of the more significant enactments need be mentioned. Among the new statutes were the Social Security Law, the National Labor Relations Act, and a Public Utilities Holding Company Act. The Security and Exchange Act of 1934, expanding an earlier measure of 1933, set up the Securities and Exchange Commission to enforce numerous restrictions on trading in corporation stocks. The first Minimum Wage Law was passed in 1936, followed by a Fair Labor Standards Act in 1938. There were a number of other laws and executive actions that might be noted if space permitted. The significant thing was that, in the Second New Deal, emphasis shifted from emergency measures, intended to stop the downward spiral of depression, to reforms that were intended to be permanent and to improve many features of American society. Some of these measures have been modified since, but none has been abandoned entirely.

LONG RANGE EFFECTS

General. Looked at from a general, as distinct from strictly an American point of view, the principal long range effect of the Great Depression was to help set the stage for World War II. In Germany, as already noted, it was a major factor in enabling Hitler to rise to power. In Spain, it was largely responsible for the failure of the Republic, which swung ever farther toward Communism in its effort to cope with depressed conditions, and was overturned by a fascistic dictatorship. As we shall see in the next chapter, the Spanish Civil War was an important element in setting the stage for world war. In Britain and France, the governments were so concerned with fighting the depression that they failed to take actions which might have stopped Hitler before he became strong enough to defy the world. In the United States, the depression deepened the feeling of isolation and brought about the passage of neutrality laws, which convinced Hitler that he need not worry about America, and greatly hampered American efforts to supply the Allies when war came. It can not be said with certainty that the war would not have occurred if there had been no depression, but there is no question that the depression helped to spawn the conditions which produced the war.

The United States.   In the United States, it is impossible to disentangle the long range effects of the depression proper and of the New Deal, in shaping the course of the country's development. One obvious result was to commit the country, apparently beyond the point of no return, to the welfare state concept. The New Deal, itself a direct result of the depression, not only took up where the Progressive Era had left off, but it pushed much further into governmental paternalism than most progressives had ever dreamed of. Some have gone so far as to call the New Deal socialistic. Whether it was or not is a question of semantics. Certainly, Marxist doctrine had nothing to do with it. Socialists usually advocate the nationalization of major industries. The New Deal, instead, carried forward the scheme of regulation of business already begun by the progressives. Norman Thomas, the perennial Socialist candidate for President, said that the only socialistic thing the New Deal did was to set up the Tennessee Valley Authority. President Roosevelt always insisted that he was *saving* capitalism, not destroying it. Certainly, business has continued under New Deal regulations on what remains essentially a free enterprise basis and, for the most part, has prospered. However, the country is not the same as it was before the Great Depression, and probably never will be again.

TOPICS AND QUESTIONS FOR DISCUSSION

Chapter 16

1. What factors, domestic and international, combined to bring on the Great Depression?
2. To what extent did the Depression disrupt the American economy? Was capitalism really threatened, as some contended?
3. How did the political reaction compare with earlier so-called "panics"?
4. What were the successive phases of the New Deal? To what extent did New Deal measures remain permanent?
5. What led to the "court packing" proposal? Would it have been constitutional? Would it have been wise?
6. Was there any real connection between the New Deal and the Progressive Era?
7. How and to what extent did the Great Depression help to bring on World War II?
8. What were the long range consequences of the New Deal for the United States?

17

World War II
and World Revolution

Responsibility. There may be some room to argue about who was responsible for the First World War, but there can be no question about responsibility for World War II. The blame rests squarely on the shoulders of Adolf Hitler as dictator of Germany. To be sure, there were other contributing factors. The inequities of the Treaty of Versailles helped to make the inter-war years the "Twenty Years' Armistice" that one writer called it. The war guilt clause of that treaty, upon which Clemenceau had insisted, served no useful purpose, but so embittered the Germans that most of them were ready to follow Hitler into another struggle to erase the entire "Versailles *Diktat*." The reparations burden further inflamed the Germans. The Great Depression, in several indirect ways, helped to move events toward war. War might have been averted had the Western Powers taken a firm stand when Hitler's aggressive intentions became obvious, but before he was strong enough to risk a general war. President Roosevelt's suggestion that the powers unite to "quarantine aggression" might have worked (we can never know for sure), but Britain and

France ignored the suggestion, and American public opinion rejected it vehemently. In the light of hindsight, the Munich appeasement was a serious mistake. But when all allowance is made for these other considerations, it was Hitler's succession of aggressions, culminating in his attack on Poland, that precipitated the conflict.

Ideological Factors. During the war, it was common to think of the issues mainly in ideological terms: the Nazi variety of totalitarianism *versus* democracy. Hitler's persecution and attempted annihilation of the Jews was thought of as a part of Nazi ideology. Certainly Hitler made it so, but basically it was an old medieval prejudice running riot. When Hitler turned on Russia, with which he had made a deal (the Molotov-Ribbentrop agreement) to divide up Eurasia for conquest, and so brought the Soviet Union into the war, the interpretation of the war as totalitarianism *versus* democracy lost whatever validity it had ever had. The more significant immediate issue was aggression *versus* the actual or threatened victims of aggression.

Relation to World Power Structure. In the long range view, the big question was what effect the war would have on the world power structure. As it turned out, the old power structure was disrupted completely and a basis for new tensions between major powers was created. So long as the outcome of the war was in doubt, though, the vital issue was whether an unscrupulous, aggressive power like Nazi Germany should attain control of all of Europe, the Middle East, and most of Africa, while a similar power in the Far East, Japan, should maintain its rule over Southeast Asia and much of the Pacific Ocean. Had the aggressors succeeded, they would have created a major threat to the security of the United States and most of the rest of the world.

AMERICAN PARTICIPATION

Before Pearl Harbor. When the war began in Europe,
American public sentiment favored the Allies as against Germany—later the Axis—but the overwhelming weight of public
opinion in the United States was isolationist. Not so the President. He saw clearly what was involved and did all he could
to aid the Allies, especially to aid Britain after the fall of
France. He dutifully issued a formal proclamation of neutrality, as required by the "neutrality law" then in effect, but in
a "fireside chat" he told the people of the country that legal
neutrality did not obligate them to ignore the facts. Two rival
propaganda organizations soon appeared: the America First
Committee, which preached isolationism, and the Committee
to Defend America by Aiding the Allies. As Hitler's armies
swept over so much of Europe, the weight of public opinion
became strongly anti-Hitler and willing to support limited aid
to Britain, but it was still very much opposed to direct American participation in the war.

In the summer of 1940, President Roosevelt negotiated an
executive agreement with Britain to exchange fifty "overage"
destroyers for leases of British naval bases in the Western
Hemisphere. The British navy was badly in need of this additional strength and the naval bases would be useful to Western
Hemisphere countries who had agreed to cooperate to prevent
the seizure by Germany of French and Dutch possessions in
the Caribbean. There was strong opposition to this destroyer-
base deal, not only from avowed isolationists, but from others
who feared it might involve us in the war. The President was
also criticized for putting the deal into the form of an executive agreement instead of a treaty, although the Attorney General had ruled that it was within his legal power. The reason

for doing so was obvious. A treaty might never have received Senate approval. Even if the Senate should approve it eventually, so much time might have elapsed that Britain's defense would be imperiled by the lack of the destroyers. It is significant that, after the initial shock, the weight of American public opinion approved the deal.

Soon after the war began in Europe, a conference of Western Hemisphere foreign ministers at Panama reaffirmed hemispheric solidarity, agreed to joint defense of the hemisphere, and declared a neutral zone in the Atlantic from which belligerent war vessels should be barred. The following July, when it appeared that Germany might seize the Caribbean dependencies of the countries she had overrun in Europe, another foreign ministers' conference at Havana declared that Western Hemisphere countries, singly or jointly, might take over the administration and defense of these colonies "for the duration," and set up an Inter-American Commission to supervise such administration. When the United States entered the war, all but one of the Latin American nations declared war in our support, and several of them took an active part in war operations.

In the first months of 1941, the President was able to persuade Congress to make the United States "the arsenal of democracy" by passing the Lend-Lease Act. This authorized the President to provide war materials to anti-Axis belligerents on the basis that any used up in the war should be charged off to our national defense. Any left over at the end of hostilities were either to be returned to the United States or sold to the recipient country. Actually, most of the left-over items were sold at merely nominal prices. In the long view, lend-lease proved to be the wise course. American supplies were necessary to enable Britain, and later Russia, to go on fighting until Pearl Harbor thrust the United States into full participation.

It avoided such complications, problems, and irritations as had flowed from the war loan policy of World War I.

The most spectacular pre-Pearl Harbor act of American participation was the issuance of the Atlantic Charter by President Roosevelt and Prime Minister Churchill in August of 1941. It was called the *Atlantic* Charter because the two heads of government met on a British warship in the Atlantic off Newfoundland. This document has been likened to the "Fourteen Points" of World War I. It was much more general, but it did serve much the same propaganda purpose. It renounced any territorial ambitions by the two powers, and declared that no territorial changes should be made that did not accord with the wishes of the people concerned. It asserted the right of all peoples to choose their own form of government, and demanded the restoration of full sovereignty to countries that had lost it. The Charter also called for the destruction of the "Nazi tyranny," free access of all countries to the trade and resources of the world, freedom of the seas, and lasting peace based on the abandonment of the use of force. The document read as though the United States were already a full participant in the war. It indicated that, even without Pearl Harbor, the United States might soon have become a full belligerent.

The Effect of Pearl Harbor. The Japanese had continued their aggressions in the Far East. They talked about a "greater East Asia co-prosperity sphere," which meant that all of Southeast Asia and the islands of the Pacific were to be brought under Japanese domination. At the fall of France, they overran French Indo-China and made peremptory demands on Britain to stop supplying war material to Nationalist China. In September of 1940, Japan entered a tripartite pact with Germany and Italy under which, if any one of the three countries should go to war with the United States, the other two agreed to join in as allies. Washington had just terminated a commercial treaty with Japan which had enabled the Japanese to import scrap iron and petroleum from America.

As Japanese-American relations grew more tense, Japan sent two of her top statesmen to Washington, ostensibly to negotiate a peaceful settlement, but their demands were so exorbitant that compliance would have meant conceding all of the Far East to Japan. While these negotiations were still going on, the attack on Pearl Harbor occurred. It had been strongly suspected that the Japanese were planning an attack on American forces, but it was believed that the attack would be made on the Philippines. Some Americans charged that President Roosevelt deliberately incited the Pearl Harbor attack to make it appear that we were being forced into a war which the President wanted to enter anyway. The charge is ridiculous, and there is not one shred of real evidence to support it. There is evidence that faulty intelligence communications prevented warning of the attack from reaching Washington in time, but this was not the President's fault.

The attack almost completely destroyed the American Pacific fleet, so we could offer no real opposition as the Japanese overran the Philippines and the Dutch East Indies. It was necessary to rebuild sea and air power in the Pacific, along with supporting ground forces, before we could begin to turn back the Japanese from their ever expanding area of control. The months after Pearl Harbor marked the lowest ebb in the war. Hitler held all of Western Europe, either in subjection or as allies. His armies were overrunning Russia and the Russians seemed to be unable to stop them. Only Britain was holding out, and it was being battered by an aerial *Blitzkrieg*.

How the Tide Was Turned. As indicated earlier, in World War I it was necessary for the United States to throw in only enough strength to break a stalemate. In World War II, we had to generate enough power, economic as well as military, to turn worldwide defeat into victory. For present purposes, it is not necessary to follow the military and diplomatic events of the war. It is to the point, however, to have a look at the means by which this overwhelming strength was created.

Unlike the situation in World War I, when national mobilization was somewhat haphazard, thorough national mobilization in World War II was achieved in record time. Planning was much more careful and complete. Every industrial plant that was capable of producing any kind of war supplies was converted to war production. New plants for the production of weapons and munitions were constructed and operated by the government. Every possible labor-saving device was introduced to stretch man power. Food, gasoline, and other types of consumer goods were rationed and strict price controls were imposed. A good psychological climate was created. Almost everyone was made to feel that he must be doing something to help win the war. Nearly everyone bought war savings bonds. This not only helped to finance the war, but held down inflation. Drafting men for the armed forces worked much better and more smoothly than in the first World War, and the training of the recruits was much better planned and executed than in the other war.

We need not trace military operations. It is enough to note a few important considerations. Within two years, the United States had built up enough military strength to begin rolling back the Japanese in the Pacific, and, along with the British, to launch an attack on Hitler's forces in North Africa. Across the Atlantic, perfect cooperation was achieved between the United States and Britain. Britain, relatively safe after Hitler's air force was destroyed, was the base for all military operations. All British and American forces were under a single command, and major strategy was planned in conferences of governmental and military leaders of the two countries. When

Russia, with the help of American lend-lease equipment, was able to begin pushing the Germans back, conferences were held with Stalin to work out a basis of cooperation, though the Soviet dictator later reneged on some of his promises.

The Atom Bomb. Hitler had had his scientists working on the atom bomb, hoping to use it to knock out Britain. Before the Germans were able to produce a workable bomb, however, Germany was crushed. In the meantime, learning what the Germans were up to, the American government launched an intensive project to produce a bomb of its own. By the time the American scientists had exploded a bomb experimentally and had two others constructed, the war in Europe was over, but Japan remained to be conquered. President Truman, who had succeeded upon the sudden death of Roosevelt, was confronted with the decision whether to use the atom bomb against Japan. His decision has been criticized, but as he saw the situation at the time, the use of the bomb would shorten the war and save hundreds of thousands of American lives. It seemed certain that, although the Japanese were being driven back from their conquests, they would not capitulate until their home islands were invaded. Not only would this have been a prolonged and extremely costly operation, but it would have necessitated bringing the Soviet Union into the war in the Far East. Stalin had agreed to enter the Asian war as soon as he could transfer the necessary troops from Europe. To President Truman, however, it seemed highly desirable to avoid Soviet participation. This would have given Stalin a basis for demanding a joint Soviet-American occupation of Japan, and this promised to create serious problems.

In the long view, it was unfortunate in many ways that the atom bomb was ever invented. It brought about the later atomic arms race, with the peril of the virtual destruction of civilization. It produced the present situation in which efforts to halt the proliferation of atomic power is meeting with such little success. Recently, it has made Red China much more of a threat to world peace than that country could be without atomic weapons. It did have some advantages, but only time can tell whether the advantages outweigh the disadvantages. It has made possible the almost unlimited uses of atomic energy for peaceful purposes. In the cold war, the probability is so strong as to amount almost to certainty that American possession of the bomb was the chief deterrent in preventing Stalin from overrunning Western Europe and becoming the same kind of peril that Hitler had been. By the time Russia got the bomb, NATO had built up enough strength in Western Europe so that Stalin could not attack without risking atomic destruction in Russia. Now, the passing of Stalin, internal changes within the Soviet Union, and the atomic stalemate between Russia and the United States, have all but eliminated the possibility of a third world war being started in Europe.

"Unconditional Surrender."   President Roosevelt and Prime Minister Churchill, determined not to repeat the folly of 1918 which had left Germany with the capacity to rearm and start another war, adopted the formula of peace only by unconditional surrender. This formula avoided the mistake of 1918, but in the case of Germany, it was a mistake in the opposite direction. In Japan, where the United States was the sole occupying power, it worked out very well. Retaining the Emperor as a symbol of national unity, General MacArthur was able to guide the Japanese in the formation of a relatively democratic responsible government. In Germany, however, it meant that the war was pushed to the utter collapse of the Nazi government, and it proved impossible, partly because the Russians would not cooperate, to set up a new all-German government to take its place. This resulted in the division of

Germany which still poses the apparently insoluble problem of reunification. Each of the occupying powers set up a military government in its own area of occupation. After a period of denazification, the United States, Great Britain, and France permitted their areas to unite and to set up the Federal Republic of Germany. In their occupied area, the Russians set up the puppet Communist government of East Germany or, as it is called officially, the People's Republic of Germany. As the cold war developed, neither Russia nor the Western Powers would permit reunification on a basis that might align a reunited Germany with the other side. So the division continues, though there are some signs that it is beginning to break down.

After the collapse of Nazi Germany, the Austrians were permitted to resume their separate status and to set up an all-Austrian government. The four-power occupation worked great hardship, especially in the Russian zone, but it did not bring about a division of the country.

BY-PRODUCTS OF THE WAR

Western Hemisphere Solidarity. The war was a major factor in bringing about a much greater degree of solidarity among the nations of the Western Hemisphere. We have already noted their cooperation in setting up a neutral zone in the Atlantic and taking steps to prevent the seizure of the Caribbean dependencies of France and the Netherlands by the Nazis. Early in 1945, the United States met with all of the Latin American countries except Argentina in a conference in Mexico City (called the Chapultepec Conference because it met in the old Palace of Chapultepec) when it was agreed that the participating countries should act in close solidarity in pursuing the war and helping to set up a United Nations organization. They also stated that an attack on any one of the countries should be regarded as an act of aggression against the others also, and that, in case of such an attack or threat of attack, all of the governments should consult on joint measures to be taken to resist it. In 1948, all the governments of the hemisphere, except Canada but including Argentina, met at Bogota, Colombia, and formed the Organization of American States. When Cuba went Communist, it was excluded from the O. A. S., but the other countries have continued to cooperate, through the Alliance for Progress and otherwise, to improve conditions in the hemisphere.

The United Nations. One very important by-product of the war was the formation of the United Nations. We need not trace the steps by which the organization was formed, nor analyze its structure. Needless to say, it resembles very much the old League of Nations. Since the resemblance is so close, one might ask why a new start was made instead of reviving the old League. One reason was that the League was discredited by its failures, but a more compelling reason was that neither the United States nor the Soviet Union was a member of the League. Both of these superpowers would have to be active in any world organization that would have a chance of succeeding, and neither was willing to join the all-but-defunct League.

The United Nations has not been able to solve all the world's problems, and has not even been able to *grapple* with some of them, but it certainly has been more successful than the League ever was. One reason undoubtedly is that most of the major powers belong to it. Another reason is that the governments of the world take the United Nations more seriously than they ever took the League, and carry important questions to the Assembly or Security Council for discussion. A third factor is that the U. N. has been fortunate in having a succession of very able Secretaries General who have taken the initiative in peace-keeping operations.

Many people feel that the U. N. should have been able to accomplish far more than it has. These people may be overlooking the essential character af the organization. It is not a supergovernment, but a diplomatic association of sovereign states. It can act only by agreement of its members, and even then, in most matters, it can only recommend. Some blame the big power veto in the Security Council for all of the U. N.'s deficiencies. Actually, without the veto, neither the United States nor the Soviet Union would have ratified the Charter. Moreover, if the veto were not provided for in the Charter, it would exist in fact, because there is no way to coerce a big power without resort to war. Some feel that the United Nations should have been made a supergovernment in the beginning, with sovereign powers to enforce peace. That was politically impossible when the Charter was written, and it would be politically impossible to change the organization into such a supergovernment today. Another objection raised is to the equality of states, large and small—one member one vote. This is offset to some extent by the five permanent members of the Security Council. However desirable it might be to have the votes of member nations weighted in the General Assembly according to the size and strength of the countries, such weighting is impossible in an organization that is diplomatic in character. Sovereign equality of states is a basic principle of international law. Whatever its defects, the United Nations has rendered important service up to now, and probably will continue to do so.

Economic Depletion of Europe. Probably the most obvious by-product of the war was the economic depletion of Europe. Besides the physical destruction in many areas, industry had broken down, most kinds of consumer goods were in short supply, currency inflation was out of hand (except in Britain), and financial resources were lacking for a quick build back. The Soviet Union, partly through its own efforts and resources, and partly by plundering its satellites, was able to build back fairly quickly. For the rest of Europe, the United States stepped into the breach with the Marshall Plan. With this help, most of the countries were back to their prewar level of prosperity, or even above it, within a few years. The recovery was remarkable in view of the magnitude of the struggle.

Prosperity in America. Only the United States emerged from the war in a more prosperous condition than it was in when the war began. The enormous expansion of industry during the war carried over into the post-war period. Most of the government war plants were either shut down or sold to private capital, but the private industries were able to convert quickly to peacetime production. The national debt had skyrocketed, but national income had kept pace, so the debt did not imperil the government's financial stability. The removal of rationing and price controls brought a slight spurt of inflation, but nothing to compare with the inflation that plagued Europe. It was this prosperity which enabled the United States to assist Europe with the Marshall Plan, and later with military supplies when those countries were striving to restore their defensibility.

Scientific Advances. The war brought great scientific advances in the United States, not only in the field of atomic energy, but in automation of industry, weaponry, radar, and other fields. After the war, these advances not only continued in the United States, but spread to other countries, especially the Soviet Union. Computers, jet propulsion, and space vehicles, with rockets powerful enough to launch them into space, soon appeared. New consumer items, such as color television and new household appliances were soon on the market. Great improvements were made in automobiles, aircraft, and building construction. These changes, and others too numerous to mention, were producing a new way of life.

CHANGED POWER STRUCTURE

Eclipse of Former Great Powers. One of the most significant outcomes of the war was the shattering of the old power structure. The former equilibrium among half a dozen "great powers" was destroyed. Of the former great powers, Germany was in ruins, and emerged split into East and West. Japan, stripped of all of her dependencies, was conquered and occupied. France and Italy were economically distressed and were incapable, for the time being, of exerting strong influence in international relations. Great Britain still considered herself a great power, and tried to act like one, but she had suffered great devastation in the *Blitzkrieg,* her economy was disrupted, and her empire was crumbling.

Emergence of Two Super-Powers. In contrast with these, the United States and the Soviet Union emerged as super-powers. Not only were they stronger relatively, because of the weakening of the other powers, but each was stronger absolutely than before the war. No other country, or combination of countries, could match either of them in potential military strength. Under the best of circumstances, this would have caused serious problems.

But conditions were far from the best possible. Most obvious was the clash between democracy and communism, but this, in the public mind, was exaggerated out of all proportion to its real importance. Conflicting ideologies can live together if they have no other reason to clash. More significant was the fact that the Soviet Union, under Stalin, took up where the Tsars had left off in Russia's historic scheme of aggressive expansion. Stalin, apparently, aimed at nothing less than what Hitler had failed to achieve permanently: the subjugation of Europe, with Russian sway over many other parts of the earth. Such a course would not only defeat the purpose for which we had fought the war, but would constitute a very real threat to our national security. Inevitably, the United States sought to contain this Russian expansion.

However, we made one serious mistake which weakened our international position. After V-J Day, we hastened with unseeming speed to demobilize the vast military strength we had built up. This was done in response to a clamor of public opinion (something of the old "back to normalcy" attitude), but it was unwise nevertheless. It encouraged Stalin to push his sway over all of Eastern Europe, and he probably was deterred from advancing into Western Europe only by our possession of the atom bomb, until we had rebuilt enough strength through NATO to make such an adventure too hazardous.

There were, of course, other factors in the situation, such as the question of the extent to which Stalin should be permitted to plunder Germany under the guise of war reparations, and what should be done about organizing government in Germany. These issues would have arisen anyway, but without the threat of Russian expansionism, they would not have been so serious.

The Cold War. Under these circumstances, it was virtually inevitable that there should develop between the United States and the Soviet Union that conflict which came to be called the cold war. It was essentially a diplomatic conflict, but far from being carried on only through normal diplomatic channels, it was "fought" with every means available short of actual armed conflict. The Russians put out fantastic propaganda, and vetoed just about everything in the United Nations Security Council. The Americans played up the peril of communism *per se*, and organized NATO and SEATO to checkmate Russian military strength. The United States first gave financial aid through the Marshall Plan to rebuild the economic strength of Western Europe, and then helped to build back the military strength of the area by providing military supplies. Even the earliest stages of space exploration are to be explained more in terms of cold war rivalry than of real zest for new scientific knowledge.

THE REVOLUTION OF RISING EXPECTATIONS

World Revolution.   One important aftermath of the war has been the development of what we may characterize as world revolution. It is also called the "revolution of rising expectations." It has taken different forms in different places, but it has touched almost every part of the world. All of its variations have some features in common. People who have felt that they were underprivileged or discriminated against are demanding full equality with the most advantaged, and are resorting to various means, including violence, to attain it. Not unnaturally, such people often do not understand the responsibility that such a changed status would entail, and do not recognize their own lack of ability, without a long period of preparation, to exercise such responsibility.

New Nations.   There is nothing new about anti-colonialism, but World War II gave it a new impetus. This was due, in part, to the Allied propaganda, but it followed mainly from the weakening of the old colonial powers. The people of colonial dependencies almost everywhere, but especially in Africa, demanded immediate independence and, in most instances, the old governing powers did not feel strong enough to resist the demand. These new nations were foredoomed to trouble. Most of their people were illiterate and utterly ignorant of the processes of self-government. In many situations, the natives were more loyal to their tribe and tribal chief than to their country as a whole. Each of these new countries had only a very small group of well educated individuals who could provide leadership, and most of these were without governmental experience of any kind. Some of the countries have extensive natural resources. Some of these had been developed by nationals of the former colonial power, using natives as laborers, but rarely if ever in managerial positions.

These countries differed in their preparation for independence. In the Congo, Belgium had done almost nothing to give natives administrative experience. The French, in their possessions, had done somewhat better, and the British had done the best of all—though it was still an inadequate best. Another retarding factor was the haphazard way in which the European dependencies had been put together, often including in the same colony native groups of widely divergent cultures, differing religions, and with traditions of enmity against each other. In some cases, Communist infiltrators, both Russian and Chinese, have stoked these internal antagonisms in the hope of gaining influence for their home governments in African affairs. It is not surprising that most of these new African states have been torn by internal turmoil and have clamored for outside assistance.

Latin America. Most parts of Latin America have long had a tradition of revolutionary upheaval, but in most of the countries, prior to World War II, this usually involved only clashes among rivals for power. Since the war, though, the underprivileged people in most of these countries have became conscious of their condition and are demanding major reforms, especially in land holding. All of the governments south of Mexico (which had a real revolution half a century ago) do lip service to the need for internal reforms, and seek United States financial assistance to carry them out. We have been trying to "help them help themselves" through the Alliance for Progress. The degree of success, however, has been disappointing. Too many governments of Latin American countries are made up of members of the old land-owning aristocracy, who are anxious to preserve the privileges of their class. Many of these governments are rife with corruption, in the old Spanish colonial tradition. Real progress has been made in several countries in improving the condition of the lower classes, but protests continue and are sometimes exploited by ambitious military leaders trying to seize power. Except in Cuba, Communist efforts to take over have failed, but Communist agitators are active in many countries. In Latin America, the "revolution of rising expectations" is still going on.

Minority Protests. In countries with sizable ethnic minorities, these minority groups have been protesting discrimination and lack of opportunity. This situation has been especially acute in the United States. Some American Indian groups have been protesting against their condition. Puerto Ricans in New York City have staged "demonstrations" which have sometimes turned into riots. The most serious outbreaks have been among Negroes, though only a small portion of the Negro community has been involved. Despite all the efforts of the federal government to secure equal civil rights and to conduct a "war on poverty," several organized Negro groups continue to agitate, one or two of them openly urging violence. We all know about the "protest marches" in the South, and the race riots in Northern cities. The rioters may be, as their local leaders claim, driven by desperation, but there is no doubt that they are stirred up by extremist agitators. These extremist agitators are willing to settle for nothing less than a major social revolution. How far they will get in that direction remains to be seen.

TOPICS AND QUESTIONS FOR DISCUSSION

Chapter 17

1. Analyze the basic reasons for World War II. Could it have been averted by more daring use of power politics?
2. Why did the United States actively support the Allies before Pearl Harbor? Was this in the best national interest?
3. How was the United States able to turn Allied defeat into victory? Compare our task in World War II with our task in World War I.
4. Why was the atom bomb invented? Was its use justified?
5. In the light of later developments, was the "unconditional surrender" formula in the interest of lasting peace?
6. Evaluate the by-products of the war: the Western Hemisphere alliance; the United Nations; the economic prostration of Europe; prosperity in America; scientific advances.
7. The war altered drastically the old power structure. What effects has this had on developments since?
8. How and why did the war plunge the world into "the revolution of rising expectations"?

18 | Current History and Where It Is Leading

THE INTERNATIONAL SCENE

The Period in General. It is obviously impossible, in a short chapter, to sketch even concisely the highly involved history of the United States since the Second World War. All the major facts involved are readily available. Therefore, we must limit our treatment to some pertinent observations.

The Atomic Age. Among other things, this period has been the atomic age. After Russia and Britain had acquired the bomb, an atomic armaments race developed between the United States and Britain, on the one hand (they cooperated closely in this as in most other international matters), and the Soviet Union on the other. This race produced not only bigger and more deadly atom bombs, but the far more terrible hydrogen bomb, with intercontinental ballistic missiles capable of delivering them almost anywhere on earth. Both sides built up huge stockpiles of bombs and rockets, so that, if an atomic war should come, each side could devastate all the territory of the other, and perhaps wipe out civilization itself.

By about 1960, realization of this peril, along with changed world conditions and a changed attitude of the Soviet Union, brought Russia and the United States to engage in joint efforts to stop the expansion of atomic weapons. They made a treaty to stop atomic testing and began working on a "non-prolifera-tion" treaty, to which all countries would be asked to sub-scribe, to prevent other, and perhaps less responsible countries, from acquiring the bomb. Before such a treaty could materi-alize, however, France had acquired the bomb, and De Gaulle was using this possession diplomatically to further his goal of pushing American influence out of Europe and making France the predominant power in that continent. A few years later, Red China acquired the bomb. Obviously, a non-proliferation treaty would be meaningless without France and Red China as parties to it, and neither will even listen to such a suggestion.

There has also been great progress, especially in the United States, in applying atomic energy to peaceful uses. It can now be used to propel submarines, other types of ocean-going ships, and aircraft, and experiments are under way to apply it to other uses. The possibilities are almost boundless. No one can say with certainty where the atomic age is leading, but whether toward world destruction or a better world, the United States has played, and will continue to play, a major role.

Power Politics. Power politics has largely dominated the international scene ever since the end of the Middle Ages, but the outcome of World War II has given it several new twists. It is conducted in the United Nations, through normal di-plomacy, by propaganda, and sometimes with the use of armed force. For nearly two decades, world power politics had its focus in the cold war. Stalin, by every means at his disposal, short of direct Soviet involvement in war, was seeking to ex-pand Russian rule and Russian influence over as much of the world as possible, and the United States was taking the lead in striving to "contain" Russian expansion. Contrary to a notion that prevailed in America at the time, this "containment policy" was not an American innovation. It has been pursued by the countries of Western Europe from the downfall of Napoleon to the eve of World War I. It was the reason for the Crimean War and the crisis of 1878 which was resolved by the Congress of Berlin. It was the breakdown of this policy in 1914 that precipitated World War I. Practically all of the diplomatic crisis of the recent period represented maneuvering in power politics. Even the Marshall Plan and the Truman Doctrine (military aid to countries fighting Communists) had their overtone of power politics.

International Organizations. One device by which the United States carried on the power politics conflict was the formation of international organizations. The Organization of American States (OAS), which we have already considered, had as one of its aims the checkmating of Soviet-inspired Communist infiltration into the Western Hemisphere. The North Atlantic Treaty Organization (NATO) had as its primary purpose the consolidation of enough power to deter Soviet thrusts into Western Europe or Turkey. The Southeast Asia Treaty Organization (SEATO), a rather pallid reflection of NATO, was aimed at blocking penetration by Red China, then considered a dutiful satellite of Moscow, into Southeast Asia. NATO, with unified command of its armed forces and with a Council of Foreign Ministers to make decisions, worked smoothly as long as the threat it was created to combat continued. Since that threat has diminished almost to the vanishing point, NATO has suffered from internal friction and has become much less of a force in world affairs.

Since Stalin. The death of Stalin in 1953 marked a turning point, but not an abrupt change, in Soviet relations with the rest of the world. After an internal power struggle of several years, Khrushchev emerged as Stalin's undisputed successor. At first, he showed few signs of moderating the Soviet attitude toward the Western World, but he did "debunk" Stalin and gradually ended the police state in the Soviet Union. As late as 1961, he precipitated the Cuban missile crisis. However, as tension developed between Russia and Red China, and the fact of the atomic stalemate became obvious, Moscow's attitude toward the West began to mellow. The change became even more rapid after the retirement of Khrushchev. Cultural exchanges were arranged, and treaties were negotiated to ban atomic testing and to exchange consuls. Soviet satellites were permitted to exercise a large degree of independence and, in the United Nations, except in refusing (along with France) to help pay for peace keeping operations, Russia became cooperative.

The upshot was that, although Red China was becoming more of a threat in the Far East, the likelihood of war between the Soviet Union and the Western nations almost completely vanished. There were still points of friction between Russia and the United States, but they were not permitted to get out of hand. This changed outlook had several consequences. De Gaulle, having rid himself of the Algerian crisis and tightened his hold on France, began to be an international trouble maker. He withdrew French forces from NATO, and eventually pushed that organization's headquarters out of Paris. He vetoed Britain's admission into the European Common Market. He blocked a British-American scheme to create an international atomic naval force. He tried, successfully for a time, to create close ties between France and West Germany, in which the latter would have been definitely a junior partner. He has also been making cordial gestures toward the Soviet Union. His aim appears to be nothing less than the elimination of American influence from Europe and the creation of something like a French hegemony over most of that continent. However, recently he has been meeting with political reverses and it is questionable how much further he can go.

AMERICAN WORLD INVOLVEMENTS

The United Nations. Since its early days, when it seemed to be little more than a glorified debating society, with Soviet vetoes blocking almost every constructive action, the United Nations has been playing an ever expanding role in world affairs. It has engaged, with at least partial success, in several peace keeping operations and has been instrumental in settling a number of international disputes. The United States has supported the world organization very actively, and has made participation in its activities a major part of our foreign policy. On some occasions we have been accused of by-passing the U. N., but these were situations in which, either because of their diplomatic character or because of the certainty of a Soviet veto, the organization could not have functioned. The admission of so many new countries, most of them African, has weakened somewhat the influence the United States can exert in the General Assembly, but the U. N. continues to be a major element in our world relations.

Korea. When North Korean troops, with obvious Russian inspiration, and equipped with Russian weapons, invaded South Korea in 1950, a situation was created which the United States could not ignore. Since the Soviet delegation, at the moment, was boycotting the U. N. Security Council as a protest against refusal to seat Red China, President Truman was able to obtain Security Council action condemning the aggression and calling upon U. N. member nations to help in resisting it. A number of countries sent token forces, but the brunt of the conflict was borne by the United States. Even so, General Mac-Arthur operated under the United Nations banner.

When MacArthur drove the North Koreans back to the Yalu River (the boundary between North Korea and Manchuria), Red China entered the conflict (unofficially—her troops were called "volunteers") and temporarily drove the Americans back. When his forces had been regrouped and reinforced, General MacArthur wanted to drive the Chinese back beyond the Yalu, but he was forbidden by President Truman to undertake the move. Such an action was entirely feasible militarily, but it would have been bad power politics. Just as we could not permit all of the peninsula to come under Russian sway, the Russians could not let it all come under ours. When we drove the North Koreans beyond the Yalu, Stalin had thrown in the Red Chinese, who were still taking orders from Moscow. Had we driven *them* out, Stalin might have felt compelled to send in Russian troops, and that would have meant World War III. The President was also criticized for not permitting MacArthur to bomb the Communist air bases in Manchuria. The reason was the same. It is significant that the Reds did not bomb *our* air bases in Japan, which they could have done as readily as we could have bombed their bases in Manchuria. Both Moscow and Washington feared that Korea might mushroom into a world war, and both wanted to prevent this. Although General MacArthur obeyed the President's orders militarily, he spoke out publicly denouncing the President's war policy. This was clearly an act of insubordination, which justified his removal.

It was fortunate, in terms of world public opinion, that we were able to conduct the Korean operation under the banner of the United Nations. However, had Russia been able to block U. N. action by a veto, considerations of power politics would have required that the United States intervene anyway. To let all of Korea fall under Stalin's sway would have created a military threat to Japan, which we were obligated to defend, and would have damaged all American interests in the Far East. At the same time, though, all of Korea under American domination would have constituted a military threat to Manchuria and Eastern Siberia, and Moscow could not permit this to come about. Therefore, the conflict could end only where it began, with Korea divided along the line of the thirty-eighth parallel.

Red China. The United States had tried unsuccessfully to bolster the Nationalist regime in Mainland China. When Chiang Kai-shek fled to Taiwan (Formosa), we continued to give diplomatic recognition to his government as the legitimate government of all China, and denied recognition to the Communist government on the mainland. Naturally, we opposed the seating of this government in the United Nations. Contrary to the common expression, it was not a matter of "admitting" Red China to the U. N. China is a charter member and a permanent member of the Security Council. The question was which regime to recognize as the legitimate government of China, and so entitled to China's seat.

As Mao Tse-tung's regime gained in strength and apparent stability, it became a threat to all American interests in the Far East. When the break between Red China and Russia began to develop, the American government officially took the stand that it was none of our business, but off the record, Washington was pleased at the cracking of the monolithic structure of international Communism. This break was one factor, but only one of several, in bringing about better relations between the United States and the Soviet Union. When the Vietnam situation became critical, our government thought it saw the hand of Mao moving to extend his sway over Indo-China. That was the primary reason for our intervention. When Red China acquired the atom bomb, it became a much greater threat to American interests and to world peace.

The normal expectation would be that, in the course of a generation or so, with the fanaticism of Mao removed from the picture, China would move on around the revolutionary cycle, as the Soviet Union has done, to stability under a moderate regime that could live in peace with the rest of the world. However, things may not work out this way. Mao, in his fanaticism, if he lives until China's atomic power is great enough, might trigger a world explosion by launching an atomic attack. If that does not happen, China's history suggests that the country may break up into fragments under local war lords, with only a shadow of a central government. There are already signs that this trend is at work.

Vietnam. American involvement in Vietnam has given rise to controversy at home and abroad. Many Americans, including some influential members of both houses of Congress, have protested the growing military commitment, with its spiraling cost in money and lives. There have been street demonstrations and draft card burnings. The wisdom of bombing North Vietnam is called into question. While most Americans support the war effort, everybody, including the President, is anxious to end the conflict, but no one knows how. All concede that it is a drain on our resources, hampering the economy and using up funds that otherwise would be available for such things as the war on poverty.

Many argue that we never should have got involved in the first place. Possibly they are right; only time and the final outcome will tell. A theory has been advanced that, rather than fighting Ho Chi-minh, we should have allied with him. Ho is a Communist, but he has no love for the Chinese and does not want them to dominate his country. This theory holds that, with American support, Ho would have been a sort of Asian Tito. This scheme would have required sacrificing the military chiefs of South Vietnam, and would have precluded whatever possibility there is of building a democratic republic in the South. However, had it been tried and worked, it would have saved the United States from the heavy military involvement.

Another effect of our Vietnam conflict has been to dampen the improving relations between the United States and the Soviet Union. Russia has protested our bombing of the North, and has been sending military supplies to Ho Chi-minh, possibly more to checkmate Chinese influence than out of loyalty to a common cause with Ho. Moscow has also made our withdrawal from Vietnam a pre-condition of pending agreements with the United States.

Latin America. Little more need be said about Latin America in general. The Alliance for Progress has not worked out as well as was hoped, but except for Cuba, United States relations with the Latin countries are excellent and our influence remains strong, even though they are always clamoring for more financial aid. O. A. S. remains very much a going concern, and holds meetings from time to time to cope with hemispheric problems. Recently our government negotiated a new treaty with Panama which recognizes Panamanian sovereignty over the Canal Zone, thus ending a source of friction in that little republic.

Cuba. While Castro was overthrowing Batista, the feeling prevailed in the United States that he was just another young liberal, as Batista had been when he seized power, and that, although he might evolve into a dictator, as Batista had done, his dictatorship would be of the traditional Latin American pattern. When he announced himself a Communist, a feeling of revulsion against him swept over the United States, and our government banned all trade with Cuba. The Bay of Pigs fiasco of April, 1961, ended any early hope of getting rid of Castro. There has been considerable controversy over the responsibility for this failure. The invaders certainly expected air cover and logistic support from the United States, but these were not provided. It is unlikely that the outgoing Eisenhower administration had actually promised such aid, but someone connected with the American government must have given the leaders of the projected invasion a hint that the aid would be forthcoming. The new Kennedy administration did not have full information and did not feel justified in involving the United States.

The Missile Crisis of October, 1962, was the next major incident. Khrushchev apparently thought he could install the missiles in Cuba without the fact being discovered by Americans until they were fully in place. He could then use the presence of the missiles to extort concessions. When American authorities discovered what was going on before the missile bases were ready, President Kennedy called Khrushchev's bluff, and the missiles were removed. The President's action may have been "brinkmanship," but it worked, and smoothed the way for better Soviet-American relations.

Since the Missile Crisis, Moscow's interest in Castro has been waning, and the Cuban dictator has been flirting with the Chinese Reds. Cuba remains an uncertain trouble spot in our foreign relations, but it has become more of a nuisance than a critical problem.

The Middle East. When Britain ended its Palestine mandate in 1948, the Jewish refugees who had settled there proclaimed the State of Israel, and it was promptly recognized by the United States and the Soviet Union. A little later, it was admitted to the United Nations. The surrounding Arab states, however, denied the right of Israel to exist on what they considered Arab territory, and launched a war to exterminate it. After a time, the United Nations was able to arrange a truce, but the Arab governments maintained that a legal state of war still existed. From time to time, "border incidents" occurred, but U. N. peace-keeping forces (contributed by several smaller countries) were able to prevent major outbreaks.

In the spring of 1967, though, a five day war occurred, in which the Israelis thoroughly trounced the Arabs and overran Egyptian territory to the Suez Canal and Jordanian territory to the Jordan River (including the "old city" of Jerusalem). Nasser of Egypt claimed that American and British war planes assisted the Israelis. Both countries denied the charge and there is no basis for believing it. Nasser probably made it as propaganda, both to gloss over defeat with his own people and in the hope of influencing the Soviet Union. Once again, the United Nations was able to arrange a cease fire, and sent in observation teams to maintain it, but as this is written, neither the General Assembly nor the Security Council has been able to agree on proposals for a permanent settlement. Meanwhile, the Arab states are rearming, with Soviet help, and declare that they will make another attempt to destroy the State of Israel.

The United States is interested in stability in the Middle East and would like to see a permanent settlement brought about through the United Nations. We would be most reluctant to intervene directly, but might feel compelled to do so if the existence of Israel were seriously threatened. The great danger, of course, would be a direct confrontation with the Soviet Union, which appears to be pledged to support the Arabs.

INTERNAL DEVELOPMENTS IN THE UNITED STATES

Industrial Expansion and Transformation.   Inside the United States, the contemporary period has been characterized by great industrial expansion. Many new industries have developed to supply the needs of the Vietnam war, to produce equipment for the penetration of outer space, and to make new articles of consumer goods. There have been some setbacks, and occasional labor troubles, but on the whole, industry has prospered.

Industry has also been undergoing significant transformations. One of these is in the much more widespread ownership of its stock. Unlike the situation in "the age of big business," most of the stock of industrial corporations is now owned by thousands of relatively small investors. These investors exercise little influence on management, so that ownership and management have become separated. So far, this has worked well. Another important transformation has been increasing cybernation. This term includes both the automation of productive machinery and the use of computers, not only to do the bookkeeping, but to solve many of the problems of management.

There has also been some inflation, which has affected consumers more than producers. Prices of almost everything, but especially food, clothing, and medical care, have risen sharply, though probably no more than in the countries of Western Europe. The government has tried, with very limited success, to combat the trend through Federal Reserve Board regulations. The danger, of course, is that the inflation may became "runaway" and affect the national credit.

The Welfare State. Developments in the direction of the welfare state have continued. Congress enacted a Medicare Law, in connection with social security, to provide assistance to persons over sixty-five years of age in medical treatment and hospital care. President Johnson instituted a "war on poverty," intended to raise the living standards of persons on low incomes. A number of projects, some federal, some joint federal, state, and local, have been initiated, but progress has been hampered by the expenses of the Vietnam war. Government regulation of business is no longer questioned. Federal aid to education has been increased, and much has been done to eliminate racial segregation in schools. In general, it may be said that the United States appears to be committed to the welfare state viewpoint beyond the point of no return.

Civil Rights. This term is commonly used incorrectly to include political equality, as well as civil rights in the proper sense of that term. Congress has passed legislation and the President has instituted programs intended to improve the situation in both of these areas. Opposition has been encountered in some places, especially to integration in housing and schools, and Negro organizations have conducted protest marches which, in some cases, have led to violence. Equality in job opportunity is a more difficult problem, but progress has been made in that direction. On the whole, it appears that the United States is moving fairly rapidly toward full equality for all citizens.

The race riots in Northern cities appear to be related only incidentally, if at all, to the civil rights problem. The poor and ignorant of the Negro ghettos, aroused by extremist agitators, have burst forth in indiscriminate attacks on persons and property. Probably these riots have hurt the cause of civil rights more than they have helped it. The situation poses a serious problem for the nation, with no quick or easy solution, but the odds are strong that it will be worked out eventually.

Ecumenism. The term "ecumenical movement" originated with the Vatican Council of the Catholic Church, which modified the rules of the Church in line with twentieth century conditions, and urged cooperation instead of antagonism among religious groups. The actions of the Council were, of course, worldwide in application, but the response has been greater in the United States than in most other countries of Christendom. Actually, much progress toward religious harmony had been made in our country long before the Vatican

Council. The Protestant denominations had their Council of Churches, and a National Council of Christians and Jews had carried out many cooperative projects. Now the tempo has been stepped up and, while organic unity is not in sight, our religious climate has advanced from mere mutual toleration to a spirit of common purpose.

RELATION TO PAST AND FUTURE

The Past. Whatever the United States is today is the result of our past. This includes not only the past of the United States as a nation, but the more remote past of our people extending back into the Middle Ages. This book has attempted to trace and interpret the main trends and developments of this past, and to indicate how each succeeding era has grown out of what had gone before. It all adds up to trying to show how the United States of today, with its conditions and problems, is the outcome of centuries of history.

The Future. It is not the business of history to predict the future, though it can and should furnish a guide for facing the future. Whatever problems or crises may confront us, the evidence of history that just as serious problems and just as great crises have been weathered in the past, is at least a ground for optimism.

Without venturing into the realm of prediction, a few observations would seem to be in order. If we may project the present trends, the United States would appear to be destined, if not for an ideal society, at least for a social structure that is more equitable than any in the past. Lessons learned from the Great Depression can probably prevent a repetition of that experience, though our economy is likely to continue to have its ups and downs. In general, there is no reason to believe that, barring atomic destruction, present trends will not continue into the foreseeable future.

In world affairs, we are now one of the two strongest powers on earth, and we shall probably continue to be. If China should reverse its long history and develop into a unified great power, we shall be one of three, and that could complicate the power relations of the world. However, the chances are not strong that this will happen. The efforts of De Gaulle to create a new power structure, with France at its center, appear to be foredoomed to failure. Some years ago, a Frenchman wrote a book entitled *The Coming Caesars* in which he interpreted world trends as indicating that the United States is moving into a position in today's world much like that of the Roman Empire in the world of its day. He probably strained his point too far, but our country does seem to be moving in the direction of world preeminence.

TOPICS AND QUESTIONS FOR DISCUSSION

Chapter 18

1. Why did the "cold war" develop? Compare the influence of ideology and power politics in bringing it about.
2. What have been the various effects of atomic developments since the war?
3. Examine the expanding role of the United Nations. Evaluate its possibilities and limitations.
4. What was the Korean Conflict all about? Why did it have to end as it began with a divided Korea?
5. What has been the effect on the United States and on world affairs of the rise of Red China?

6. What was the real reason for United States involvement in Vietnam? What do you see as the ultimate outcome?
7. Where do developments in the United States (automation, civil rights agitation, enlargement of welfare state projects, inflation, anti-war activities) all seem to be leading?
8. Is the "Space age" prompted by scientific motivation or by international rivalry? Where does it appear to be leading?

BIBLIOGRAPHY

CHAPTER 1

Bury, J. B., *The Idea of Progress: An Inquiry Into Its Origin and Growth* (London, 1920).

Commager, Henry Steele, *The Search for a Usable Past* (New York, 1967).

Gardiner, Patrick, *The Nature of Historical Explanation* (London, 1952).

Hodder, Frank H., "Propaganda as a Source of American History," *Mississippi Valley Historical Review*, Vol. IX (June 1922), 3–23.

Mahan, Alfred T., *Influence of Sea Power upon History* (Boston, 1904).

Turner, Frederick Jackson, *The Frontier in American History* (New York, 1920).

Salmon, Lucy M., *Why is History Rewritten?* (New York, 1929).

Seligman, R. A., *The Economic Interpretation of History* (Second ed., New York, 1917).

Semple, Ellen, and Jones, Clarence F., *American History and Its Geographic Conditions* (Boston, 1935).

CHAPTER 2

Bourne, Edward G., *Spain in America 1450–1580* [Vol. 3, American Nation Series] (New York, 1904).
Cheyney, Edward P., *European Background of American History* [Vol. 1, American Nation Series] (New York, 1904).
Morison, Samuel E., *Admiral of the Ocean Sea* (Boston, 1942).
Richman, I. B., *The Spanish Conquerors* [Vol. 2, Chronicles of America] (New Haven, 1921).

CHAPTER 3

Abbott, Wilbur C., *The Expansion of Europe* (2 volumes, New York, 1918).
Chitwood, Oliver P., *A History of Colonial America* (New York, 1931).
Tyler, Lyon G., *England in America* [Vol. 4, American Nation Series] (New York, 1904).

CHAPTER 4

Andrews, Charles M., *Colonial Self-Government 1652–1689* [Vol. 5, American Nation Series] (New York, 1904).
Beer, George L., *The Old Colonial System 1660–1754* (Part I, 2 volumes, New York, 1933).
Greene, E. B., *Provincial America 1689–1740* [Vol. 6, American Nation Series] (New York, 1905).
Parrington, V. L., *The Colonial Mind, 1620–1800* [Vol. I, Main Currents in American Thought, 3 vols.] (New York, 1927).

CHAPTER 5

Becker, Carl, *The Declaration of Independence* (New York, 1945).

Becker, Carl, *The Eve of Revolution* [Vol. 11, Chronicles of America] (New Haven, 1918).

Bemis, Samuel F., *The Diplomacy of the American Revolution* (Bloomington, Ind., 1957).

Edwards, L. P., *Natural History of Revolution* (Chicago, 1927).

Egarton, H. E., *The Causes and Character of the American Revolution* (Oxford, England, 1923).

Friedenwald, Herbert, *The Declaration of Independence* (New York, 1904).

McIlwain, Charles H., *The American Revolution: A Constitutional Interpretation* (New York, 1923).

Schlesinger, Arthur M., *New Viewpoints in American History*, Chapter VII (New York, 1922).

VanTyne, Claude H., *The Causes of the War of Independence* (Boston, 1922).

CHAPTER 6

Beard, Charles A., *An Economic Interpretation of the Constitution of the United States* (New ed., New York, 1960).

Fiske, John, *The Critical Period of American History* (Boston, 1888).

Morris, Richard B., *The Peacemakers: The Great Powers and American Independence* (New York, 1965).

Schuyler, Robert L., *The Constitution of the United States* (New York, 1923).

CHAPTER 7

Hodder, Frank H., "Side Lights on the Missouri Compromise,"
American Historical Association, *Report for 1909*, 153–161.
Pratt, Julius W., *Expansionists of 1812* (New York, 1925).
Reddaway, W. F., *The Monroe Doctrine* (Cambridge, Eng-
land, 1898).
Turner, Frederick Jackson, *Rise of the New West* [Vol. 14,
American Nation Series] (New York, 1906).

CHAPTER 8

Bowers, Claude G., *Party Battles of the Jackson Period* (Bos-
ton, 1922).
Fish, Carl Russell, *The Civil Service and the Patronage* (New
York, 1905).
James, Marquis, *Andrew Jackson, the Border Captain* (New
York, 1940).
Minnigerode, Meade, *The Fabulous Forties* (New York, 1924).
Norton, A. B., *The Great Revolution of 1840* (Mount Vernon,
Ohio, 1888).
Ostrogorsky, M., *Democracy and the Party System* (New
York, 1910).
Schlesinger, Arthur M., Jr., *The Age of Jackson* (Boston,
1946).

CHAPTER 9

Carpenter, Jesse T., *The South as a Conscious Minority, 1789–
1861* (Gloucester, Mass., 1963).

Cole, Arthur C., *The Irrepressible Conflict 1850–1865* [Vol. VII, Schlesinger and Fox, History of American Life] (New York, 1934).

Corwin, Edward S., "The Dred Scott Decision in the Light of Contemporary Legal Doctrines," *American Historical Review*, Vol. XVII (1911), 52–69.

Crandall, Andrew W., *The Early History of the Republican Party, 1854–1856* (Boston, 1930).

DeVoto, Bernard, *The Year of Decision, 1846* (Boston, 1943).

Hodder, Frank H., "The Railroad Background of the Kansas-Nebraska Act" *Mississippi Valley Historical Review*, Vol. XII (June 1925), 3–22.

Johnson, Samuel A., *The Battle Cry of Freedom* (Lawrence, Kansas, 1954).

Milton, George Fort, *The Eve of Conflict* (Boston, 1934).

Russel, Robert R., "The Pacific Railway Issue in Politics Prior to the Civil War," *Mississippi Valley Historical Review*, Vol. XII (Sept., 1925), 187–201.

Simms, Henry H., *A Decade of Sectional Controversy, 1851–1861* (Chapel Hill, North Carolina, 1942).

Stenberg, Richard R., "The Motivation of the Wilmot Proviso," *Mississippi Valley Historical Review*, Vol. XVIII (March, 1932), 535–548.

Stenberg, Richard R., "Some Political Aspects of the Dred Scott Case," *Mississippi Valley Historical Review*, Vol. XIX (March, 1933), 571–577.

CHAPTER 10

Beale, Howard K., "On Rewriting Reconstruction History," *American Historical Review*, Vol. 45 (1940), 807–827.

Bowers, Claude G., *The Tragic Era* (Boston, 1929).

Daniels, Jonathan, *A Southerner Discovers the South* (New York, 1938).

Flack, Horace E., *The Adoption of the Fourteenth Amendment* (Baltimore, 1908).

Kirkland, Edward C., *The Peacemakers of 1864* (New York, 1927).

Milton, George Fort, *The Age of Hate* (New York, 1930).

Pressly, Thomas J., *Americans Interpret Their Civil War* (Princeton, 1954).

Randall, J. G., "The Blundering Generation," *Mississippi Valley Historical Review*, Vol. XXVII (June, 1940), 3–28.

Randall, J. G., *The Civil War and Reconstruction* (Boston, 1937).

Seitz, Don C., *The Dreadful Decade, 1869–1879* (Indianapolis, 1926).

Stryker, L. P., *Andrew Johnson: A Study in Courage* (New York, 1929).

Woodward, William E., *Years of Madness* (New York, 1951).

CHAPTER 11

Beer, Thomas, *The Mauve Decade* (New York, 1926).

Fetter, Frank A., *The Masquerade of Monopoly* (New York, 1931).

Haynes, F. E., *Third Party Movements Since the Civil War* (Iowa City, 1916).

Hicks, John D., *The Populist Revolt* (Minneapolis, 1931).

Hendrick, Burton J., *The Age of Big Business* [Vol. 39, Chronicles of America] (New Haven, 1921).

Josephson, Matthew, *The Politicos, 1865–1896* (New York, 1938).

Josephson, Matthew, *The Robber Barons* (New York, 1934).

Knauth, Oswald W., *The Policy of the United States Towards Industrial Monopoly* (New York, 1914).

Malin, James C., *An Interpretation of Recent American History* (New York, 1926).

Orth, Samuel P., *The Boss and the Machine* [Vol. 43, Chronicles of America] (New Haven, 1921).

Ross, E. D., *The Liberal Republican Movement* (New York, 1919).

CHAPTER 12

Jenks, L. H., *Our Cuban Colony* (New York, 1928).

Millis, Walter, *The Martial Spirit* (Cambridge, 1931).

Nearing, Scott, and Freeman, Joseph, *Dollar Diplomacy* (New York, 1926).

Perkins, Dexter, *Hands Off: A History of the Monroe Doctrine* (Boston, 1941).

Pratt, J. W., *Expansionists of 1898* (Baltimore, 1936).

Roosevelt, Theodore, *Theodore Roosevelt: An Autobiography* (New York, 1913).

Wells, Sumner, *Naboth's Vineyard: The Dominican Republic* (New York, 1928).

CHAPTER 13

Chamberlain, John, *Farewell to Reform* (New York, 1933).

Filler, Louis, *Crusaders for American Liberalism* (New York, 1939).

Hechler, Kenneth W., *Insurgency: Personalities and Politics of the Taft Era* (New York, 1964).

Josephson, Matthew, *The President Makers, 1896–1919* (New York, 1940).

LaFollette, Robert M., *Autobiography* (Madison, Wis., 1913).

Mowry, George E., *Theodore Roosevelt and the Progressive Movement* (Madison, Wis., 1947).

Regier, C. C., *The Era of the Muckrakers* (Chapel Hill, North Carolina, 1932).

Roosevelt, Theodore, *Autobiography* (cited for Chapter XII).

CHAPTER 14

Bailey, Thomas A., *Woodrow Wilson and the Lost Peace* (New York, 1944).

Baker, Newton D., *Why We Went to War* (New York, 1936).

Birdsall, Paul, *The Versailles Treaty Twenty Years After* (New York, 1941).

Grattan, C. Hartley, *Why We Fought* (New York, 1929).

Millis, Walter, *Road to War* (Boston, 1935).

Mock, James R., and Larson, Cedric, *Words That Won the War* (Princeton, 1940).

Peterson, Horace C., *Propaganda for War* (Norman, Okla., 1937).

Slosson, Preston W., *The Great Crusade and After*, 1914–1928 [Vol. XII, Schlesinger and Fox, History of American Life] (New York, 1930).

CHAPTER 15

Allen, Frederick L., *Only Yesterday* (New York, 1931).

Beard, Charles A., and Mary, *America in Midpassage* [Vol. III of Rise of American Civilization] (New York, 1940).

Merz, Charles, *The Dry Decade* (New York, 1931).

Moulton, Harold G., and Pasvolsky, Leo, *War Debts and World Prosperity* (New York, 1932).

Nevins, Allen, and Hacker, Louis M., Eds., *The United States and Its Place in World Affairs, 1918–1943* (Boston, 1943).

White, William Allen, *A Puritan in Babylon* (New York, 1938).

CHAPTER 16

Allen, Frederick L., *Since Yesterday* (New York, 1940).

Beard, Charles A., *American Foreign Policy in the Making, 1932–1940* (New Haven, 1946).

Hanson, Alvin, *Fiscal Policy and Business Cycles* (New York, 1941).

Pearson, Drew, and Allen, Robert, *The Nine Old Men* (New York, 1936).

Robey, Ralph, *Roosevelt versus Recovery* (New York, 1934).

Schlesinger, Arthur M., *The New Deal in Action, 1933–1938* (New York, 1939).

Seldes, Gilbert, *The Years of the Locust* (Boston, 1933).

Wallace, Henry A., *Century of the Common Man* (pamphlet, New York, 1942).

Willkie, Wendell, *One World* (New York, 1943).

CHAPTER 17

Beard, Charles A., *A Foreign Policy for America* (New York, 1940).

Buell, Raymond Leslie, *Isolated America* (New York, 1940).

Welles, Sumner, *The Time for Decision* (New York, 1944).

CHAPTER 18

Bloomfield, Lincoln P., *The United Nations and U.S. Foreign Policy* (Boston, 1960).

Dallin, David J., *The Big Three* (New Haven, 1945).

Dean, Vera Micheles, *The Four Cornerstones of Peace* (New York, 1946).

Lippmann, Walter, *U.S. Foreign Policy: Shield of the Republic* (Boston, 1943).

Steel, Ronald, *Pax Americana* (New York, 1967).

SOME SOURCES OF INTERPRETATION

Abbott, Wilbur C., *The Expansion of Europe: A History of the Foundations of the Modern World* (2 vols. New York, Holt, 1918).

In the preface, the author calls this book "a new synthesis of modern history." It not only traces colonization and colonial development in America, but shows the relation to conditions and developments in Europe. This treatment illustrates the unity of history.

Allen, Frederick L., *Only Yesterday* (New York, Harper, 1931).

An entertaining evaluation of the 1920's, in a somewhat satirical vein.

Allen, Frederick L., *Since Yesterday* (New York, Harper, 1940).

Sequel to *Only Yesterday*, covering the depression years in much the same manner.

Andrews, Charles M., *Colonial Self-Government* [Vol. 5, American Nation Series] (New York, Harper, 1904).

Mainly a narrative account of the launching of colonial institutions, but has some interpretative description.

Bailey, Thomas A., *Woodrow Wilson and the Lost Peace* (New York, Macmillan, 1944).

A compendium of views, contemporary with the Versailles Treaty, mostly unfavorable to Wilson.

Baker, Newton D., *Why We Went to War* (New York, Harper, 1936).

An official version of reasons for entering World War I, by President Wilson's Secretary of War.

Beale, Howard K., "On Rewriting Reconstruction History," *American Historical Review*, Vol. 45 (1940), 807–827.

This article, written by a faculty member of the University of North Carolina, calls for a more objective evaluation of Radical reconstruction, pointing out some positive values.

Beard, Charles A., *A Foreign Policy for America* (New York, Knopf, 1940).

Traces the controversy between interventionists and isolationists during the period of American neutrality in World War II.

Beard, Charles A., *An Economic Interpretation of the Constitution of the United States* (New York, Macmillan, new ed., 1960).

Interprets the making and adoption of the Constitution as primarily an expression of economic group interests. Valid as far as it goes, but minimizes other factors that were also important.

Beard, Charles A., and Mary, *America in Midpassage* [Vol. III of Rise of American Civilization] (New York, Macmillan, 1940).

An entertaining account of the decade of the 1920's, the depression, and the New Deal. A generally "leftist" viewpoint, with much space devoted to social and cultural history.

Beard, Charles A., *American Foreign Policy in the Making, 1932–1940* (New Haven, Yale University Press, 1946).

A very critical review of New Deal foreign policy by an eminent historian.

Beard, Charles A., and Mary, *The Rise of American Civilization* (1 vol ed., New York, Macmillan, 1930).

Sketches the whole scope of American history down to the date of publication, with the Beards' own interpretation: a bit left of center, and with heavy stress on economic influence.

Becker, Carl, *The Declaration of Independence* (New York, Knopf, 1945).

A clear analysis of the Declaration, with illuminating discussion of the factors involved in its making.

Becker, Carl, *The Eve of Revolution* [Vol. 11, Chronicles of America] (New Haven, Yale University Press, 1918).

More an analysis than an interpretation, much of it in the form of pseudo-quotations from contemporary characters. Conveys the feeling of the period very effectively.

Beer, George L., *The Old Colonial System 1660–1754* [Part I, 2 vols.] (New York, Peter Smith, 1933).

An excellent description of colonial institutions valuable in interpreting their influence on later history.

Beer, Thomas, *The Mauve Decade* (New York, Garden City Pub. Co., 1926).

An interesting description of American life at the close of the nineteenth century. Useful in interpreting popular reaction to events and developments.

Bemis, Samuel F., *The Diplomacy of the American Revolution* (Bloomington, University of Indiana Press, 1957).

A detailed account of intrigue among the great powers in connection with the American Revolution. It helps to explain how independence was achieved.

Birdsall, Paul, *The Versailles Treaty Twenty Years After* (New York, Reynal and Hitchcock, 1941).

An interpretative account of peace making after World War I. Very favorable to Woodrow Wilson.

Bloomfield, Lincoln P., *The United Nations and U.S. Foreign Policy* (Boston, Little, Brown, 1960).

The sub-title, *A New Look at the National Interest*, indicates the approach of the book. It analyzes the capacities and weaknesses of the United Nations and suggests a proper role for the U.N. in United States foreign policy.

Bourne, Edward G., *Spain in America* [Vol. 3, American Nation Series] (New York, Harper, 1904).

A narrative account of Spanish exploration and colonization, but useful as a basis for interpretation.

Bowers, Claude G., *Party Battles of the Jackson Period* (Boston, Houghton, Mifflin, 1922).

A lively discussion of the politics of the period, but strongly biased in favor of Jackson.

Bowers, Claude G., *The Tragic Era* (Boston, Houghton, Mifflin, 1929).

One of several books of the time rewriting the story of Radical reconstruction, with a view to rehabilitating the reputation of President Andrew Johnson.

Buell, Raymond Leslie, *Isolated America* (New York, Knopf, 1940).

An anti-isolationist discussion of the situation of the time by an eminent historian.

Bury, J. B., *The Idea of Progress: An Inquiry Into Its Origin and Growth* (London, Macmillan, 1920).

The author, a British scholar, sketches several past interpretations of history, and traces the idea of progress as a current interpretation. He stresses, however, that progress is a *doctrine*, not an objective fact.

Carpenter, Jesse T., *The South as a Conscious Minority, 1789–1861: A Study in Political Thought* (Gloucester, Mass., Peter Smith, 1963).

Traces the development of Southern attitudes through successive periods from the beginning of the federal government to secession. It can contribute to an understanding of why the South seceded.

Chamberlain, John, *Farewell to Reform: The Rise, Life and Decay of the Progressive Mind in America* (New York, Day, 1933).

Written in a spirit of disillusionment, this book stresses progressivism as a broad cultural movement rather than just a matter of political reform.

Cheyney, Edward P., *European Background of American History* [Vol. 1, American Nation Series] (New York, Harper, 1904).

Mainly narrative, but shows the relation of developments in Europe to the beginnings of America.

Chitwood, Oliver P., *A History of Colonial America* (New York, Harper, 1931).

A good narrative and descriptive account of colonial history and colonial institutions. Does not contain much interpretation as such.

Cole, Arthur C., *The Irrepressible Conflict 1850–1865* [Vol. VII of Schlesinger and Fox, Eds., History of American Life] (New York, Macmillan, 1934).

A good account of the sectional conflict, with stress on social and cultural factors. Takes the view that the conflict was unavoidable.

Commager, Henry Steele, *The Search for a Usable Past* (New York, Knopf, 1967).

Twenty-two essays on different aspects of historiography.

Corwin, Edward S., "The Dred Scott Decision in the Light

of Contemporary Legal Doctrines," *American Historical Review*, Vol. XVII (1911), 52–69.

The writer contends that the decision was not *obiter dicta*, as alleged at the time and since, and was not based on Calhounist premises.

Crandall, Andrew W., *The Early History of the Republican Party, 1854–1856* (Boston, Gorham Press, 1930).

This is the most thorough study available of the rise of the Republican Party and the first two years of its history. It shows the relation of this development to the Kansas Conflict and to other sectional issues.

Dallin, David J., *The Big Three: The United States, Britain and Russia* (New Haven, Yale University Press, 1945).

Traces and analyzes relations among these countries between world wars, and during World War II. Is pessimistic regarding immediate future, but this was before rift developed between the Soviet Union and Red China.

Daniels, Jonathan, *A Southern Discovers the South* (New York, Macmillan, 1938).

Daniels, a Southerner, advocates a more liberal view of race relations than prevailed in the South at the time he wrote.

Dean, Vera Micheles, *The Four Cornerstones of Peace* (New York, Whittlesey House, 1946).

Mrs. Dean, of the Foreign Policy Association, analyzes the development of the United Nations, and evaluates its future possibilities.

DeVoto, Bernard, *The Year of Decision, 1846* (Boston, Houghton, Mifflin, 1943).

Considers the year 1846, the beginning of the Mexican War, a vital turning point in American history.

Edwards, L. P., *Natural History of Revolution* (Chicago, Univ. of Chicago Press, 1927).

This study examines the major revolutions of history and finds that, though no two are exactly alike, all of them follow a discernible pattern. This helps to interpret the meaning and predict the course of any particular revolution.

Egarton, H. E., *The Causes and Character of the American Revolution* (Oxford, England, Clarendon Press, 1923).

An objective evaluation by a British scholar. He considers the Revolution to have been virtually inevitable.

Fetter, Frank A., *The Masquerade of Monopoly* (New York, Harcourt, 1931).

The author considers monopoly as a "shifting gentleman criminal," always masquerading to hide its real character. He traces unsuccessful efforts to deal with it in various stages. He believes that a deeper understanding of the economics involved is necessary to a solution.

Filler, Louis, *Crusaders for American Liberalism* (New York, Harcourt, 1939).

An excellent discussion of the "muckrakers" and their influence in furthering liberalism.

Fish, Carl Russell, *The Civil Service and the Patronage* (New York, Longmans, 1905).

An analytical and historical study of appointments to public office from 1759 to 1904. Helpful in interpreting some phases of national history.

Fiske, John, *The Critical Period of American History* (Boston, Houghton, Mifflin, 1888).

The book that first applied the term "critical period" to the time of the Confederation. It shows how the situation really was critical for the future of the United States.

Flack, Horace E., *The Adoption of the Fourteenth Amendment* (Baltimore, Johns Hopkins Univ. Press, 1908).

A rather dry but detailed account of the adoption of the amendment. For present purposes, only Chapter V, "Congressional Interpretation of the Amendment," is significant.

Friedenwald, Herbert, *The Declaration of Independence* (New York, Macmillan, 1904).

A generally good analysis and interpretation of the Declaration, but very lauditory.

Gardiner, Patrick, *The Nature of Historical Explanation* (London, Oxford Univ. Press, 1952).

The author, an Oxford University scholar, calls his little book a philosophy of history. Rather, it is an analysis of various approaches in explaining the meaning of history.

Gooch, G. P., *History and Historians of the Nineteenth Century* (New York, Longmans, 1913).

This book sketches historical writings and interpretations from the beginning of the modern era. Very good as an orientation in interpretation.

Grattan, C. Hartley, *Why We Fought* (New York, Vanguard, 1929).

An appraisal of the reasons for United States entry into World War I. The author attempts to be completely objective, discarding assumptions and rationalizations that prevailed during and immediately after the war.

Greene, E. B., *Provincial America* [Vol. 6, American Nation Series] (New York, Harper, 1905).

This book takes up where Andrews, *Colonial Self-Government* leaves off. It is narrative and descriptive, but does some interpreting by implication.

Hanson, Alvin, *Fiscal Policy and Business Cycles* (New York, Norton, 1941).

An interpretation by a Harvard economist of business cycles in relation to the Great Depression. He argues that basing government fiscal policy on what is known of the economics of business cycles could prevent such depressions.

Haynes, F. E., *Third Party Movements Since the Civil War* Iowa City, Iowa State Historical Society, 1916).

The only systematic study of third party movements down to the date of writing. Can aid interpretation by throwing new light on several political movements.

Hechler, Kenneth W., *Insurgency: Personalities and Politics of the Taft Era* (New York, Russell and Russell, 1964).

A sympathetic account of the successive stages of insurgency, 1909–1912. Interprets the movement as preliminary steps to Wilsonian liberalism and the New Deal.

Hendrick, Burton J., *The Age of Big Business* [Vol. 39, Chronicles of America] (New Haven, Yale Univ. Press, 1921).

Sketches the development of the principal monopolistic combinations after the Civil War. The author tries to be completely objective, but can not hide his "anti-trust" feelings.

Hicks, John D., *The Populist Revolt* (Minneapolis, Univ. of Minnesota Press, 1931).

The most thorough study of the Populist movement. Hicks sees it as the last stand of the old agrarianism rather than as the foreshadowing of the Progressive movement.

Hodder, Frank H., "Propaganda as a Source of American History," *Mississippi Valley Historical Review*, Vol. IX (June 1922), 3–23.

This article shows, by a number of examples, how using propaganda as a source has often distorted the meaning of history.

Hodder, Frank H., "The Railroad Background of the Kansas-Nebraska Act," *Mississippi Valley Historical Review*, Vol. XII (June 1925), 3–22.

A detailed account of the enactment of the measure, showing how railroad considerations influenced each step in its passage through Congress.

Hodder, Frank H., "Side Lights on the Missouri Compromise," American Historical Association, *Report for 1909*, 153–161.

Presents some details of the enactment of the compromise that are not usually available, and indicates reasons for certain steps.

James, Marquis, *Andrew Jackson, the Border Captain* (New York, Garden City Pub. Co., 1940).

Tells the intimate story of Jackson and his home life down to the time when he entered politics.

Jenks, L. H., *Our Cuban Colony* (New York, Vanguard, 1928).

Describes, and condemns by implication, United States dominance over Cuba in the 1920's.

Johnson, Samuel A., *The Battle Cry of Freedom* (Lawrence, Univ. of Kansas Press, 1954).

Interprets the role of the New England Emigrant Aid Company in the Kansas Conflict and the establishment of the Republican Party.

Josephson, Matthew, *The Politicos, 1865–1896* (New York, Harcourt, 1938).

Shows how corrupt professional politicians worked hand in glove with the big business interests to suppress the South and the West, and so to dominate the life of the country.

Josephson, Matthew, *The President Makers, 1896–1919* (New York, Harcourt, 1940).

A provocative discussion of Presidential politics during the period covered.

Josephson, Matthew, *The Robber Barons* (New York, Harcourt, 1934).

Shows how the tycoons of big business operated to establish and maintain monopolies.

Kirkland, Edward C., *The Peacemakers of 1864* (New York, Macmillan, 1927).

This book looks into the various peace efforts of 1864 by politicians, journalists and others. It is useful as a sampling of cross currents of opinion at the time.

Knauth, Oswald W., *The Policy of the United States Towards Industrial Monopoly* (New York, Longmans, 1914).

Traces in detail the legislation, actions of Presidents, Supreme Court decisions, and analysis of government policy. The author concludes that, as of 1913 (date of writing), the United States had not developed a consistent policy for curbing monopoly.

Kraus, Michael, *The Writing of American History* (Norman, Univ. of Oklahoma Press, 1953).

The writer sketches the principal writings on American history during the nineteenth century and first half of the twentieth century, with very little interpretation.

LaFollette, Robert M., *Autobiography* (Madison, Wis., LaFollette Co., 1913).

More reliable than Theodore Roosevelt's autobiography. Throws light on many phases of the Progressive movement.

Lippmann, Walter, *U.S. Foreign Policy: Shield of the Republic* (Boston, Little, Brown, 1943).

Lippmann, a leading commentator, analyzes American foreign policy as of the early 1940's, and makes suggestions for adapting it to changing needs.

Mahan, Alfred T., *Influence of Sea Power upon History* (18th ed., Boston, Little, Brown, 1904).

Sets forth Admiral Mahan's doctrine that sea power is the great determinant of the course of history.

Malin, James C., *An Interpretation of Recent American History* (New York, Century, 1926).

An interpretative account of the period from the Civil

War to World War I. Malin considers the year 1887, passage of the Interstate Commerce Act, as dividing the era of *laissez faire* from the era of the development of the welfare state.

McIlwain, Charles H., *The American Revolution: A Constitutional Interpretation* (New York, Macmillan, 1923).

A good analysis of the constitutional issues in the Revolution and their influence in shaping the institutions of the United States.

Merriam, C. Edwards, *A History of American Political Theories* (New York, Macmillan, 1903).

This book describes prevailing political theories in successive eras, and relates theories to historical events.

Merz, Charles, *The Dry Decade* (Garden City, N.Y., Doubleday, Doran, 1931).

A factual account of national prohibition and its working down to 1930 (the eve of repeal). Useful in interpreting the significance of the prohibition experiment.

Millis, Walter, *The Martial Spirit* (Cambridge, Riverside, 1931).

A somewhat cynical account of how the United States was pushed into the Spanish-American War. It contains some significant revelations.

Millis, Walter, *The Road to War* (Boston, Houghton, Mifflin, 1935).

Emphasizes the influence of propaganda and newspapers in bringing United States involvement in World War I. The author calls it an interpretation.

Milton, George Fort, *The Age of Hate* (New York, Coward, McCann, 1930).

An account of Radical reconstruction that is very hostile to the Radicals and highly favorable to President Andrew Johnson.

Milton, George Fort, *The Eve of Conflict. Stephen A. Douglas and the Needless War* (Boston, Houghton, Mifflin, 1934).

This book argues that the Civil War could have been averted by following the ideas of Stephen A. Douglas.

Minnegerode, Meade, *The Fabulous Forties* (New York, Putnam, 1924).

A very entertaining book on the 1840's, devoted mainly to the private life and unusual happenings of the decade, but excellent on the election of 1840.

Mock, James R., and Larson, Cedric, *Words That Won the War* (Princeton, Princeton Univ. Press, 1940).

The story of the Committee on Public Information in World War I, with the strong implication that American propaganda was the decisive factor in the Allied victory.

Morison, Samuel E., *Admiral of the Ocean Sea* (Boston, Little, Brown, 1942).

An interpretative biography of Christopher Columbus, suggesting factors that determined his ideas and his aims.

Morris, Richard B., *The Peacemakers: The Great Powers and American Independence* (New York, Harper and Row, 1965).

This book examines the intrigue and power politics involved in making the peace that ended the War for Independence.

Moulton, Harold G., and Pasvolsky, Leo, *War Debts and World Prosperity* (New York, Century, 1932).

A good discussion of the war debt issue by two eminent economists.

Mowry, George E., *Theodore Roosevelt and the Progressive Movement* (Madison, Univ. of Wisconsin Press, 1947).

A discussion, sympathetic to Roosevelt, of Theodore Roosevelt's influence on the Progressive movement.

Nearing, Scott, and Freeman, Joseph, *Dollar Diplomacy: A*

Study of American Imperialism (New York, Huebsch and Viking, 1926).

This is an account of the expansion of American investment in Latin America and Asia, and of government action supporting it, in the first fourth of the twentieth century.

Nevins, Allen, and Hacker, Louis M., Eds., *The United States and Its Place in World Affairs, 1918–1943* (Boston, Heath, 1943).

A compilation of documents tracing and interpreting the history of the inter-war years in terms of its relation to and influence on the United States.

Norton, A. B., *The Great Revolution of 1840: Reminiscences of the Log Cabin-Hard Cider Campaign* (Mount Vernon, Ohio, A. B. Norton & Co., 1888).

A strongly anti-Jackson account of conditions and of the political campaign of 1840. "Revolution" is far too strong a term.

Orth, Samuel P., *The Boss and the Machine* [Vol. 43, Chronicles of America] (New Haven, Yale Univ. Press, 1921).

An enlightening account of the corrupt "machine" politics that prevailed in the last half of the nineteenth century, with explanations and reports of reactions.

Ostrogorsky, M., *Democracy and the Party System* (New York, Macmillan, 1910).

A penetrating analysis of political party developments.

Parrington, Vernon L., *The Colonial Mind 1620–1800* [Vol. I, Main Currents in American Thought, 3 vols.] (New York, Harcourt, 1927).

An interpretative account of events and developments of the colonial period, with emphasis on the attitudes and viewpoints associated with each.

Paxson, Frederick L., *History of the American Frontier, 1763–1893* (Boston, Houghton, Mifflin, 1924).

A good narrative history, reflecting, in part, Turner's frontier hypothesis.

Paxson, Frederick L., *The Last American Frontier* (New York, Macmillan, 1915).

Sketches the advance of the frontier from the Mississippi River to the Pacific Ocean. A narrative account, but shows influence of the advancing frontier on the country as a whole.

Pearson, Drew, and Allen, Robert, *The Nine Old Men* (Garden City, N.Y., Doubleday, Doran, 1936).

A very hostile account of the Supreme Court's handling of New Deal measures hinting that something drastic should be done about the Court.

Perkins, Dexter, *America's Quest for Peace* (Bloomington, Indiana Univ. Press, 1962).

Traces the history of the quest for peace over the last century. One essay each on "Peace through Law," "Peace through Collective Security," and "Peace through Disarmament."

Perkins, Dexter, *Hands Off: A History of the Monroe Doctrine* (Boston, Little, Brown, 1941).

Explains how the Monroe Doctrine has been reinterpreted repeatedly to make it fit changing United States policy.

Peterson, Horace C., *Propaganda for War. The Campaign Against American Neutrality*, (Norman, Univ. of Oklahoma Press, 1937).

A scholarly study of the background of United States entry into World War I, but overstresses the role of propaganda in pushing us into war.

Pollard, A. F., *Factors in Modern History* (London, Constable and Co., 1926).

An analytical survey of English history to show factors at work in shaping developments. Some of this is "pre-

history" of the United States and is useful in seeking an
interpretation of American history.

Pratt, Julius W., *Expansionists of 1812* (New York, Macmillan,
1925).

This book discusses the "War Hawks," who desired the
annexation of Canada, in pushing the United States into the
War of 1812. This is a neglected aspect of the subject.

Pratt, Julius W., *Expansionists of 1898* (Baltimore, Johns Hopkins Univ. Press, 1936).

This is considered by many to be the best analytical study
of the rise of late nineteenth century imperialism.

Pressly, Thomas J., *Americans Interpret Their Civil War*
(Princeton, Princeton Univ. Press, 1954).

A compilation, with author's comments, of excerpts from
and summaries of different writings, showing various interpretations of the Civil War.

Randall, J. G., "The Blundering Generation," *Mississippi Valley Historical Review*, Vol. XXVII (June, 1940), 3–28.

A somewhat satirical discussion of how the United States
blundered into the Civil War.

Randall, J. G., *The Civil War and Reconstruction* (Boston,
Heath, 1937).

Mainly an excellent factual account, but does some interpreting by implication. The author thinks the Civil War
might have been averted by better statesmanship.

Reddaway, W. F., *The Monroe Doctrine* (Cambridge, Eng.,
Cambridge Univ. Press, 1898).

An analysis, by an English scholar, of the development
and real significance of the Monroe Doctrine down to approximately the time of the Spanish-American War.

Regier, C. C., *The Era of the Muckrakers* (Chapel Hill, Univ.
of North Carolina Press, 1932).

A critical study of writers of the early 1900's who were

called "muckrakers." The author is generally sympathetic with their aims, but is critical of their methods.

Richman, I. B., *The Spanish Conquerors* [Vol. II, Chronicles of America] (New Haven, Yale Univ. Press, 1921).

A very readable account of the major Spanish conquerors and explorers, showing their motives and aspirations.

Robey, Ralph, *Roosevelt versus Recovery* (New York, Harper, 1934).

A severely critical commentary on the early stages of the New Deal.

Roosevelt, Theodore, *Theodore Roosevelt: an Autobiography* (New York, Macmillan, 1913).

Roosevelt wrote what he wanted people to believe. His reports of facts are not fully reliable.

Ross, E. D., *The Liberal Republican Movement* (New York, Holt, 1919).

A good account of the Liberal Republican movement of 1872, with some analysis of its influence.

Russel, Robert R., "The Pacific Railway Issue in Politics Prior to the Civil War," *Mississippi Valley Historical Review*, Vol. XII (Sept. 1925), 187–201.

Sketches the story of the Pacific Railroad issue before the Kansas-Nebraska Act. Mentions Hodder's article, "The Railroad Background of the Kansas-Nebraska Act."

Salmon, Lucy M., *Why is History Rewritten?* (New York, Oxford Univ. Press, 1929).

Miss Salmon, an eminent historian, examines several changing factors in the writing of history. Chapter VII, "Interpretation," is especially useful.

Schlesinger, Arthur M., Jr., *The Age of Jackson* (Boston, Little, Brown, 1946).

Basically narrative, but brings out the author's strongly pro-Jackson interpretation of Jacksonian democracy.

Schlesinger, Arthur M., *The New Deal in Action, 1933–1938* (New York, Macmillan, 1939).

A sympathetic account of the New Deal by an eminent historian.

Schlesinger, Arthur M. *New Viewpoints in American History* (New York, Macmillan, 1922).

Each of the twelve chapters is an essay on one significant aspect or development. Especially good is Chapter VII, "The American Revolution."

Schlesinger, Arthur M., *Paths to the Present* (New York, Macmillan, 1949).

Twenty-three essays which explain the development of different American traits. Not exactly interpretation, but may help the student arrive at his own interpretations.

Schuyler, Robert L., *The Constitution of the United States. An Historical Survey of Its Formation* (New York, Macmillan, 1923).

A good factual account.

Seldes, Gilbert, *The Years of the Locust. America 1929–1932* (Boston, Little, Brown, 1933).

A somewhat philosophical analysis of the Great Depression and of reactions to it, including a temporary upsurge of Communism.

Seligman, R. A., *The Economic Interpretation of History* (2nd ed., New York, Macmillan, 1917).

Author does not limit his consideration to the United States. He stresses the predominant role of economic factors in shaping the course of history, but is not as extreme as Marx.

Semple, Ellen, and Jones, Clarence F., *American History and Its Geographic Conditions* (Boston, Houghton, Mifflin, 1935).

Traces the major developments in American history to show the influence of geography on each. Not exactly a "geographic interpretation, but close to it.

Seitz, Don C., *The Dreadful Decade, 1869–1879* (Indianapolis, Bobbs, Merrill, 1926).

Describes the developments of this decade, showing how high finance and corruption dominated public life.

Simons, A. M., *Social Forces in American History* (New York, Macmillan, 1911).

This is definitely a Marxian interpretation.

Simms, Henry H., *A Decade of Sectional Controversy, 1851–1861* (Chapel Hill, Univ. of North Carolina Press, 1942).

This study covers the period analytically, but overstresses slavery as the basic issue.

Slosson, Preston W., *The Great Crusade and After* [Vol. XII, Schlesinger and Fox, eds., History of American Life] (New York, Macmillan, 1930).

A social and idealistic account of World War I and the post-war era (the 1920's).

Steel, Ronald, *Pax Americana* (New York, Viking, 1967).

A critique of the foreign policy of the last two decades which, by accident, has created a global empire.

Stenberg, Richard R., "The Motivation of the Wilmot Proviso," *Mississippi Valley Historical Review*, Vol. XVIII (March, 1932), 535–548.

An examination (partly speculation) of Wilmot's motives in proposing to bar slavery from territory acquired from Mexico. Stenberg takes into account the influence of tariff and other political considerations.

Stenberg, Richard R., "Some Political Aspects of the Dred Scott Case," *Mississippi Valley Historical Review*, Vol. XIX (March, 1933), 571–577.

This article examines the influence of the Benton fight on the courts in Missouri. It also examines political elements in the Supreme Court decision.

Stryker, L. P., *Andrew Johnson: A Study in Courage* (New York, Macmillan, 1929).

A narrative of President Andrew Johnson's hopeless struggle against Radical reconstruction. One of several books that appeared at about the same time intended to rehabilitate the reputation of Andrew Johnson.

Thompson, Walker, *Federal Centralization* (New York, Harcourt, 1923).

An extended discussion of the centralization of more and more control in the federal government, thus threatening the very foundation of the federal system in the United States.

Turner, Frederick Jackson, *The Frontier in American History* (New York, Holt, 1920).

Contains, along with several other essays on various aspects of the frontier, the essay "The Significance of the Frontier in American History," which sets forth Turner's frontier hypothesis.

Turner, Frederick Jackson, *Rise of the New West* [Vol. 14, American Nation Series] (New York, Harper, 1906).

A narrative account of the settlement and development of the West from 1815 through 1830. It also points out the effects of Western development on national events and politics, in line with Turner's frontier hypothesis.

Tyler, Lyon G., *England in America* [Vol. 4, American Nation Series] (New York, Harper, 1904).

A good detailed narrative account of English colonization, with very little interpretation.

VanTyne, Claude H., *The Causes of the War of Independence* (Boston, Houghton, Mifflin, 1922).

VanTyne, considered a top authority on the Revolutionary War, analyzes the conditions and developments that led to the outbreak of the war. He summarizes his thesis in a sectional heading, "The Freest of Peoples Were the First to Revolt."

Wallace, Henry A., *Century of the Common Man* [Two speeches in pamphlet form] (New York, International Workers Order, 1942).

A left-of-center argument, by the then Vice President of the United States, that a new economic democracy, growing out of the New Deal, will provide peace and prosperity for the common man.

Welles, Sumner, *Naboth's Vineyard: The Dominican Republic* (New York, Payson and Clark, 1928).

An indictment of American Caribbean policy in the 1920's by a prominent public figure, later Assistant Secretary of State under Roosevelt.

Welles, Sumner, *The Time for Decision* (New York, Harper, 1944).

A good discussion of American policy during the first years of World War II by an Assistant Secretary of State.

White, William Allen, *A Puritan in Babylon* (New York, Macmillan, 1938).

An interesting discussion by a famous country editor of Calvin Coolidge and his era.

Willkie, Wendell, *One World* (New York, Simon and Schuster, 1943).

A commentary on Willkie's trip around the world, following his defeat for the Presidency, which convinced him of the need for worldwide cooperation: "One world or none."

Woodward, William E., *Years of Madness. A Reappraisal of the Civil War* (New York, Putnam, 1951).

    This book argues that the Civil War was unnecessary, and did far more harm than good.

DECLARATION OF INDEPENDENCE

IN CONGRESS, JULY 4, 1776.

The unanimous Declaration of the thirteen united States of America,

When in the Course of human events, it becomes necessary for one people to dissolve the political bands which have connected them with another, and to assume among the Powers of the earth, the separate and equal station to which the Laws of Nature and of Nature's God entitle them, a decent respect to the opinions of mankind requires that they should declare the causes which impel them to the separation.

We hold these truths to be self-evident, that all men are created equal, that they are endowed by their Creator with certain unalienable Rights, that among these are Life, Liberty and the pursuit of Happiness. That to secure these rights, Governments are instituted among Men, deriving their just powers from the consent of the governed, That whenever any Form of Government becomes destructive of these ends, it is the Right of the People to alter or to abolish it, and to institute new Government, laying its foundation on such principles and organizing its powers in such form, as to them shall seem most likely to effect their Safety and Happiness. Prudence, indeed, will dictate that Governments long established should not be changed for light and transient causes; and accordingly all experience hath shown, that mankind are more disposed to suffer, while evils are sufferable, than to right themselves by abolishing the forms to which they are accustomed. But when a long train of abuses and usurpations, pursuing invariably the same Object evinces a design to reduce them under absolute Despotism, it is their right, it is their duty, to throw off such Government, and to provide new Guards for their future security. — Such has been the patient sufferance of these Colonies; and such is now the necessity which constrains them to alter their former Systems of Government. The history of the present King of Great Britain is a history of repeated injuries and usurpations, all having in direct object the establishment of an absolute Tyranny over these States. To prove this, let Facts be submitted to a candid world.

He has refused his Assent to Laws, the most wholesome and necessary for the public good.

He has forbidden his Governors to pass Laws of immediate and pressing importance, unless suspended in their operation till his Assent should be obtained; and when so suspended, he has utterly neglected to attend to them.

He has refused to pass other Laws for the accommodation of large districts of people, unless those people would relinquish the right of Representation in the Legislature, a right inestimable to them and formidable to tyrants only.

He has called together legislative bodies at places unusual, uncomfortable, and distant from the depository of their Public Records, for the sole purpose of fatiguing them into compliance with his measures.

He has dissolved Representative Houses repeatedly, for opposing with manly firmness his invasions on the rights of the people.

He has refused for a long time, after such dissolutions, to cause others to be elected; whereby the Legislative Powers, incapable of Annihilation, have returned to the People at large for their exercise; the State remaining in the mean time exposed to all the dangers of invasion from without, and convulsions within.

He has endeavored to prevent the population of these States; for that purpose obstructing the Laws for Naturalization of Foreigners; refusing to pass others to encourage their migrations hither, and raising the conditions of new Appropriations of Lands.

He has obstructed the Administration of Justice, by refusing his Assent to Laws for establishing Judiciary Powers.

He has made Judges dependent on his Will alone, for the tenure of their offices, and the amount and payment of their salaries.

He has erected a multitude of New Offices, and sent hither swarms of Officers to harass our people, and eat out their substance.

He has kept among us, in times of peace, Standing Armies without the Consent of our legislatures.

He has affected to render the Military independent of and superior to the Civil Power.

He has combined with others to subject us to a jurisdiction foreign to our constitution, and unacknowledged by our laws; giving his Assent to their acts of pretended Legislation:

For quartering large bodies of armed troops among us:

For protecting them, by mock Trial, from Punishment for any Murders which they should commit on the Inhabitants of these States:

For cutting off our Trade with all parts of the world:

For imposing taxes on us without our Consent:

For depriving us in many cases, of the benefits of Trial by Jury:

For transporting us beyond Seas to be tried for pretended offences:

For abolishing the free System of English Laws in a neighbouring Province, establishing therein an Arbitrary government, and enlarging its Boundaries so as to render it at once an example and fit instrument for introducing the same absolute rule into these Colonies:

For taking away our Charters, abolishing our most valuable Laws, and altering fundamentally the Forms of our Governments:

For suspending our own Legislatures, and declaring themselves invested with Power to legislate for us in all cases whatsoever.

He has abdicated Government here, by declaring us out of his Protection and waging War against us.

He has plundered our seas, ravaged our Coasts, burnt our towns, and destroyed the lives of our people.

He is at this time transporting large armies of foreign mercenaries to compleat the works of death, desolation and tyranny, already begun with circumstances of Cruelty & perfidy scarcely paralleled in the most barbarous ages, and totally unworthy the Head of a civilized nation.

He has constrained our fellow Citizens taken Captive on the high Seas to bear Arms against their Country, to become the executioners of their friends and Brethren, or to fall themselves by their Hands.

He has excited domestic insurrections amongst us, and has endeavoured to bring on the inhabitants of our frontiers, the merciless Indian Savages, whose known rule of warfare, is an undistinguished destruction of all ages, sexes and conditions.

In every stage of these Oppressions We have Petitioned for Redress in the most humble terms: Our repeated Petitions have been answered only by repeated injury. A Prince, whose character is thus marked by every act which may define a Tyrant, is unfit to be the ruler of a free people.

Nor have We been wanting in attentions to our Brittish brethren. We have warned them from time to time of attempts by their legislature to extend an unwarrantable jurisdiction over us. We have reminded them of the circumstances of our emigration and settlement here. We have appealed to their native justice and magnanimity, and we have conjured them by the ties of our common kindred to disavow these usurpations which, would inevitably interrupt our connections and correspondence. They too have been deaf to the voice of justice and of consanguinity. We must, therefore, acquiesce in the necessity, which denounces our Separation, and hold them, as we hold the rest of mankind, Enemies in War, in Peace Friends.

We, therefore, the Representatives of the united States of America, in General Congress, Assembled, appealing to the Supreme Judge of the world for the rectitude of our intentions, do, in the Name, and by authority of the good People of these Colonies, solemnly publish and declare, That these United Colonies are, and of Right ought to be Free and Independent States; that they are Absolved from all Allegiance to the British Crown, and that all political connection between them and the State of Great Britain, is and ought to be totally dissolved; and that as Free and Independent States, they have full power to levy War, conclude Peace, contract Alliances, establish Commerce, and to do all other Acts and Things which Independent States may of right do. And for the support of this Declaration, with a firm reliance on the Protection of Divine Providence, we mutually pledge to each other our Lives, our Fortunes and our sacred Honor.

JOHN HANCOCK.

BUTTON GWINNETT.
LYMAN HALL.
GEO. WALTON.
WM. HOOPER.
JOSEPH HEWES.
JOHN PENN.
EDWARD RUTLEDGE.
THOS. HEYWARD, Junr.
THOMAS LYNCH, Junr.
ARTHUR MIDDLETON.
SAMUEL CHASE.
WM. PACA.
THOS. STONE.
CHARLES CARROLL OF
   CARROLLTON.
GEORGE WYTHE.
RICHARD HENRY LEE.
TH. JEFFERSON.
BENJ. HARRISON.
THOS. NELSON, JR.
FRANCIS LIGHTFOOT LEE.
CARTER BRAXTON.
ROBT. MORRIS.
BENJAMIN RUSH.
BENJA. FRANKLIN.
JOHN MORTON.
GEO. CLYMER.
JAS. SMITH.

GEO. TAYLOR.
JAMES WILSON.
GEO. ROSS.
CAESAR RODNEY.
GEO. READ.
THO. M'KEAN.
WM. FLOYD.
PHIL. LIVINGSTON.
FRANS. LEWIS.
LEWIS MORRIS.
RICHD. STOCKTON.
JNO. WITHERSPOON.
FRAS. HOPKINSON.
JOHN HART.
ABRA. CLARK.
JOSIAH BARTLETT.
WM. WHIPPLE.
SAML. ADAMS.
JOHN ADAMS.
ROBT. TREAT PAINE.
ELBRIDGE GERRY.
STEP. HOPKINS.
WILLIAM ELLERY.
ROGER SHERMAN.
SAM'EL. HUNTINGTON.
WM. WILLIAMS.
OLIVER WOLCOTT.
MATTHEW THORNTON.

CONSTITUTION OF THE UNITED STATES

WE THE PEOPLE of the United States, in Order to form a more perfec Union, establish Justice, insure domestic Tranquility, provide fo the common defence, promote the general Welfare, and secure th Blessings of Liberty to ourselves and our Posterity, do ordain an establish this CONSTITUTION for the United States of America

ARTICLE. I.

SECTION. 1. All legislative Powers herein granted shall be vested ii a Congress of the United States, which shall consist of a Senate anc House of Representatives.

SECTION. 2. [1] The House of Representatives shall be composed of Members chosen every second Year by the People of the several States, and the Electors in each State shall have the Qualifications requisite for Electors of the most numerous Branch of the State Legislature.

[2] No person shall be a Representative who shall not have attained to the Age of twenty five Years, and been seven Years a Citizen of the United States, and who shall not, when elected, be an Inhabitant of that State in which he shall be chosen.

[3] [Representatives and direct Taxes shall be apportioned among the several States which may be included within this Union, according to their respective Numbers, which shall be determined by adding to the whole Number of free Persons, including those bound to Service for a Term of Years, and excluding Indians not taxed, three fifths of all other Persons.].* The actual Enumeration shall be made within three Years after the first Meeting of the Congress of the United States, and within every subsequent Term of ten Years, in such Manner as they shall by Law direct. The Number of Representatives shall not exceed one for every thirty Thousand, but each State shall have at Least one Representative; and until such enumeration shall be made, the State of New Hampshire shall be entitled to chuse three, Massachusetts eight, Rhode-Island and Providence Plantations one, Connecticut five, New-York six, New Jersey four, Pennsylvania eight, Delaware one, Maryland six, Virginia ten, North Carolina five, South Carolina five, and Georgia three.

[4] When vacancies happen in the Representation from any State, the Executive Authority thereof shall issue Writs of Election to fill such Vacancies.

[5] The House of Representatives shall chuse their Speaker and other Officers; and shall have the sole Power of Impeachment.

[1] SECTION. 3. The Senate of the United States shall be composed of two Senators from each State, [chosen by the Legislature thereof,]** for six Years; and each Senator shall have one Vote.

NOTE.—This text of the Constitution follows the engrossed copy signed by Gen. Washington and the deputies from 12 States. The superior number preceding the paragraphs designates the number of the clause; it was not in the original.
*The part included in heavy brackets was changed by section 2 of the fourteenth amendment.
**The part included in heavy brackets was changed by section 1 of the seventeenth amendment

² Immediately after they shall be assembled in Consequence of the first Election, they shall be divided as equally as may be into three Classes. The Seats of the Senators of the first Class shall be vacated at the Expiration of the second Year, of the second Class at the Expiration of the fourth Year, and of the third Class at the Expiration of the sixth Year, so that one third may be chosen every second Year; [and if Vacancies happen by Resignation, or otherwise, during the Recess of the Legislature of any State, the Executive thereof may make temporary Appointments until the next Meeting of the Legislature, which shall then fill such Vacancies].*

³ No Person shall be a Senator who shall not have attained to the Age of thirty Years, and been nine Years a Citizen of the United States, and who shall not, when elected, be an Inhabitant of that State for which he shall be chosen.

⁴ The Vice President of the United States shall be President of the Senate, but shall have no Vote, unless they be equally divided.

⁵ The Senate shall chuse their other Officers, and also a President pro tempore, in the Absence of the Vice President, or when he shall exercise the Office of President of the United States.

⁶ The Senate shall have the sole Power to try all Impeachments. When sitting for that Purpose, they shall be on Oath or Affirmation. When the President of the United States is tried, the Chief Justice shall preside: And no Person shall be convicted without the Concurrence of two thirds of the Members present.

⁷ Judgment in Cases of Impeachment shall not extend further than to removal from Office, and disqualification to hold and enjoy any Office of honor, Trust or Profit under the United States: but the Party convicted shall nevertheless be liable and subject to Indictment, Trial, Judgment and Punishment, according to Law.

SECTION. 4. ¹ The Times, Places and Manner of holding Elections for Senators and Representatives, shall be prescribed in each State by the Legislature thereof; but the Congress may at any time by Law make or alter such Regulations, except as to the Places of chusing Senators.

² The Congress shall assemble at least once in every Year, and such Meeting shall [be on the first Monday in December,]** unless they shall by Law appoint a different Day.

SECTION. 5. ¹ Each House shall be the Judge of the Elections, Returns and Qualifications of its own Members, and a Majority of each shall constitute a Quorum to do Business; but a smaller Number may adjourn from day to day, and may be authorized to compel the Attendance of absent Members, in such Manner, and under such Penalties as each House may provide.

² Each House may determine the Rules of its Proceedings, punish its Members for disorderly Behavior, and, with the Concurrence of two thirds, expel a Member.

³ Each House shall keep a Journal of its Proceedings, and from time to time publish the same, excepting such Parts as may in their Judgment require Secrecy; and the Yeas and Nays of the Members of either House on any question shall, at the Desire of one fifth of those Present, be entered on the Journal.

---

*The part included in heavy brackets was changed by clause 2 of the seventeenth amendment.
**The part included in heavy brackets was changed by section 2 of the twentieth amendment.

⁴ Neither House, during the Session of Congress, shall, without the Consent of the other, adjourn for more than three days, nor to any other Place than that in which the two Houses shall be sitting.

SECTION. 6. ¹ The Senators and Representatives shall receive a Compensation for their Services, to be ascertained by Law, and paid out of the Treasury of the United States. They shall in all Cases, except Treason, Felony and Breach of the Peace, be privileged from Arrest during their Attendance at the Session of their respective Houses, and in going to and returning from the same; and for any Speech or Debate in either House, they shall not be questioned in any other Place.

² No Senator or Representative shall, during the Time for which he was elected, be appointed to any civil Office under the Authority of the United States, which shall have been created, or the Emoluments whereof shall have been encreased during such time; and no Person holding any Office under the United States, shall be a Member of either House during his Continuance in Office.

SECTION. 7. ¹ All Bills for raising Revenue shall originate in the House of Representatives; but the Senate may propose or concur with Amendments as on other Bills.

² Every Bill which shall have passed the House of Representatives and the Senate, shall, before it become a Law, be presented to the President of the United States; If he approve he shall sign it, but if not he shall return it, with his Objections to that House in which it shall have originated, who shall enter the Objections at large on their Journal, and proceed to reconsider it. If after such Reconsideration two thirds of that House shall agree to pass the Bill, it shall be sent, together with the Objections, to the other House, by which it shall likewise be reconsidered, and if approved by two thirds of that House, it shall become a Law. But in all such Cases the Votes of both Houses shall be determined by yeas and Nays, and the Names of the Persons voting for and against the Bill shall be entered on the Journal of each House respectively. If any Bill shall not be returned by the President within ten days (Sundays excepted) after it shall have been presented to him, the Same shall be a Law, in like Manner as if he had signed it, unless the Congress by their Adjournment prevent its Return, in which Case it shall not be a Law.

³ Every Order, Resolution, or Vote to which the Concurrence of the Senate and House of Representatives may be necessary (except on a question of Adjournment) shall be presented to the President of the United States; and before the Same shall take Effect, shall be approved by him, or being disapproved by him, shall be repassed by two thirds of the Senate and House of Representatives, according to the Rules and Limitations prescribed in the Case of a Bill.

SECTION. 8. The Congress shall have Power To lay and collect Taxes, Duties, Imposts and Excises, to pay the Debts and provide for the common Defence and general Welfare of the United States; but all Duties, Imposts and Excises shall be uniform throughout the United States;

² To borrow Money on the credit of the United States;

³ To regulate Commerce with foreign Nations, and among the several States, and with the Indian Tribes;

⁴ To establish an uniform Rule of Naturalization, and uniform Laws on the subject of Bankruptcies throughout the United States;

⁵ To coin Money, regulate the Value thereof, and of foreign Coin, and fix the Standard of Weights and Measures;

⁶ To provide for the Punishment of counterfeiting the Securities and current Coin of the United States;

⁷ To establish Post Offices and post Roads;

⁸ To promote the Progress of Science and useful Arts, by securing for limited Times to Authors and Inventors the exclusive Right to their respective Writings and Discoveries;

⁹ To constitute Tribunals inferior to the supreme Court;

¹⁰ To define and punish Piracies and Felonies committed on the high Seas, and Offences against the Law of Nations;

¹¹ To declare War, grant Letters of Marque and Reprisal, and make Rules concerning Captures on Land and Water;

¹² To raise and support Armies, but no Appropriation of Money to that Use shall be for a longer Term than two Years;

¹³ To provide and maintain a Navy;

¹⁴ To make Rules for the Government and Regulation of the land and naval Forces;

¹⁵ To provide for calling forth the Militia to execute the Laws of the Union, suppress Insurrections and repel Invasions;

¹⁶ To provide for organizing, arming, and disciplining the Militia, and for governing such Part of them as may be employed in the Service of the United States, reserving to the States respectively, the Appointment of the Officers, and the Authority of training the Militia according to the discipline prescribed by Congress;

¹⁷ To exercise exclusive Legislation in all Cases whatsoever, over such District (not exceeding ten Miles square) as may, by Cession of particular States, and the Acceptance of Congress, become the Seat of the Government of the United States, and to exercise like Authority over all Places purchased by the Consent of the Legislature of the State in which the Same shall be, for the Erection of Forts, Magazines, Arsenals, dock-Yards, and other needful Buildings;—And

¹⁸ To make all Laws which shall be necessary and proper for carrying into Execution the foregoing Powers, and all other Powers vested by this Constitution in the Government of the United States, or in any Department or Officer thereof.

SECTION. 9. ¹ The Migration or Importation of such Persons as any of the States now existing shall think proper to admit, shall not be prohibited by the Congress prior to the Year one thousand eight hundred and eight, but a Tax or duty may be imposed on such Importation, not exceeding ten dollars for each Person.

² The Privilege of the Writ of Habeas Corpus shall not be suspended, unless when in Cases of Rebellion or Invasion the public Safety may require it.

³ No Bill of Attainder or ex post facto Law shall be passed.

*⁴ No Capitation, or other direct, Tax shall be laid, unless in Proportion to the Census or Enumeration herein before directed to be taken.

⁵ No Tax or Duty shall be laid on Articles exported from any State.

⁶ No Preference shall be given by any Regulation of Commerce or Revenue to the Ports of one State over those of another: nor shall Vessels bound to, or from, one State be obliged to enter, clear, or pay Duties in another.

* See also the sixteenth amendment.

⁷ No Money shall be drawn from the Treasury, but in Consequence of Appropriations made by Law; and a regular Statement and Account of the Receipts and Expenditures of all public Money shall be published from time to time.

⁸ No Title of Nobility shall be granted by the United States: And no Person holding any Office of Profit or Trust under them, shall, without the Consent of the Congress, accept of any present, Emolument, Office, or Title, of any kind whatever, from any King, Prince, or foreign State.

SECTION. 10. ¹ No State shall enter into any Treaty, Alliance, or Confederation; grant Letters of Marque and Reprisal; coin Money; emit Bills of Credit; make any Thing but gold and silver Coin a Tender in Payment of Debts; pass any Bill of Attainder, ex post facto Law, or Law impairing the Obligation of Contracts, or grant any Title of Nobility.

² No State shall, without the Consent of the Congress, lay any Imposts or Duties on Imports or Exports, except what may be absolutely necessary for executing it's inspection Laws: and the net Produce of all Duties and Imposts, laid by any State on Imports or Exports, shall be for the Use of the Treasury of the United States; and all such Laws shall be subject to the Revision and Controul of the Congress.

³ No State shall, without the Consent of Congress, lay any Duty of Tonnage, keep Troops, or Ships of War in time of Peace, enter into any Agreement or Compact with another State, or with a foreign Power, or engage in War, unless actually invaded, or in such imminent Danger as will not admit of delay.

ARTICLE. II.

SECTION. 1. ¹ The executive Power shall be vested in a President of the United States of America. He shall hold his Office during the Term of four Years, and, together with the Vice President, chosen for the same Term, be elected as follows

² Each State shall appoint, in such Manner as the Legislature thereof may direct, a Number of Electors, equal to the whole Number of Senators and Representatives to which the State may be entitled in the Congress: but no Senator or Representative, or Person holding an Office of Trust or Profit under the United States, shall be appointed an Elector.

[The Electors shall meet in their respective States, and vote by Ballot for two Persons, of whom one at least shall not be an Inhabitant of the same State with themselves. And they shall make a List of all the Persons voted for, and of the Number of Votes for each; which List they shall sign and certify, and transmit sealed to the Seat of the Government of the United States, directed to the President of the Senate. The President of the Senate shall, in the Presence of the Senate and House of Representatives, open all the Certificates, and the Votes shall then be counted. The Person having the greatest Number of Votes shall be the President, if such Number be a Majority of the whole Number of Electors appointed; and if there be more than one who have such Majority, and have an equal Number of Votes, then the House of Representatives shall immediately chuse by Ballot one of them for President; and if no Person have a Majority, then from the five highest on the List the said House shall in like Manner chuse the President. But in chusing the President, the Votes shall be taken by States, the Representation from each State having one Vote; A quorum for this Purpose shall consist of a Member or Members from two thirds of the States, and a Majority of all the States shall be necessary to a Choice. In every Case, after the Choice of the President, the Person having the greatest Number of Votes of the Electors shall be the Vice President. But if there should remain two or more who have equal Votes, the Senate shall chuse from them by Ballot the Vice President.]*

³ The Congress may determine the Time of chusing the Electors, and the Day on which they shall give their Votes; which Day shall be the same throughout the United States.

⁴ No Person except a natural born Citizen, or a Citizen of the United States, at the time of the Adoption of this Constitution, shall be eligible to the Office of President; neither shall any Person be eligible to that Office who shall not have attained to the Age of thirty five Years, and been fourteen Years a Resident within the United States.

⁵ In Case of the Removal of the President from Office, or of his Death, Resignation, or Inability to discharge the Powers and Duties of the said Office, the Same shall devolve on the Vice President, and the Congress may by Law provide for the Case of Removal, Death, Resignation or Inability, both of the President and Vice President, declaring what Officer shall then act as President, and such Officer shall act accordingly, until the Disability be removed, or a President shall be elected.

⁶ The President shall, at stated Times, receive for his Services, a Compensation, which shall neither be encreased nor diminished during the Period for which he shall have been elected, and he shall not receive within that Period any other Emolument from the United States, or any of them.

⁷ Before he enter on the Execution of his Office, he shall take the following Oath or Affirmation:—"I do solemnly swear (or affirm) that I will faithfully execute the Office of President of the United States, and will to the best of my Ability, preserve, protect and defend the Constitution of the United States."

SECTION. 2. ¹ The President shall be Commander in Chief of the Army and Navy of the United States, and of the Militia of the several States, when called into the actual Service of the United States; he may require the Opinion, in writing, of the principal Officer in each of the executive Departments, upon any Subject relating to the Duties of their respective Offices, and he shall have Power to grant Reprieves and Pardons for Offences against the United States, except in Cases of Impeachment.

² He shall have Power, by and with the Advice and Consent of the Senate, to make Treaties, provided two thirds of the Senators present concur; and he shall nominate, and by and with the Advice and Consent of the Senate, shall appoint Ambassadors, other public Ministers and Consuls, Judges of the supreme Court, and all other Officers of the United States, whose Appointments are not herein otherwise provided for, and which shall be established by Law: but the Congress may by Law vest the Appointment of such inferior Officers, as they

---

*This paragraph has been superseded by the twelfth amendment.

think proper, in the President alone, in the Courts of Law, or in the Heads of Departments.

³ The President shall have Power to fill up all Vacancies that may happen during the Recess of the Senate, by granting Commissions which shall expire at the End of their next Session.

SECTION. 3. He shall from time to time give to the Congress Information of the State of the Union, and recommend to their Consideration such Measures as he shall judge necessary and expedient; he may, on extraordinary Occasions, convene both Houses, or either of them, and in Case of Disagreement between them, with Respect to the Time of Adjournment, he may adjourn them to such Time as he shall think proper; he shall receive Ambassadors and other public Ministers; he shall take Care that the Laws be faithfully executed, and shall Commission all the Officers of the United States.

SECTION. 4. The President, Vice President and all civil Officers of the United States, shall be removed from Office on Impeachment for, and Conviction of, Treason, Bribery, or other high Crimes and Misdemeanors.

ARTICLE. III.

SECTION. 1. The judicial Power of the United States, shall be vested in one supreme Court, and in such inferior Courts as the Congress may from time to time ordain and establish. The Judges, both of the supreme and inferior Courts, shall hold their Offices during good Behaviour, and shall, at stated Times, receive for their Services a Compensation, which shall not be diminished during their Continuance in Office.

SECTION. 2. ¹ The judicial Power shall extend to all Cases, in Law and Equity, arising under this Constitution, the Laws of the United States, and Treaties made, or which shall be made, under their Authority;—to all Cases affecting Ambassadors, other public Ministers and Consuls;—to all Cases of admiralty and maritime Jurisdiction;—to Controversies to which the United States shall be a Party;—to Controversies between two or more States;—between a State and Citizens of another State;*—between Citizens of different States,—between Citizens of the same State claiming Lands under Grants of different States, and between a State, or the Citizens thereof, and foreign States, Citizens or Subjects.

² In all Cases affecting Ambassadors, other public Ministers and Consuls, and those in which a State shall be Party, the supreme Court shall have original Jurisdiction. In all the other Cases before mentioned, the supreme Court shall have appellate Jurisdiction, both as to Law and Fact, with such Exceptions, and under such Regulations as the Congress shall make.

³ The Trial of all Crimes, except in Cases of Impeachment shall be by Jury; and such Trial shall be held in the State where the said Crimes shall have been committed; but when not committed within any State, the Trial shall be at such Place or Places as the Congress may by Law have directed.

SECTION. 3. ¹ Treason against the United States, shall consist only in levying War against them, or in adhering to their Enemies, giving them Aid and Comfort. No Person shall be convicted of Treason unless on the Testimony of two Witnesses to the same overt Act, or on Confession in open Court.

*This clause has been affected by the eleventh amendment.

² The Congress shall have Power to declare the Punishment of Treason, but no Attainder of Treason shall work Corruption of Blood, or Forfeiture except during the Life of the Person attainted.

ARTICLE. IV.

SECTION. 1. Full Faith and Credit shall be given in each State to the public Acts, Records, and judicial Proceedings of every other State. And the Congress may by general Laws prescribe the Manner in which such Acts, Records and Proceedings shall be proved, and the Effect thereof.

SECTION. 2. ¹ The Citizens of each State shall be entitled to all Privileges and Immunities of Citizens in the several States.

² A Person charged in any State with Treason, Felony, or other Crime, who shall flee from Justice, and be found in another State, shall on Demand of the executive Authority of the State from which he fled, be delivered up, to be removed to the State having Jurisdiction of the Crime.

³ [No Person held to Service or Labour in one State, under the Laws thereof, escaping into another, shall, in Consequence of any Law or Regulation therein, be discharged from such Service or Labour, but shall be delivered up on Claim of the Party to whom such Service or Labour may be due.]*

SECTION. 3. ¹ New States may be admitted by the Congress into this Union; but no new State shall be formed or erected within the Jurisdiction of any other State; nor any State be formed by the Junction of two or more States, or Parts of States, without the Consent of the Legislatures of the States concerned as well as of the Congress.

² The Congress shall have Power to dispose of and make all needful Rules and Regulations respecting the Territory or other Property belonging to the United States; and nothing in this Constitution shall be so construed as to Prejudice any Claims of the United States, or of any particular State.

SECTION. 4. The United States shall guarantee to every State in this Union a Republican Form of Government, and shall protect each of them against Invasion; and on Application of the Legislature, or of the Executive (when the Legislature cannot be convened) against domestic Violence.

ARTICLE. V.

The Congress, whenever two thirds of both Houses shall deem it necessary, shall propose Amendments to this Constitution, or, on the Application of the Legislatures of two thirds of the several States, shall call a Convention for proposing Amendments, which, in either Case, shall be valid to all Intents and Purposes, as Part of this Constitution, when ratified by the Legislatures of three fourths of the several States, or by Conventions in three fourths thereof, as the one or the other Mode of Ratification may be proposed by the Congress: Provided, [that no Amendment which may be made prior to the Year One thousand eight hundred and eight shall in any Manner affect the first and fourth Clauses in the Ninth Section of the first Article; and]** that no State, without its Consent, shall be deprived of its equal Suffrage in the Senate.

---

*This paragraph has been superseded by the thirteenth amendment.
**Obsolete.

ARTICLE. VI.

[1] All Debts contracted and Engagements entered into, before the Adoption of this Constitution shall be as valid against the United States under this Constitution, as under the Confederation.

[2] This Constitution, and the Laws of the United States which shall be made in Pursuance thereof; and all Treaties made, or which shall be made, under the Authority of the United States, shall be the supreme Law of the Land; and the Judges in every State shall be bound thereby, any Thing in the Constitution or Laws of any State to the Contrary notwithstanding.

[3] The Senators and Representatives before mentioned, and the Members of the several State Legislatures, and all executive and judicial Officers, both of the United States and of the several States, shall be bound by Oath or Affirmation, to support this Constitution; but no religious Test shall ever be required as a Qualification to any Office or public Trust under the United States.

ARTICLE. VII.

The Ratification of the Conventions of nine States, shall be sufficient for the Establishment of this Constitution between the States so ratifying the Same.

DONE in Convention by the Unanimous Consent of the States present the Seventeenth Day of September in the Year of our Lord one thousand seven hundred and Eighty seven and of the Independence of the United States of America the Twelfth   IN WITNESS whereof We have hereto subscribed our Names,

Gº WASHINGTON—
Presidᵗ. and deputy from Virginia.

[Signed also by the deputies of twelve States.]

New Hampshire.

JOHN LANGDON,	NICHOLAS GILMAN.

Massachusetts.

NATHANIEL GORHAM,	RUFUS KING.

Connecticut.

WM. SAML. JOHNSON,	ROGER SHERMAN.

New York.

ALEXANDER HAMILTON.

New Jersey.

WIL: LIVINGSTON,	WM. PATERSON,
DAVID BREARLEY,	JONA: DAYTON.

Pennsylvania.

B FRANKLIN,	THOMAS MIFFLIN,
ROBᵀ MORRIS,	GEO. CLYMER,
THOS. FITZSIMONS,	JARED INGERSOLL,
JAMES WILSON,	GOUV MORRIS.

Delaware.

GEO: READ,   GUNNING BEDFORD, jun,
JOHN DICKINSON,   RICHARD BASSETT.
JACO: BROOM,

Maryland.

JAMES MCHENRY,   DAN OF ST THOS. JENIFER,
DANL CARROLL.

Virginia.

JOHN BLAIR—   JAMES MADISON Jr.

North Carolina.

WM. BLOUNT,   RICH'D DOBBS SPAIGHT,
HU WILLIAMSON.

South Carolina.

J. RUTLEDGE,   CHARLES COTESWORTH PINCKNEY,
CHARLES PINCKNEY,   PIERCE BUTLER.

Georgia.

WILLIAM FEW,   ABR BALDWIN.

Attest: WILLIAM JACKSON, *Secretary.*

RATIFICATION OF THE CONSTITUTION

The Constitution was adopted by a convention of the States on September 17, 1787, and was subsequently ratified by the several States, on the following dates: Delaware, December 7, 1787; Pennsylvania, December 12, 1787; New Jersey, December 18, 1787; Georgia, January 2, 1788; Connecticut, January 9, 1788; Massachusetts, February 6, 1788; Maryland, April 28, 1788; South Carolina, May 23, 1788; New Hampshire, June 21, 1788; Virginia, June 25, 1788; New York, July 26, 1788; North Carolina, November 21, 1789; Rhode Island, May 29, 1790.

ARTICLES IN ADDITION TO, AND AMENDMENT OF, THE CONSTITUTION OF THE UNITED STATES OF AMERICA, PROPOSED BY CONGRESS, AND RATIFIED BY THE LEGISLATURES OF THE SEVERAL STATES PURSUANT TO THE FIFTH ARTICLE OF THE ORIGINAL CONSTITUTION

ARTICLE [I]*

Congress shall make no law respecting an establishment of religion, or prohibiting the free exercise thereof; or abridging the freedom of speech, or of the press, or the right of the people peaceably to assemble, and to petition the Government for a redress of grievances.

ARTICLE [II]

A well regulated Militia, being necessary to the security of a free State, the right of the people to keep and bear Arms, shall not be infringed.

ARTICLE [III]

No Soldier shall, in time of peace be quartered in any house, without the consent of the Owner, nor in time of war, but in a manner to be prescribed by law.

ARTICLE [IV]

The right of the people to be secure in their persons, houses, papers, and effects, against unreasonable searches and seizures, shall not be violated, and no Warrants shall issue, but upon probable cause, supported by Oath or affirmation, and particularly describing the place to be searched, and the persons or things to be seized.

ARTICLE [V]

No person shall be held to answer for a capital, or otherwise infamous crime, unless on a presentment or indictment of a Grand Jury, except in cases arising in the land or naval forces, or in the Militia, when in actual service in time of War or public danger; nor shall any person be subject for the same offence to be twice put in jeopardy of life or limb, nor shall be compelled in any criminal case to be a witness against himself, nor be deprived of life, liberty, or property, without due process of law; nor shall private property be taken for public use without just compensation

ARTICLE [VI]

In all criminal prosecutions, the accused shall enjoy the right to a speedy and public trial, by an impartial jury of the State and district wherein the crime shall have been committed; which district shall

*Only the 13th, 14th, 15th, and 16th articles of amendment had numbers assigned to them at the time of ratification.

have been previously ascertained by law, and to be informed of the
nature and cause of the accusation; to be confronted with the witnesses
against him; to have compulsory process for obtaining Witnesses in
his favor, and to have the Assistance of Counsel for his defence.

ARTICLE [VII]

In Suits at common law, where the value in controversy shall
exceed twenty dollars, the right of trial by jury shall be preserved,
and no fact tried by a jury shall be otherwise reexamined in any
Court of the United States, than according to the rules of the common law.

ARTICLE [VIII]

Excessive bail shall not be required, nor excessive fines imposed,
nor cruel and unusual punishments inflicted.

ARTICLE [IX]

The enumeration in the Constitution, of certain rights, shall not
be construed to deny or disparage others retained by the people.

ARTICLE [X]

The powers not delegated to the United States by the Constitution,
nor prohibited by it to the States, are reserved to the States respectively, or to the people.

ARTICLE [XI]

The Judicial power of the United States shall not be construed to
extend to any suit in law or equity, commenced or prosecuted against
one of the United States by Citizens of another State, or by Citizens
or Subjects of any Foreign State.

ARTICLE [XII]

The electors shall meet in their respective states and vote by ballot
for President and Vice-President, one of whom, at least, shall not be an
inhabitant of the same state with themselves; they shall name in their
ballots the person voted for as President, and in distinct ballots the
person voted for as Vice-President, and they shall make distinct lists
of all persons voted for as President, and of all persons voted for as
Vice-President, and of the number of votes for each, which lists they
shall sign and certify, and transmit sealed to the seat of the government of the United States, directed to the President of the Senate;—
The President of the Senate shall, in presence of the Senate and House
of Representatives, open all the certificates and the votes shall then
be counted;—The person having the greatest number of votes for
President, shall be the President, if such number be a majority of the
whole number of Electors appointed; and if no person have such
majority, then from the persons having the highest numbers not exceeding three on the list of those voted for as President, the House of
Representatives shall choose immediately, by ballot, the President.

But in choosing the President, the votes shall be taken by sta[
representation from each state having one vote; a quorum f[
purpose shall consist of a member or members from two-thirds [
states, and a majority of all the states shall be necessary to a c[
[And if the House of Representatives shall not choose a Presi[
whenever the right of choice shall devolve upon them, before the fou[
day of March next following, then the Vice-President shall act[
President, as in the case of the death or other constitutional disabili[
of the President.]* The person having the greatest number of vot[
as Vice-President, shall be the Vice-President, if such number be [
majority of the whole number of Electors appointed, and if no person
have a majority, then from the two highest numbers on the list, the
Senate shall choose the Vice-President; a quorum for the purpose shall
consist of two-thirds of the whole number of Senators, and a majority
of the whole number shall be necessary to a choice. But no person
constitutionally ineligible to the office of President shall be eligible
to that of Vice-President of the United States.

ARTICLE XIII

SECTION 1. Neither slavery nor involuntary servitude, except as a
punishment for crime whereof the party shall have been duly convicted, shall exist within the United States, or any place subject to
their jurisdiction.

SECTION 2. Congress shall have power to enforce this article by
appropriate legislation.

ARTICLE XIV

SECTION 1. All persons born or naturalized in the United States,
and subject to the jurisdiction thereof, are citizens of the United States
and of the State wherein they reside. No State shall make or enforce
any law which shall abridge the privileges or immunities of citizens of
the United States; nor shall any State deprive any person of life,
liberty, or property, without due process of law; nor deny to any
person within its jurisdiction the equal protection of the laws.

SECTION 2. Representatives shall be apportioned among the several
States according to their respective numbers, counting the whole number of persons in each State, excluding Indians not taxed. But when
the right to vote at any election for the choice of electors for President
and Vice President of the United States, Representatives in Congress,
the Executive and Judicial officers of a State, or the members of the
Legislature thereof, is denied to any of the male inhabitants of such
State, being twenty-one years of age, and citizens of the United States,
or in any way abridged, except for participation in rebellion, or other
crime, the basis of representation therein shall be reduced in the proportion which the number of such male citizens shall bear to the whole
number of male citizens twenty-one years of age in such State.

SECTION 3. No person shall be a Senator or Representative in Congress, or elector of President and Vice President, or hold any office,
civil or military, under the United States, or under any State, who,
having previously taken an oath, as a member of Congress, or as an

*The part included in heavy brackets has been superseded by section 3 of the twentieth amendment.

_r as a member of any State legislature,
l officer of any State, to support the Con-
ates, shall have engaged in insurrection or
ne, or given aid or comfort to the enemies
may by a vote of two-thirds of each House,

alidity of the public debt of the United States,
including debts incurred for payment of pensions
services in suppressing insurrection or rebellion, shall
d.   But neither the United States nor any State shall
any debt or obligation incurred in aid of insurrection
against the United States, or any claim for the loss or
on of any slave; but all such debts, obligations and claims
eld illegal and void.

on 5. The Congress shall have power to enforce, by appro-
legislation, the provisions of this article.

339

ARTICLE XV

SECTION 1. The right of citizens of the United States to vote shall
not be denied or abridged by the United States or by any State on
account of race, color, or previous condition of servitude.

SECTION 2. The Congress shall have power to enforce this article
by appropriate legislation.

ARTICLE XVI

The Congress shall have power to lay and collect taxes on incomes,
from whatever source derived, without apportionment among the
several States, and without regard to any census or enumeration.

ARTICLE [XVII]

The Senate of the United States shall be composed of two Senators
from each state, elected by the people thereof, for six years; and each
Senator shall have one vote.   The electors in each State shall have
the qualifications requisite for electors of the most numerous branch
of the State legislatures.

When vacancies happen in the representation of any State in the
Senate, the executive authority of such State shall issue writs of
election to fill such vacancies: _Provided_, That the legislature of any
State may empower the executive thereof to make temporary appointments until the people fill the vacancies by election as the legislature
may direct.

This amendment shall not be so construed as to affect the election
or term of any Senator chosen before it becomes valid as part of the
Constitution.

[ARTICLE [XVIII]

[SECTION 1. After one year from the ratification of this article the
manufacture, sale, or transportation of intoxicating liquors within,
the importation thereof into, or the exportation thereof from the
United States and all territory subject to the jurisdiction thereof for

beverage purposes is hereby prohibited.

[SECTION 2. The Congress and the several States shall have concurrent power to enforce this article by appropriate legislation.

[SECTION 3. This article shall be inoperative unless it shall have been ratified as an amendment to the Constitution by the legislatures of the several States, as provided in the Constitution, within seven years from the date of the submission hereof to the States by the Congress.]*

ARTICLE [XIX]

The right of citizens of the United States to vote shall not be denied or abridged by the United States or by any State on account of sex.

Congress shall have power to enforce this article by appropriate legislation.

ARTICLE [XX]

SECTION 1. The terms of the President and Vice President shall end at noon on the 20th day of January, and the terms of Senators and Representatives at noon on the 3d day of January, of the years in which such terms would have ended if this article had not been ratified; and the terms of their successors shall then begin.

SECTION 2. The Congress shall assemble at least once in every year, and such meeting shall begin at noon on the 3d day of January, unless they shall by law appoint a different day.

SECTION 3. If, at the time fixed for the beginning of the term of the President, the President elect shall have died, the Vice President elect shall become President. If a President shall not have been chosen before the time fixed for the beginning of his term, or if the President elect shall have failed to qualify, then the Vice President elect shall act as President until a President shall have qualified; and the Congress may by law provide for the case wherein neither a President elect nor a Vice President elect shall have qualified, declaring who shall then act as President, or the manner in which one who is to act shall be selected, and such person shall act accordingly until a President or Vice President shall have qualified.

SECTION 4. The Congress may by law provide for the case of the death of any of the persons from whom the House of Representatives may choose a President whenever the right of choice shall have devolved upon them, and for the case of the death of any of the persons from whom the Senate may choose a Vice President whenever the right of choice shall have devolved upon them.

SECTION 5. Sections 1 and 2 shall take effect on the 15th day of October following the ratification of this article.

SECTION 6. This article shall be inoperative unless it shall have been ratified as an amendment to the Constitution by the legislatures of three-fourths of the several States within seven years from the date of its submission.

---

*Repealed by section 1 of the twenty-first amendment.

ARTICLE [XXI]

Section 1. The eighteenth article of amendment to the Constitution of the United States is hereby repealed.

Section 2. The transportation or importation into any State, Territory, or possession of the United States for delivery or use therein of intoxicating liquors, in violation of the laws thereof, is hereby prohibited.

Section 3. This article shall be inoperative unless it shall have been ratified as an amendment to the Constitution by conventions in the several States, as provided in the Constitution, within seven years from the date of the submission hereof to the States by the Congress.

ARTICLE [XXII]

Section 1. No person shall be elected to the office of the President more than twice, and no person who has held the office of President, or acted as President, for more than two years of a term to which some other person was elected President shall be elected to the office of the President more than once. But this article shall not apply to any person holding the office of President when this Article was proposed by the Congress, and shall not prevent any person who may be holding the office of President, or acting as President, during the term within which this Article becomes operative from holding the office of President or acting as President during the remainder of such term.

Section 2. This article shall be inoperative unless it shall have been ratified as an amendment to the Constitution by the legislatures of three-fourths of the several States within seven years from the date of its submission to the States by the Congress.

ARTICLE [XXIII]

Section 1. The District constituting the seat of Government of the United States shall appoint in such manner as the Congress may direct:

A number of electors of President and Vice President equal to the whole number of Senators and Representatives in Congress to which the District would be entitled if it were a State, but in no event more than the least populous State; they shall be in addition to those appointed by the States, but they shall be considered, for the purposes of the election of President and Vice President, to be electors appointed by a State; and they shall meet in the District and perform such duties as provided by the twelfth article of amendment.

Section 2. The Congress shall have power to enforce this article by appropriate legislation.

ARTICLE [XXIV]

Section 1. The right of citizens of the United States to vote in any primary or other election for President or Vice President, for electors for President or Vice President, or for Senator or Representative in Congress, shall not be denied or abridged by the United States or any State by reason of failure to pay any poll tax or other tax.

Sec. 2. The Congress shall have power to enforce this article by appropriate legislation.

ARTICLE [XXV]

SECTION 1. In case of the removal of the President from office or of his death or resignation, the Vice President shall become President.

SEC. 2. Whenever there is a vacancy in the office of the Vice President, the President shall nominate a Vice President who shall take office upon confirmation by a majority vote of both Houses of Congress.

SEC. 3. Whenever the President transmits to the President pro tempore of the Senate and the Speaker of the House of Representatives his written declaration that he is unable to discharge the powers and duties of his office, and until he transmits to them a written declaration to the contrary, such powers and duties shall be discharged by the Vice President as Acting President.

SEC. 4. Whenever the Vice President and a majority of either the principal officers of the executive departments or of such·other body as Congress may by law provide, transmit to the President pro tempore of the Senate and the Speaker of the House of Representatives their written declaration that the President is unable to discharge the powers and duties of his office, the Vice President shall immediately assume the powers and duties of the office as Acting President.

Thereafter, when the President transmits to the President pro tempore of the Senate and the Speaker of the House of Representatives his written declaration that no inability exists, he shall resume the powers and duties of his office unless the Vice President and a majority of either the principal officers of the executive department or of such other body as Congress may by law provide, transmit within four days to the President pro tempore of the Senate and the Speaker of the House of Representatives their written declaration that the President is unable to discharge the powers and duties of his office. Thereupon Congress shall decide the issue, assembling within forty-eight hours for that purpose if not in session. If the Congress, within twenty-one days after receipt of the latter written declaration, or, if Congress is not in session, within twenty-one days after Congress is required to assemble, determines by two-thirds vote of both Houses that the President is unable to discharge the powers and duties of his office, the Vice President shall continue to discharge the same as Acting President; otherwise, the President shall resume the powers and duties of his office.

INDEX